UNDER EIGHT FLAGS

UNDER EIGHT FLAGS

Anthony (Tony) F. Winstanley

Navigator Books

Published by Navigator Books
Ringwood, Hampshire

ISBN 0 902830 60 0

Typeset by Moorhouse Typesetter
Printed by The Cromwell Press, Melksham, Wiltshire

Foreword

On November 4th, 1993, Tony Winstanley, my father-in-law, arrived to stay with us in Jakarta. His mission was to complete this book, but at the time I'm not sure he believed it was possible. Tony had written over a hundred pages in a scribbler and quickly set out to write a hundred more. We bought a small computer and after a few short lessons Tony started typing in what he had written. Days passed with Tony entering the computer room early each morning and exiting only for meals and tea breaks. It may sound like his time spent here was nothing but hours locked away struggling with the computer. In fact it was much worse than that.

Our blind dog, "Lucky", was kept in the computer room and had the habit of attaching himself to one of Tony's legs. This would have been catastrophic had he been writing in longhand, but with two free fingers Tony typed on. Then, there were his nightly thrashings at the ping-pong table. It didn't seem to bother him much though, as we had a lot of laughs and he did manage the odd victory. Our night-watchman, part-time ping-pong ball retriever and sole fan, Sugito, was a boon to these gruelling matches in the hot night air. A swim was often required afterwards, followed by one of Bernadette's meals, and then back to the computer, or a bit of the BBC on T.V. He often told us of his desire to study the flora and, particularly, fauna of this enchanting land, and finally his chance came.

One afternoon Bernadette went with him to "Taman Safari", and there in the damp mountain air he encountered Miss O. Tang. News and photos of his exploits quickly made it back to Canada where stories began circulating. Gossip about "Pops" began making the rounds here, too. Soon, he became known as the man who would take to the pools of unsuspecting hosts and hostesses in the strangest of manners. I myself witnessed him entering pools in several ways: after stripping down to his underwear, down a slide fully clothed (including shoes) and simply falling backward from a conversation, again fully clothed. These fits of silliness, his propensity for appalling puns and his inclination towards Asian fauna quickly gained him the central place in party photos, adorned with clinging females. I don't remember him complaining.

Tony has completed his mission. Perhaps now instead of listening to his endless stories of life at sea, we will simply be referred to this weighty tome, *Under Eight Flags*. But then, this is only the first volume, and Tony, or "Ant" as his friends in England like to call him, has more than enough amusing stories to fill another two.

Scott Leaney
Jakarta,
Indonesia
May, 1994.

Table of Contents

Preface

From time to time during the last few years my children have asked me about my life at sea. I felt flattered that they might find that anything I had to tell them was of interest. Some of the stories may have sounded far-fetched because they happened so long ago in circumstances which are difficult to relate to modern times. Perhaps they got tired of hearing these yarns. At any rate, about a year ago, Veronica, my eldest child, suggested that instead of talking about my sea experiences, I should think about writing an account of them. I was reminded of the sobering fact that I might not be around for very much longer, and all the stories would be lost if I did not save them for posterity!

I was fortunate that during my last term at school I was encouraged to keep a diary, and this propensity to put things down on paper stayed with me for the first years at sea. When I read these daily accounts now, my observations and impressions seem childish and naive, but they have been invaluable in helping to write an accurate account of events which happened more than half a century ago.

When I set out to write this account, I had to decide whether to include some of the seamy episodes which occurred from time to time. I could write an accurate account and thus run the risk of offending someone's sensibilities. On the other hand, an expurgated version might lack conviction. Those of my children with whom I broached this subject unanimously opted for the former. "Write it as it really happened, warts and all!" they said. I was inclined to agree and thought that if my already-tarnished reputation suffered further, well so be it! Because of inhibitions resulting from a strict Catholic upbringing, I was unable as a young man to write in my diary about some of the experiences I had. I was ashamed of myself. Now, supposedly in my dotage, I could write about them without batting an eyelid! I could write of the events that concerned members of the opposite sex and my experiences with them.

While still at school any association with or knowledge of the opposite sex was extremely limited. Laxton College was a small boarding school for boys. The Dominican Fathers who bought the old Georgian mansion in the last century must have decided that the boys should be as far removed from the outside world as was possible in England. The mansion lay in the middle of its own grounds of over 100 acres, and the only way to reach it by car was through the imposing lodge gates, where the porter queried visitors on their reasons for wanting to enter. Then there was a winding cattle track with frequent stops to open gates before reaching the stone fortress which was Laxton College. The nearest village was over a mile away, and Stamford, a sizeable town, was 8 miles off. No wonder we felt isolated. Indeed, while I was there the only female we saw at regular intervals was the matron, a formidable figure not likely to arouse any emotion other than fear. But we did get fleeting glimpses of the Irish maids who delivered great pots of mostly inedible food to the refectory. They scurried about in the distance - visions in their white and blue uniforms. Their domain was strictly out of bounds - even a look in their direction was considered sinful and to engage them in conversation was almost impossible. I recall a strange feeling of exhilaration at the sight of legs encased in black stockings viewed from at least fifty feet away. I toiled dismally at Latin and Greek while the subjects which would have proved useful were not included in the curriculum. The word "sex" was never mentioned either at home or at school. A feeble attempt was made to prepare boys for life outside. Shortly before leaving Laxton, the house master called me to his room for what was called "A Going-away Chat". Other boys who had been subjected to this had come away with knowing smirks on their faces and I wondered what I was in for. It made very little impression on me, because as I recall the house master looked as uncomfortable as I felt. He began by warning me of the dangers of keeping bad company; of the temptations of the flesh; of unbridled passion coupled with evil thoughts. He skirted around the subject sincerely enough without telling me anything meaningful. It was quite possible that his knowledge and experience were as meagre as my own. His parting advice was, "Save yourself for marriage."

Not very long afterwards I was aboard my first ship with a crew of hard-bitten seamen whose ideas about "saving themselves for the future" were not the same as those of my former house master! I heard a lot of ribald humour about girls in foreign ports particularly in dens of iniquity like Marseilles and Buenos Aires. Much of what was said went over my head, but I soon realized that there was a mysterious, exciting world out there with pleasures of which I knew nothing, and which were now about to become available.

Quite recently it occurred to me that not only was I fortunate to have experienced the sort of seafaring which no longer exists, but had I been successful in passing my exams during the time that I was serving in the British merchant service, I would not have had such a varied and interesting life at sea. Most of my contemporaries in Britain gained their masters' tickets by the time they were thirty. They went on to join well-known companies, and by the time they were fifty, they were in command of their own ships. In the early sixties, the merchant fleet was in rapid decline and men were forced to retire early, some as young as fifty. My main reason for emigrating to Canada in 1948 was because of repeated failures to pass exams and, hence, I had poor prospects in the British merchant service. I now realize that my continually changing from one shipping company to another was not only necessary at the time, but it enabled me to see far more of the world than would have been the case had I stuck with one company.

I have often been asked whether I was seasick during the many years I have been at sea. The answer is "Yes, frequently." It was an affliction which I was never able to completely overcome, although it affected me less frequently during my later years at sea. I always found the heavy pitching of a ship more upsetting than the heavy rolling. Fortunately the attitude of people in recent years has changed to more tolerance for sufferers of "mal de mer". In the bad old days they were regarded with scorn by some seamen. During my first year at sea aboard the "Burma" when I was dogged by seasickness, I was looked upon as a slacker avoiding work on the pretense of illness. I was told that the only way to get over it was to dangle a piece of fatty pork down my throat in order to bring up everything and thus end the problem. The theory being that if there was nothing left inside, the sickness would cease immediately. The general opinion was that seasickness was entirely in one's head and that if a more positive attitude was taken it would simply go away. We now know that this is nonsense — seasickness is very real. I sailed with a mate aboard a small research ship on the West Coast of Canada who suffered from chronic seasickness. He was a big, strapping fellow who did his job efficiently, but once we were out in the open Pacific and the ship began to pitch and roll in the heavy swell, he became prostrate with sickness. He would lie inert and paralyzed by the motion and there was nothing we could do to help him. If he had remained at sea for any length of time his condition would have worsened and he would have died. I still find myself becoming a little irritated by such remarks as "Seasick? Of course not, never been seasick in my life!"

My initial difficulties at sea can be attributed to the fact that the education I received did little or nothing to prepare me for the "rough and tumble" of life aboard ship. One of the masters at school said, "Winstanley, if you had twice as much sense as you have now, you'd still be a half-wit!" My father's reaction to yet another poor school report can be imagined. The last had read, "This boy seems to have only the vaguest notion of the reason for his being at Laxton!" However I did gain one distinction — I held the record for receiving more whackings in one term than any other boy!

By the time I was sixteen, it had become painfully obvious to my parents that further education at Laxton College was a waste of my grandmother's money. I left after the summer term in 1936, and it was decided that I should attend a school in Birmingham to see whether I could learn enough to be able to pass the school certificate. I caught the early train from Redditch every morning. It took an hour to reach New Street station and from there I walked to Lawrence's College which was right in the middle of the city. It had been recommended as a school which could bring backward pupils to an acceptable level of intelligence where they could pass exams. At first I began to show some promise, but this happy state of affairs was short-lived and as the weeks went by, I fell behind and as test results came in, my performance became increasingly disappointing. In desperation my father sent me to a tutor who lived in a house near ours. I would return from Birmingham late in the afternoon, have a hurried supper and walk to Mr. Watson's house for an hour's tuition. He had a lot of patience, but before long it ran out along with my father's willingness to spend any more money. So a few weeks before Christmas everyone, including me, had had enough, and any further schooling ceased abruptly. Considered academically hopeless, I was now about to enter a career for which I was singularly ill-equipped. It must have been the final straw for my father who, like any man, wanted his son to enter a worthwhile profession. He may have thought I would take an interest in farming, and for a few weeks I did accompany him on his visits to farms around Worcestershire. I thoroughly enjoyed the wonderful hospitality of the farmers and their wives who would never let us leave without giving us a meal of the finest farm food. But I was never "cut out" to be a farmer. What was to be done with me? The answer to that question must have been heard in many British households — "Send him to sea." "The rest is history," as they say!

By the summer of 1993, I had written about 150 pages of my memoirs into a note book, but was at a loss as to how I would complete a book, having failed to master the use of a lap-top computer. My daughter Bernadette and her husband, Scott, were visiting us in Canada and became aware of my difficulties. They suggested that I spend the winter with them in Indonesia where they would give me the help I needed. I immediately saw that this was too good an opportunity to miss. As I gathered my work together I realized that I had enough material in my first eleven years at sea to fill a book and that my complete memoirs would have to be written at a later date. Soon after my arrival in Jakarta, Scott purchased a Macintosh computer. This acquisition proved most timely for, oddly enough, I was able to overcome my prejudice against such "gadgets" and began tapping in the words, albeit slowly.

My sincere thanks to Bernie who spent many gruelling hours editing the manuscript; her patience was sorely tried by my continual lapses into the present tense! My special thanks to Scott for his expert advice in the use of the computer and for his time spent on lay-out and format. This book would not have been completed without their generosity and encouragement. I am particularly indebted to Gertrude and John in England, who for some years have been telling me that I must get down to writing my story. My deep gratitude also goes to Veronica and Roy, who finally got me going on it and to my children, relatives, and good friends Captain Roy Harrington and Mr James Robertson who spurred me on. I will need you all again in the near future when I begin the next volume!

Victoria May 1995.

After the first edition of this book had circulated among my relatives and friends it soon became apparent that it needed some polishing-up. There were some glaring errors which were spotted by seamen who politely reminded me that I should have known better. For example a single screw ship driven by a steam reciprocating engine has only one crankshaft! Boners like this have been corrected and this book is as accurate as it is possible to be after a lapse of fifty years. I have added a few paragraphs of events which have come to mind in the past year.

I am indebted to those who have assisted in making this a better book. My sincere thanks to Roy Diment who has so generously donated his time and talents in designing a more eye-catching cover. In order to create the now defunct Canadian Red Ensign, he deftly removed the emblem from the flag of the province of Manitoba, and placed the appropriate one on the old Red Duster. My thanks to Captains Roy Harrington, Norman Collett, and Bernie Crooks for their assistance in tidying-up the loose ends in the script. I am most grateful to Bob Bell who offered to make drawings of two ships of which I had no good photographs. I wasn't sure what the result would be, particularly in the case of the "Mandalay". All he had to go by was a set of builders' plans. I am more than pleased with the pictures, and am impressed by the accuracy of detail, but then he is a skilled draftsman.

Tony Winstanley

Chapter 1. The "Burma"

In 1936, Great Britain had the largest merchant fleet in the world. Ships flying the Red Ensign could be seen in every major port and ones so little known that it would have been difficult to find them on a map. There were great ocean liners, tankers, troopships, nondescript tramp steamers and coasters around the British Isles. As far away as China and India, there was hardly a stretch of water on the globe not churned up by the passage of a British ship.

The depression was over, world trade was increasing and in spite of ominous signs of war in Europe, vast amounts of cargo had to be moved across the oceans. Most of it would be carried under the "Red Duster". For any youth with thoughts about going to sea as a way of life, it was a good time to start. I had no such ideas having left school at sixteen with an undistinguished scholastic record. My future held no particular promise and I had no idea what I wanted to do. It was my mother Violet who suggested that a life at sea might do me some good. She looked at the shipping section in the London papers to find the companies who might be willing to take a boy with no knowledge of the sea. I was too old to be accepted by the Training Ships, and we had no sea connections. We lived in the Midlands, as far from salt water as it is possible to be in England. The only time I had seen the sea was on infrequent holidays to the crowded resort of Weston-Super-Mare. I wrote several letters of application to shipping companies whose notices seemed appealing — "Regular sailings to ports in Brazil and the west coast of South America" and "Fast cargo ships to Australia and New Zealand." It all sounded like the sort of adventure I needed.

It was something of a surprise when just before Christmas 1936, a letter came from the Henderson Line of Glasgow, who it seemed might be reckless enough to employ me. I took the train to London for an interview with one of the company's senior masters. Captain Thompson was a tall man with a severe expression caused perhaps by having to interview a callow youth. However, a letter soon came from the company instructing me to join the S/S "Burma" on December 29th, 1936 at Queen's Dock, Liverpool. Enclosed was a Kit List with the required gear for a cadet. It caused my father, Alfred, to frown at the outlay of more than £100 for uniform, dungarees (overalls), oil skins (rain gear), and copies of Nicholls's Concise Guide and Nicholls's Seamanship. My father insisted on accompanying me to Liverpool. As we sat in the train compartment he impressed upon me the importance of settling down and doing my best. Possibly some doubts lingered in his mind and now he had a vested interest in me.

There were three ways in which a boy could enter the Merchant Service and eventually qualify to become a ship's officer. The best and easiest route was to go on one of the training ships which took cadets as young as thirteen. The training was rigorous and the life spartan, but by the time he was seventeen a boy had a good grounding in seamanship and navigation. The top cadets were sent to the best companies. Another way was via the lower deck to serve four years as ordinary seaman in the foc'sle. Conditions were such that very few made it. There was very little encouragement and there existed the nasty snobbery which seemed to bar the way for any aspiring fo'c'sle-hand to better himself. It was a good man indeed who rose above his lot. It was known as "coming up through the hawse pipe." I learned later that some of the very best mates and masters came via that route. Then there were those such as I who went straight to sea without benefit of any pre-sea training. If one were lucky enough to be with mates who had some interest in teaching an apprentice the elements of seamanship and navigation, it was fortunate indeed. In most cases they were far too busy and had neither the patience nor the inclination. I found that among some men there was resentment that a boy should come aboard with ideas about becoming a deck officer without roughing it in the foc'sle for four years.

Distinctions of class existed aboard ship as they did ashore. Companies like Cunard and Union Castle took the top cadets from the training ships "Worcester" and "Conway". They were the old "wooden walls" dating from Nelson's day. Then there was the P & O, (Peninsula & Oriental) Line which had a reputation for being the snootiest of all. It was the oldest shipping line, having evolved from the East India Company whose beautiful ships were so much a part of the traditions of Empire in India and The East. For readers of Kipling or Forster, a passage to India almost certainly meant by P & O Line. There was a popular story at the time about officers in the P & O applying to the Admiralty for permission to wear swords for special occasions. The reply came back, "Permission granted on condition that swords are worn on right side only!" But there was one shipping company with an outstanding reputation for excellent ships and good conditions. This was Alfred Holt's Blue Funnel Line of Liverpool. They established the "Conway" as a means of assuring a supply of trained boys known as midshipmen. At the other end of the scale were the hard-case tramps out of Cardiff and Newcastle who took apprentices without benefit of pre-sea training., although in most cases they were the sons of masters and mates, and thus had some ideas about ships and the sea. On many of these ships conditions were deplorable but for the men who manned them it was no different from the privations of life ashore.

The days of Board of Trade rations at sea, or "whack", had for the most part disappeared. This was the regimen that stipulated so many ounces of bread, tea and condensed milk per day per man. It meant that the ships' crews were half-starved. It was said that Lady Astor, a wealthy American, had been asked to make up a subsistence diet for seamen. When someone had the temerity to remark that the amount seemed niggardly, she replied, "Seamen should not expect more. After all, they have the pleasure of seeing the world free of charge!" Some ship owners had reputations for poor conditions aboard their ships and seamen had their own titles for them. The Lamport and Holt Line became known as "Lousy and Hungry", the Hogarth Baron Line became known as "Hungry Hogarth's" and P. Henderson & Co the company I was about to join, became "Poverty, Hunger and Corruption". I was to discover later that Scandinavian, German and Dutch ships were far more advanced in providing good conditions for their seamen. And possibly the best were the American ships in which the whole crew was usually housed amidships instead of being crammed in the fore-end or stern.

My father and I arrived at the dock in Liverpool to find the "Burma" unloading cargo from Rangoon, Burma. At 8,000 gross tons, she was the largest ship I had seen at close quarters. I stood in awe and wonderment. The rattle and clatter of steam winches and the shouts and curses of the dockers as the loads were lifted out of the hatches only served to increase my feeling of apprehension. This was the vessel which was to be my home for the next year. Built by Dennys of Dumbarton in 1914, she was one of the oldest in a fleet of twelve ships in the U.K.-Burma-India trade. Like any Clyde-built ship, the "Burma" was strongly constructed, and what she lacked in appearance was compensated for by the assurance that she was a "good sea boat". With a tall, black funnel, white superstructure and old-fashioned counter stern, she was a typical cargo-passenger ship of her day. She had accommodation for 112 passengers. Her holds were filled with thousands of sacks of bran, lead ingots and teak wedges destined by the million for use on the railway lines. Bales of wax, chests of tea and foul-smelling animal hides were also part of the cargo.

The "Burma". I spent my first year at sea aboard this ship. She was built on the Clyde in 1914 for the U/K to Burma trade, and carried 112 passengers, 100 crew members and 8000 tons of cargo. She survived the war and finished her days carrying mules between ports on the east coast of Africa.

My father and I went up the gangway and stood on deck. A dark-skinned man spoke to us. He was one of the lascars, (general term for Indian seamen), recruited in Rangoon but originally from the Chittagong area of India, and sometimes referred to as "jungli wallahs". Others hailed from Bombay and Madras, and were known as "Bombay or Madras wallahs". We were taken to the chief officer's cabin. Mr. McIntosh was a busy man. He was poring over manifests and a cargo plan when we walked in, but found time to tell my father what the company expected of me. He then instructed me to go on deck in search of the senior cadet while he spoke a few words in confidence to my father. The senior cadet, a boy named Turnbull, had been at sea for three years, part of it in the Royal Navy as a midshipman on a battleship. This had given him a superior air, and I soon discovered that he was apt to remind anyone willing to listen that, should war break out, the senior service would immediately claim his talents.

I was taken to a small cabin that I was to share with another boy who would join the ship later. Turnbull's cabin was next to the ship carpenter's, all in a house on the boat deck between No. 3 cargo hatch and the ship's tall, black funnel. A tall, young man appeared wearing one gold stripe. His name was Wyn-Thomas and he had just got his second mate's certificate and was anxious to assert his authority. He told me to put on dungarees and he put me to work immediately. My first job was in the 'tween deck of No. 2 hold, piling dunnage wood into neat piles. Before long, I was called on deck to say farewell to my father who then disappeared down the gangway. An elderly man in white overalls came up to me. He was the 2nd engineer, and it was evident from his manner that he wished to help me. "Take my advice, son, before it's too late. Go back down the gangway. This is a wasted life. Stay away from the sea and find a shore job!"

The "Burma" all lit up to celebrate the King's 25th year on the throne.

On New Year's Eve, the "Burma" was finally unloaded and we prepared to leave for Glasgow, the ship's home port. It was a bitterly cold night and with the aid of tugs, fore and aft, we moved from one dock to another, past a line of other cargo and passenger ships. At midnight, the air was shattered by a chorus of steam whistles and sirens to announce the arrival of the new year, 1937. My station was on the fo'c'sle head with the chief officer, the serang (bosun) and several kallassees (Indian deck seamen) who handled the ropes. Chips, (the carpenter), stood by the anchor windlass, and I was instructed to relay orders shouted from the bridge. This became difficult as I did not yet know nautical terminology and could only repeat what I heard as closely as it sounded. The order "vast heaving" sounded like "fast heaving", and that is what I called out. It was too dark to see the expression on the mate's face, which was just as well. Once out in the river, the "Burma" blew a series of blasts on the whistle to signal that the tugs could leave, we increased speed and the lights of Liverpool began to disappear astern.

At the Bar lightship we dropped the pilot and headed out into the Irish Sea, a nasty place to be at that time of year. Never having been aboard any vessel larger than a river steamer I soon began to feel queasy as the bows started to rise and fall in the swell. I was on the 12 to 4 watch with the second mate, who stood in the wheel house while I stood out in the open on the weather side. I was buffeted by a strong, cold wind and tried to keep my footing as the ship rolled and plunged about. Every so often the sea would catch her and the bows would scoop a mass of foaming water onto the foredeck. My duty was to report lights as they appeared, but I spent most of the watch vomiting over the side. The watch seemed endless and to add to my misery I received a bawling out from the second mate for not cleaning up my mess. He quite rightly set me swilling with a bucket which kept me from my bunk until 5 am. The accommodation inside the "Burma" was constructed of teak, and as she pitched and rolled there was a great deal of creaking and groaning inside the ship as these wooden components worked together. The sight of land as we approached the Clyde the following afternoon was very welcome for I had already begun to have doubts whether the sea life was for me.

The "Burma" stayed in Glasgow for almost two weeks. During that time I learnt something about the ship and her crew, and I was beginning to settle down when one day I was called to the chief officer's cabin. He was holding a telegram in his hand. My mother was seriously ill and I must go home at once. The overnight train took me to Birmingham where my father met me and we drove in silence to the hospital. My mother was unconscious and slipping fast and a few hours later she died. I left the hospital in a state of shock. My mother had never been sick a day in her life, but flu had developed into septic-pneumonia. Penicillin would probably have saved her life but it had not yet been discovered. In those days the only treatment was sulfa drugs. The loss of my mother was devastating for all of us, particularly for my father. After the funeral, my sister, Gertrude, returned to her job as a governess in France, my brother, Bernard, returned to school, and I returned to the "Burma". It was a sad and lonely time for the family.

Upon my return to the ship I met the third cadet, Bob Greenall. He was a burly lad of eighteen, the son of a customs officer from Dover, and already a competent seaman having had some pre-sea experience in small vessels in the channel. During our stay in Glasgow we were kept busy from dawn until dusk; there was no such thing as an eight hour day. The longer the ship remained in port, the dirtier she became. The afterdeck was piled high with ashes from the stoke-hold mixed with the foul-smelling refuse from the galleys and the whole mess was made worse by rain. The once well-scrubbed, white teak decks were filthy, but the ship would remain that way until we got to sea and could dump it over the side. I spent many hours down in the holds cleaning out the bilges and strainers known as "rose boxes". They became clogged with foul-smelling material and the occasional dead rat, but at least it was warmer work than being on deck.

The crew numbered about a hundred men of whom twenty-three were European. The master, Captain Lusk, was a white-haired solemn man from the Hebrides. All the deck officers including the radio officer, (Sparks), were Scottish with the exception of the 4th mate who was Welsh. The carpenter, (Chips), was an Aberdonian who liked to remind us that the ship could sail without a fourth mate and apprentices but certainly not without him. Indeed, apprentices were considered the lowest form of life aboard. There were five engineers whose rooms were on the main deck below the passenger accommodation.

My room-mate aboard the "Burma", Bob Greenall, standing outside our cabin on inspection day. We had to clear everything moveable from our cabin and put it on to No.3 hatch before the old man and mate made their rounds.

The Old Man (Captain) was seldom seen as his accommodation was abaft the bridge. I never saw the inside of his cabin but if it was anything like the rest of the officers' quarters it was devoid of much comfort. Such luxury as running water was limited to a tin tank inside a commode which the steward kept topped up and this led to a basin via a tap, (cold only). The water was then tipped into another tank underneath for disposal over the side. This arrangement was the same for the passengers also and was considered adequate. Communication to and from the old man's room was via a voice pipe, a rubber tube with a brass speaking end to which a whistle was attached. One blew down the pipe and this activated a whistle at the other end which alerted the old man that there was a call.

The same thing was possible from his end. One of the mates on the bridge was in the habit of flicking ashes from his cigarette down the voice pipe. When the old man, lying in his bunk, heard the whistle he put his face to the end of the voice pipe and received a blast of noxious ash in his face. Thereafter, smoking on the bridge was strongly discouraged. One mate with a particular grudge against the captain was reputed to have once relieved himself into the voice pipe!

If the living conditions for officers were spartan, they were plush in comparison with the crew's quarters. Over eighty men were crammed into the fo'c'sle which was in the bows of the vessel. In later years, the practice of housing men in such a vulnerable place was changed to the after part, or stern, although it was still referred to as the fo'c'sle. The kallassees (seamen) were on the starboard side. The tindal, (assistant bosun), along with the other men made do with bunks, two-high, lining the bare steel-plating of the hull. The cassab (lamp-trimmer) was in charge of the lamp-locker. The lowest ranked man aboard was the topaz, (a low-caste Indian) who did the dirty jobs such as cleaning toilets and because of this, was not allowed to eat with the other men or touch their eating utensils. A coal-fired bogey provided heat of sorts. One night I was sent to call a man for duty. At the entrance to the fo'c'sle (crew's quarters I stepped over a high sill which prevented water from getting in. The lighting was so dim men appeared like shadows. The air was fetid — a mixture of coal and tobacco smoke, curried food and human sweat. Working clothes were hanging from lines stretching from stanchions. Fresh water was obtained from a pump which was in constant use. The clank and squeak of the handle, along with the din made by the slamming of steel doors, must have made life very uncomfortable. In rough weather, the pounding and plunging as the bows slammed into walls of water, made conditions even worse. The firemen, coal-trimmers, donkeymen and cooks had similar squalid accommodation on the port side.

The entire non-European crew were broadly referred to as lascars. Well-known shipping lines, such as the P & O and British India, had agreements with the Indian government to employ men from the sub-continent. A kallassee on the "Burma" was paid about 50 rupees a month but due to the baksheesh system was only able to keep half of that. The other half went into the serang's pocket.The serang, who was both bosun and a kind of "Godfather" to the crew was, by Indian standards, a fairly rich man. When the ship reached Rangoon it was his responsibility to find new seamen when required. Not a very difficult task as for every man working at sea there were hundreds ashore willing to replace him. Strangely enough there was little resentment at having to pay for their jobs and it was generally accepted. The British Raj tried to stamp out this iniquitous practice but met with little success. The baksheesh system was so deeply entrenched into Indian society that it was virtually impossible to get anything accomplished without first offering baksheesh. Our serang was a pleasant man, who found time to show me some of the elements of seamanship, which was more than any of the officers did. The officers had their own servants. I was on deck outside their quarters one day when I heard one of the mates shout, "Boy!" I thought for a moment he was calling me. To my surprise, an elderly Indian with white hair shuffled towards him. This was his “Boy”!

During our stay in Glasgow I learnt something about life in the area around Queens Dock, which had changed little in over a hundred years. The dreary cobblestone streets were lined with tenement houses. It was a poor section of the city and once clear of the dock gates it was a five minute walk to the streetcars on Argyle street. We had to run the gauntlet through a crowd of street urchins. Seamen were viewed as a target — a source of easy money. Ragged boys and girls, some no older than four or five years, would lie in wait for men emerging from the docks. On my first walk ashore a cluster surrounded me. They clutched my coat, crying, “Hey, ‘Mista’, gimme a penny!” They were not so much aggressive as persistent, and I wondered whether it was better to run for it or to stop and hand out a few precious pennies. My monthly wage was £1 a month and one shilling was enough to pay for a good night ashore, so I was not exactly flush. I soon learnt that the best strategy was to throw a couple of pennies in the air, and while they scrambled for them make a quick getaway.

In Glasgow I discovered that it was wise to remain silent, when possible, as an English accent seemed to provoke hostility among some Scots. One day, in a dockside cafe I asked the waitress for my cheque. I heard her say sarcastically to another girl, “Oi, ’e wants ’is cheque ’e does!” I should have asked for the “bill”. Apart from the occasional taunts and derisive glances, I never once felt physically threatened as I walked the grimy streets of Glasgow. In fact, as I got to know the city better, I found Glaswegians to be a generous, helpful people. Two years later, when I suffered a bout of pneumonia and had to be carried ashore on a stretcher and subsequently spend three weeks in Ruchill Hospital, the parents of one of the other cadets took me into their home and treated me as one of the family until I could return to the ship.

We began loading cargo. A large consignment of the best Scotch whisky was to be stowed in the locked cage of No. 2 hold. For obvious reasons, this had to be closely guarded and I was sent down to watch the dockers. But being canny Glaswegians, they had methods of broaching the precious liquid. The cases were lifted off the dock by means of a rope sling on a cargo hook at the end of a winch wire. The load would be snatched up from the dock and swung over the hatch, then lowered to the men waiting below. At a critical point, the winch man would bring the load to a sudden stop, the rope would bite deeply into the wooden boxes thus cracking a few bottles and, before long, a stream of good scotch whisky would dribble into the cans and cups readily held out. There wasn’t much I could do except shout at the winch man to be more careful, and he laughed and told me where to go.

Pilfering cargo was commonplace in most of the world’s ports, and I was to see a lot of it in the coming years. When loading or discharging goods that were particularly susceptible to theft, we would be sent down to watch but it went on anyway. It wasn’t until the war started that the penalties for theft of cargo became stiffer. There was an incident in 1941 when I was aboard the "Mandalay" when the police were called after cases of food were broken into. A man was arrested and taken away. The apprentice in the hold was called as a witness to the theft and the man received a lengthy prison sentence. But dockers were not the only ones to broach cargo. I heard of a chief officer who was in the habit of making frequent trips down a hold to look at the cargo. An apprentice had emerged from the hatch wearing a new pair of shoes, leaving his old ones behind in the shoe box. The chief officer went down to take a look and subsequently complained that he couldn't find a pair to fit him! The shippers of footwear soon became aware that not all of their shoes were reaching their destination. They solved the problem by sending a consignment of left-foot shoes on one ship, and right-foot shoes on another!

The day before we were due to sail, the mate told me to put on my uniform and go to the shipping office on James Watt Street. It was signing-on day. I stood self-consciously in a uniform which did not fit well. There had been no time for a made-to-measure suit, so it had to be one "off the hook" which was cheaper anyway. I was directed to a wicket where a clerk began to interrogate me in a rude and abusive manner common to shipping clerks. I was issued with a blue book called a " Seaman's Discharge Book" and although I didn't realize it at the time, this document was more valuable than a passport. It would be the means of securing employment in later years. I signed the articles which stated that I would be paid the sum of one pound per month.

When I returned aboard, I was ordered to stand at the gangway as the Marine Superintendent was coming aboard. Captain Cattenach had been the senior master and had now earned a good shore job. He could not stand the sight of idle apprentices and as soon as he saw me, asked what I was doing. I gave the only answer possible — "I am standing at the gangway, Sir." But it was not a wise reply and he was annoyed. The 4th mate was standing nearby and he was told to put me to work immediately — there would be no "swinging the lead" when he was around. I was soon to learn that the cardinal sin aboard ship was to appear idle. The important thing was always to appear to be doing something. So, if an officer was around it was good to have a bucket or length of rope in one's hand!

With the cargo loaded we left the dock and accompanied by a tug at the bow and one at the stern, we steamed slowly down the Clyde. As we approached the shipyards the clatter of riveting guns grew louder. A year earlier the mighty "Queen Mary" had been completed in the John Brown Yard, and now the keel of another super liner had been laid down, later named the "Queen Elizabeth." By the time we reached the mouth of the Clyde, night had fallen. The engines were put on full speed and we made for Birkenhead which lay across the Mersey from Liverpool. We reached there the following day. The area around the docks was seedy, but not as squalid as in Glasgow, and no children were begging in the streets. The "Burma" was to be fully loaded. A fifty-ton locomotive, destined for the Egyptian State Railway, was among the last loads hoisted aboard. It was placed on the foredeck and lashed down. Alongside it lay a motor launch for the

Liverpool, January 1937. Loading a 50 ton loco onto the foredeck of the "Burna" for the Egyptian State railways.

use of the Suez Canal pilots. Our cargo consisted of everything from shoes to car parts, including boxes of tinned food for the Europeans in Burma who yearned for delicacies not obtainable in the Orient. Joining the cases of whisky in the strong room, or cage as it was called, were boxes of Burmese currency filled with millions of rupees in note form, plus several bars of gold bullion. On the evening before our departure, the passengers arrived. For the most part they were members of the Civil Service in Burma, military people and their families. This was a time before the age of air travel when people leaving their home shores knew it could be years before they would return, and for some, never.

Our most unusual passengers were a group from the remote Shan State of Upper Burma. Among them were three giraffe-necked women. They were colourful curiosities who had been brought to England to be viewed by those who went to the Bertram Mills Circus. The giraffe-necked ladies were very proud to be regarded as oddities. They wore their brightly-coloured clothes with grace and charm, and the fact that their necks had been elongated by the addition of brass rings didn't seem to bother anyone. It was believed that their neck muscles had become atrophied, and that if the rings were removed, their heads, lacking support, would fall to the side with fatal results. There were two older women, one with a young child named Olympia after the hall in London where the circus had been held. The third was a girl in her teens who would have additional rings added as she grew older. Two men accompanied the troupe. I watched them as their heap of new trunks were unloaded at dockside. They had made a lot of money and had gone on a shopping spree in London and were now making sure that their treasures would be put aboard safely.

Prior to departure I had incurred the wrath of the master by hoisting the company flag upside down. It was made fast to a stick, which device was supposed to allow it to flutter free in the breeze without becoming entangled in the rigging. Not understanding this, and in some hurry, I had attached it to the halyard in the wrong place. I had also hoisted the P flag, or the "Blue Peter", to the yard. This signified that the "Burma" would sail within 24 hours. Despite my error we sailed for Rangoon, Burma with over a hundred passengers and a hundred crew, about 8,000 tons of general cargo and the ship down to her load marks. The weather was typical for January — a south-westerly gale and rough seas as the "Burma" ran down the coast towards Lands End. Our next port of call would be Marseilles to pick up a few passengers who by joining the ship there would avoid the dreaded Bay of Biscay and gain an extra day or two in England. Naturally enough we apprentices were curious about the mix of our passengers. Were there any pretty girls aboard? Someone had seen an attractive Chee-Chee, (Anglo-Indian), girl coming up the gangway. It was strictly forbidden for any of us to fraternize with the passengers and unless duty took us there, the passenger accommodation was off-limits.

One day I was working on an outside deck with Turnbull, the senior apprentice, when we heard a lot of shouting coming from inside the accommodation. Normally the steward would deal with such disturbances but he was nowhere to be seen. Feeling some trepidation on entering a forbidden area, Turnbull and I went along the passage towards the commotion. We came upon a white memsahib trying to separate an ayah and a topaz who were shouting at each other. We managed to separate them but not before the topaz had received a nasty gash on his face inflicted by a knife. The dispute was over a religious taboo which forbade the topaz from handling any cooking utensils because of his caste. The chief steward arrived, there was a lot of shouting and Turnbull and I left.

I was on the 12 to 4 watch with Mr. Peggie, the second mate. He was a large man with a grim expression and had a reputation for having a nasty temper. I was to discover that he had little use for apprentices whom he considered as boys from privileged backgrounds who had taken an easy route that had been denied him. He had risen from the lower deck — no mean feat in those days, and had "come up through the hawse pipe". He was a hard man and he didn't like me. As we steamed south in increasingly rough seas, the crew were called out to tighten the lashings on the deck cargo, particularly the 50-ton locomotive, which would create havoc if heavy rolling caused the wires to part. Lifelines were rigged across the fore and afterdeck which was normal practice in rough weather. When I was called to go on watch, I realized by the motion that the weather had worsened and it was difficult to dress and hold on at the same time. The ship lifted to the oncoming sea and then would make a sickening, corkscrew dive into the trough. The woodwork around the cabins creaked and the wind howled. It was bitterly cold, especially on the weather side of the bridge where I spent the watch clinging to a rail and trying to keep a good lookout. As the long watch wore on I became increasingly uncomfortable — a combination of seasickness, tiredness and the cold. With every lurch of the ship I was thrown against the nearest solid object. I managed to find the best vantage point to get out of the worst of the icy blast. Huddled in this wretchedness I momentarily drifted off to sleep. Suddenly, I felt myself gripped by strong hands, lifted off my feet and flung roughly into the corner of the bridge. Mr. Peggie's voice roared above the noise of the elements, "Never let me find you asleep again on watch!" This rude awakening produced the desired effect and miserable as I was, I finished the watch with my eyes glued to the horizon. There seems to have been three strikes against me, I was a Sassenach, a Catholic, and I was useless.

News of my serious dereliction of duty reached Wyn-Thomas, the 4th mate, and he continued to make life miserable by constantly checking on my whereabouts to make sure I had not sneaked away from any job I had been given. It was surely an infuriating thing for him to find aboard ship someone who was so obviously useless! You could not fool seamen for very long. No amount of "bull" about experience elsewhere counted for much. You were soon found out — either you could do the job, or you couldn't! I was told to take in the log. A wire ran from the clock on the wing of the bridge to the universal joint fitted on the end of a 15 ft. boom. The log line, with a rotator at its end, ran from there into the sea. This device measured the ship's speed through the water. Once the line was brought aboard, the boom was swung inboard. It took two of us to perform this operation. I was tending the forward guy and instead of easing it past the cleat, removed too many turns. The heavy boom took charge and it crashed against the ship's side. This had the effect of enraging Wyn-Thomas who shouted abuse in my direction, came closer and jabbed me in the side with his fist, yelling, "You useless bastard!" Nobody liked Wyn-Thomas, I least of all, but personal likes and dislikes had little bearing on the running of a ship. Fortunately I had one good ally in Greenall, who took the trouble to explain how things were done. He had the good sense and understanding to say that I could hardly be expected to know unless I was shown how to do a job first.

Once past Cape Ushant we entered the Bay of Biscay. A westerly gale had churned up a rough sea and there was the ever-present swell sweeping across the vast expanse of the Atlantic which added to the turbulence. The weather worsened by the hour until storm force winds forced us to heave to. Added to seasickness were feelings of apprehension. I had heard talk of rough weather but had never dreamed it would be like this. I stood on deck, gripping a rail as the sheer force of the wind made it impossible to stand upright. The ship lay with her bows facing the sea, the propeller turning with sufficient speed to maintain this position. In all respects we were stopped. I watched in awe as the bow fell into the deep troughs between the seas, then we would rise quickly to meet the next onslaught of another steep-sided sea, lift over, and slide down into the trough. Some way off I could see an even higher sea approaching, its crest foaming. Someone shouted, "Hold on! That one will catch us!" It seemed that every sixth or seventh wave would be the one she could not rise over. A wall of water, perhaps 40 to 50 feet high, was a frightening spectacle as it approached the ship. The "Burma", like a tired old horse in a steeplechase, lifted her bows, but it was not enough. There was a sickening thump as the fo'c'sle disappeared under a mass of water and foam. Hundreds of tons of cold Atlantic cascaded over the fo'c'sle head. The foredeck was filled to the gunwales. Had anyone been there it would have meant either being swept overboard or bashed against the unyielding steel of the hatches. The sea climbed up the ship's side and lifted a lifeboat off its chocks and pushed it against the house. A shout from the bridge told us to look lively and secure the boat and any other loose gear before it all went overboard. The wind was so strong that movement about the deck was difficult and hazardous. I was not of much assistance as I grasped a rope to take a turn around a solid object and was promptly told that I had not done it correctly!

Eventually the weather began to moderate. The mate and some of the seamen ventured out onto the foredeck to check the lashings on the deck load which, miraculously, had not shifted. There was talk about going into Gibraltar to repair any damage. The radio officer told us that a Portuguese ship not far from us had sent out distress calls, and we heard later that she had gone down with all hands. Cape St. Vincent was a welcome sight about 10 miles off the port bow and once past it, the weather improved quickly and the temperature rose when the sun appeared. It was almost balmy; the engines were put at full speed and we resumed our proper course. When the mighty rock appeared on our port bow we knew the calm waters of the Meddy were ahead. Passengers began to appear on the outside decks and I heard snatches of conversation as they spoke of their ordeal during the storm. One little girl had received a gash on her head and the ship's doctor was reported to be too seasick to be of assistance. He was a man of advanced years, who, in retirement, had accepted the post thinking that a cruise would be beneficial to his health!

The port of Marseilles looked picturesque as we steamed in to pick up the pilot but we had been told that there would be no shore leave for anyone. It was a city with an evil reputation among seafarers and was known as one of the three most wicked ports in the world, which left me wondering exactly what that meant. The other apprentices, being more worldly-wise, described the dubious pleasures available ashore. But shore leave was out of the question which was probably as well because Marseilles, then as now, could be a dangerous place in which to wander about. We heard about knifings and general mayhem, particularly in the Arab quarter. My first introduction to the wicked ways of man was in Marseilles. I spent most of our brief stay in port down a cargo hold ostensibly to see that the dockers did not pilfer cargo. These burly men must have seen me as an object of ridicule for one of them thrust a grubby package into my hand. Flustered but curious, I opened it to find a series of cards. At first I could not make out what they meant. They were black and white photos of naked men and women in scenes of frenzied passion that I had never dreamed possible. So this was what sex was all about. I must have looked uncomfortable as I handed them back and the men shrieked with laughter. I thought of my "going away" chat with the house master at school and wondered what he would have to say about this. Those images stayed with me for sometime — a mixture of disgust and curiosity.

The day was not without excitement of another kind. Ahead of us lay another company ship that had lost her rudder in a storm in the Gulf of Lyons. She was the "Kemmendine" and although she had taken rolls of 40 degrees the three railway engines on deck had not shifted. A good lashing job!. While I watched her replacement rudder being lifted off our deck, I noticed a passenger ship moving towards us. A strong onshore wind was pushing her towards us and her tugs were unable to stop her drift. It was obvious that this ship would hit us. Her decks were packed with refugees from the war in Spain and as most of them were standing on one side, their weight was sufficient to give the ship a list. A clamour of shouts arose from both ships. Several of our seamen ran along the decks with fenders in an effort to cushion the impact wherever it might occur. One of the tugs managed to swing the stern of the refugee ship clear with the result that the "Imerite's" midship section fell across our bow. There were cries of anguish from the pilot on her bridge and shrieks from the refugees who no doubt had had enough excitement in their recent lives. Her pilot could be seen standing on the bridge waving his arms and screeching orders. As the "Imerite" scraped past the bow of the "Burma", one of her lifeboats became entangled and was torn from its cradle and left draped across our bows. Chips pounced upon the splintered remains of the lifeboat, carrying away the name board, "Imerite", in triumph. He considered it a worthwhile memento.

Chips, whose cabin was next to ours, was a dour Scot who didn't like Catholics. He referred to them as "Dogans", and when he discovered that I was one, he began to taunt me with questions and remarks which I was unable to answer. When we were at anchor in the Mersey he pointed ashore to a cathedral under construction and said, "The bastards exploit the poor of Liverpool to pay for that." He liked whisky and always kept a bottle under the mattress at the foot of his bunk. The assistant carpenter was a tall Burmese youth whom Chips suspected of helping himself to a drink from the bottle. Because there was no toilet nearby, (ours was two decks down in the steward's accommodation — a long walk!), Chips was in the habit of relieving himself into an empty whisky bottle. He was determined to "turn the tables" on his assistant and substituted a full bottle of urine for the one of whisky. One day he was all smiles as he said, "I caught the bugger!" He had looked at the bogus bottle and found it down two or three drams! Later, I was standing on deck looking at a French passenger ship which lay across the dock from us. She had seen better days and had the appearance of a ship which was not being used for the purpose for which she was built. Someone noticed my interest in her and said, "She is a convict ship. She takes them to Devil's Island and they never return to France!"

We steamed out of Marseilles harbour into the teeth of a gale. We were bound for the Suez canal. Our route took us between Corsica and Sardinia and through the Straits of Messina. A day later, I was on watch when we approached Sicily in darkness. I reported a light on the port bow, but by the time the second mate looked in that direction, the light had disappeared. He laughed and said it was the volcano on Stromboli. I didn't believe him until it flared up again and continued to do so at intervals. It was daylight as we entered the Straits of Messina and the passengers lined the rail. The town of Messina was close enough to see signs which read in large black letters, "Il Duce" and "Mare Nostrum" — the Italians considered the Meddy as theirs.

Meeting another company ship was an event which brought people out on deck if it occurred during the hours of daylight. The mates consulted the Henderson Line schedule and knew with some accuracy when and where we would meet. A smudge of smoke appeared fine on the port bow and soon the tall black funnel and white super structure of the "Amarapoora" rose above the horizon. Course was altered slightly to bring the ships closer and the captain told the mate to get the apprentice on watch up on monkey island (upper bridge) with semaphore flags. He may have heard that I had been practising signalling by Morse Code and Semaphore Flags. When I was ordered to stand up on top with the flags, my heart sank and I began to feel uncomfortable, realizing that my proficiency was not up to expectations. The senior apprentice, who no doubt foresaw what would happen and probably wore a nasty smirk on his face, stood beside me with a message in his hand. The "Amarapoora" drew closer and it was clear that another apprentice aboard her was going through a similar ordeal as his tiny figure could be seen standing on top of her bridge. The two ships travelling at 12 knots would pass each other too quickly for very much exchange of information via flags. When Turnbull estimated that signals could be read, he told me to begin and I waved the flags in the prescribed manner to announce the beginning of a message. The text was the usual one between vessels: "Captain Lusk to Master" followed by words of greeting, weather experienced, and ending with, "Bon Voyage". I started off well enough, fluffed a word and had to repeat it. I was beginning to think that things were going well, when a sudden, unexpected blast of the ship's whistle threw my concentration completely off and the next few words were badly bungled. It was customary for company ships to exchange whistle salutes but nobody had told me about this. Before I could gather my wits to complete the signal, it was evident that the captain was very displeased, and Turnbull was ordered to take over before the "Amarapoora" got out of range.

News of my ineptitude reached the quartermasters, men from the Hebrides, who then found a nickname for me. Turnbull was disliked because of his cockiness, Greenall was recognized as a promising boy, and then there was me! So we three became known as "Know-all", "Greenall" and "Fuck-all!" Indeed, there were times when I was addressed as such which did little for my self-confidence and soon my dislike for Turnbull turned to hatred. One evening, matters came to a head when he called me a "useless bastard" and I grabbed him by the throat. We fell to the deck, each trying to deliver a telling blow, but the commotion caused by this unseemly scuffle brought one of the Mates to the scene and we were soon separated and told in no uncertain terms to go below. I suffered a thick lip but Turnbull had a bloody nose which gave me some satisfaction!

The steam reciprocating engine was a wondrous thing to behold. I had seen this monster in silent repose when the ship was in Glasgow, and I could hear the swish and clumping sound coming from below and wanted to see the machine in action. The 3rd engineer, a hefty Scot, invited me down to the engine room. It was a thrilling sight with the pistons thrusting mightily to turn the crankshaft which flashed round at about 60 revs a minute. It was a triple expansion engine of about 3,000 h.p. powered by steam at a pressure of 240 lbs. per square inch, which was sufficient to push the ship at 12 knots. A blast of hot air enveloped us as we entered the stokehold where a dozen firemen were tending the furnaces. They were stripped to the waists, their bodies streaked with sweat and coal dust. A large can of water stood on the floor from which the men could slake their thirst and next to it stood a box of salt tablets to replace what was lost through sweat. Twenty firemen and trimmers were needed on each four hour watch to feed the hungry furnaces which consumed 60 tons of coal a day. Conditions in the stokehold were hellish in the tropics when the temperature would rise to 140 degrees. Some fresh air was caught by the large cowl ventilators on deck but these had to be trimmed constantly into the wind.

As we drew closer to the Suez Canal, the weather became warmer and we were ordered to change our uniforms from "blues" to "whites", (white tropical gear). These items of clothing caused me many problems. Among the required gear my father had bought in Liverpool were two tropical white suits and as he was anxious to cut costs he had chosen the cheapest available. I removed a white suit from the drawer and when I attempted to put in on, I realized what a wretched, ill-fitting garment it was. The cloth was so coarse it could very well have been canvas. It took considerable effort to bend the material in order to get the trousers on. The jacket could have been a suit of light armour and brass buttons had to be attached by means of pegs! The total effect was ludicrous. The suit was so stiff that walking was not only restrained but produced an odd scraping sound like sandpaper on a board! No wonder people laughed but it certainly wasn't funny to me. I was trying to appear like officer material and instead I felt like a sandwich-board man. Our headgear also changed east of Suez. The naval cap known as a cheese cutter was substituted for a khaki-coloured topee. It was useless aboard ship except on a calm day. But there was a strict rule that we were never to appear on deck in the hot sun without wearing this particular headpiece. Sure enough it was blowing hard in the Gulf of Suez as I stepped on deck and much to the amusement of the kallassees my topee went sailing over the side. My father would not have found it so funny as he had paid five shillings for it!

Keeping the white suits clean was next to impossible. Many times, having just put on a white suit, I would hear a whistle from the bridge which demanded my presence promptly. The mate would order me to trim the ventilators. The "Burma" had ten cowl ventilators which turned to allow air to ventilate the cargo holds, (the weather side vents back to wind, and the lee side ones into the wind). I would scramble some 20 feet up a ladder and with both hands grasp the handles. Often the cowl would be difficult to budge and had to be shaken vigorously. My stomach would be pressed against the flange which was covered in black grease and naturally a lot of it stuck to my lovely white jacket! As apprentices we were supposed to have our meals in the main dining saloon (though never at the same time as the passengers) and we had to be in uniform. We hated this. It sometimes meant quite unnecessary rapid changes of clothing when we were hot and filthy from working on deck. One time, after having had to trim the ventilators in my whites, I refused to change and walked defiantly into the saloon wondering what reaction there would be. The pompous steward waved me aside and told me to go to the galley to eat out of sight of the passengers. Because of interruptions to our meal time we would sometimes arrive in the saloon and be told by the steward that we were too late to eat and so would miss our meal.

It wasn't long before both white suits were filthy. There was no such thing as a washing machine aboard ship. It was a question of drawing a bucket of water from the pump, and with a bar of red carbolic soap I would sit on the door sill doing my washing. After some time, the white suits treated in this manner produced results that were comical. The starch had been removed but the creases had a corrugated effect and the trouser length had shrunk so that the cuffs reached midway between my knees and my ankles! The oilskins became a problem of another kind. They too were difficult to get into. Suiting up before venturing on deck in winter conditions took all of twenty minutes, so once we were in warm weather I was glad to throw them in the cupboard. Three months later and back in wintry weather, I searched for my oilskins. The hot, humid climate had reduced them to a black, gluey ball. It took some effort to claw this mess apart. The cloth had been treated with some substance like asphalt and smelt like it. As I pulled it, the cloth tore until finally in disgust I threw it overboard, which is where it should have gone in the first place!

Passengers sometimes needed access to their baggage which was stored in a room in the stern. It fell to me to drag the heavy trunks from a pile as directed by the owners. This baggage was labeled, "Wanted On Voyage". The giraffe-necked ladies and their entourage were particularly anxious to check their possessions, but I was more interested in another group. The Williams family included two beautiful daughters who came and asked me to find their baggage. I was assisted by a kallassee and was surprised when the girls began speaking to him in fluent Hindustani. I had noticed that there was something different about the Williams family. They spoke with an accent that sounded Welsh. They were friendly in a guarded way and I was to learn later why this was so. Being Anglo-Indians, they belonged to a class which was treated with contempt by the white sahibs and Indians alike. These unfortunates seemed to go to extreme lengths to appear as British as possible in their manners and appearance. Being educated they were indispensable to the administration of colonial India. They held minor posts in the Customs, Police, Government and Railways. Indeed, the Government Services would have ceased to function without the Anglos. My friendship with the Williams family was short-lived. Someone had observed that I spent too much time talking and not enough time working, and I was told to cease idling!

There was one job in particular which I did not enjoy. I was ordered to polish the ship's whistle. It was positioned high on the funnel, some 30 feet above deck and access was by ladder. The cleaning material was bath brick and oil contained in a large can which I slung over my shoulder. At the top of the ladder a steel ring was located at the base of the 6-ft. long brass whistle. "Make sure you do it properly!" warned the 4th mate. Knees trembling and sweating profusely, I wriggled up through the steel ring, the can over my shoulder making upward progress difficult. The whistle was a frightening object. There was very little to hold onto and it hissed ominously as a jet of steam escaped from the base. One slip or careless move on the wire leading to the bridge would release a deafening roar and scalding steam. I had been told that the way to clean this monster was to climb up to the steel braces holding it, and stand between it and the funnel. The only way to do this was by grasping one of the guy wires. It was impossible to reach the top of the whistle by merely standing at the top of the ladder. The general maxim at sea when going aloft was, "One hand for the company and one hand for yourself!" But that didn't always apply, and it certainly didn't in this case. Two hands were required and so by bracing myself between the whistle and the funnel, I was able to reach the difficult parts. Removing weeks of salt-encrusted grime meant lots of elbow grease and liberal applications of colza oil. As we were steaming at 12 knots into a head wind it was inevitable that some of the oil was swept away onto the funnel and, even worse, some landed on the newly-scrubbed teak deck below. Half an hour in such a cramped position was bad enough, however my physical discomfort, together with anxiety about the difficult descent plus the possibility of a row when I finished, all served to increase my determination to put a shine on the brute! But it seemed to resist my best efforts and when I eventually returned to the deck and glanced upwards to view the results of my labour, it did not look any better than before.

The 2nd mate had become tired of my presence on his watch so I was put on the 4 to 8 watch and came under the scrutiny of the chief officer. He kept me busy for almost the entire morning polishing brass. The bridge and chartroom on the "Burma" were furnished with clocks, barometers, telegraph, compass binnacle — all made of brass which had to be brought to a high shine. It seemed a great waste of time and energy to put in every day. When working on deck I would hear the shrill sound of a whistle blown by the mate on watch calling me to the bridge. This usually meant one of three things — he wanted a cup of tea, I was to trim the hold ventilators due to a shift in the direction of the wind, or I had to deliver a "chit" to the old man or chief engineer. As there was no telephone connecting the bridge with the engine room, any requests for alterations of speed had to be made by written messages or chits. After being given the chit I was curious as to its contents, and when out of sight I would open it. It usually read, "Compliments from the master, reduce speed to 50 revs." On one ship I was aboard, the master and chief engineer were not on speaking terms even though they sat within a few feet of each other in the dining saloon. If the old man had a message to give to the chief, rather than break the silence, he would send him a chit!

The passage from Marseilles to Port Said had taken 5 days and the prospect of seeing Egypt was exciting. It would be the first really foreign country I had seen and it promised to be an experience very different from any I could have imagined. I stood on the bows of the ships as we steamed up past the breakwater where the statue of Ferdinand de Lesseps stood, his outstretched hand pointing in the direction of the canal he had built. We dropped anchor in a crowded harbour. It was a grand spectacle. Passenger liners, cargo ships and a myriad of small craft vied for space. Bumboats, propelled by oars, darted back and forth across the harbour. Passengers lined the decks of the big white ships which were surrounded by bumboats selling carpets and souvenirs of all kinds. Port Said was where East met West and the buildings lining the water's edge included the renowned emporium of Simon Arzt which provided for the needs of the traveller on his way to the East. Further along was the white-domed Canal Suez Building with the French tri-colour flying. The Eastern Exchange Hotel overlooking the Mediterranean was the favourite watering-hole for Europeans and Egyptians who could afford to pay three times what whisky was worth elsewhere. A tree-lined road ran along the waterside on which horse-drawn gharry carts competed for space with cars and pedestrians. Many of the men wore red fezzes and the women were dressed in voluminous robes with their faces covered in veils. The sound of hawkers touting their wares to British Tommies, the blaring of car horns and raucous shouting from the boatmen mingled with the toots from ships, big and small, created a cacophony of noise. It was a rousing introduction to the gateway of the East and I longed to step ashore, but once again, shoreleave was not authorized!

The company sometimes hired an Egyptian watchman while the ship was in Port Said in an attempt to stop the theft of ship's gear. Often the watchmen were scoundrels. I heard about the scruffy individual who went aboard one Henderson Line ship and approached the chief officer and assured him that he was a very good watchman and he had a letter of reference to prove it. The letter was written in English on the notepaper of a well-known shipping company and signed by the chief officer. It read, "The bearer of this letter, Achmed Abdulla, is an unreliable blackguard, a thief and a liar. Therefore I have no hesitation in saying that under no circumstances should he be employed as a watchman." Brass fittings were apt to disappear. The brass dogs that secured ports were easily removed. One of the mates was lying on his settee when he heard a sound from the open port above his head. An arm was reaching in to unscrew a dog. The mate was quick enough to slip the chain off the heavy port and it fell on the would-be thief's arm. A popular story concerned the mate of a ship in Port Said who was upset by the disappearance of several brass sounding pipe caps. He called the labour foreman and complained about this apparent dishonesty. While the foreman was protesting his innocence he unscrewed a sounding cap with his bare toes and walked off with it held in the ball of his foot!

I was put to work with the other boys under the supervision of Chips to assemble the large searchlight on the bow. Most ships hired searchlights from the Suez Canal Company but Paddy Henderson's, being a parsimonious Scottish firm, carried their own light. The canal was 84 miles long and for most of its length, ships could not pass without one being stopped and secured to the bank. Homeward-bound passenger ships, tankers and naval craft had priority over us and there would be frequent stops. A small boat, manned by natives, was lifted aboard and suspended over the ship's side in readiness for when the ship had to be tied up. The canal pilots were French, German and British. They were highly-paid and considered themselves among the nautical elite. Even without the widespread use of ship-to-ship radio, the movement of traffic went remarkably smoothly. This was achieved by a series of signal stations situated along the banks of the canal. As we proceeded along the canal the pilot would scan the masts to see what signal was flying and would thus learn about oncoming traffic.

It seemed strange indeed to be steaming through this narrow ditch cut through the desert with an endless vista of sand on both sides. A railway ran parallel with the canal and it was a grand sight to watch the steam locomotives come rattling down the track right alongside us. Half-way through the canal at Ishmalia we changed pilots and by that time it was dark. I was sent onto the bows of the vessel with a grumpy carpenter who was in charge of the light for the entire transit of the canal. He was anxious to sneak away for a break and explained the workings of the light to me. My job was to keep two carbons at a correct distance apart. I peered through a small, smoked-glass window. The bluish beam of light was directed on the banks of the canal, and orders from the bridge directed me to put the light where ever it was most needed. A bright light in the distance indicated a ship travelling in the opposite direction. The ship was stopped, the boat was lowered over the side and rowed to the bank. The crewmen scrambled to the shore to take the ship's lines and secure them. The approach of a large passenger ship was an impressive sight — a great bulk of over 20,000 tons, a black hull surmounted by a white super-structure and two large funnels. She proved to be the "Mooltan", a P & O liner homeward-bound from India. She

P.O Liner "Mooltan" in Suez Canal, 1938

made a strange, rustling sound as she came alongside and passed so close one could hear the passengers chatting on deck. She was followed by several lesser vessels and as their passage took all of half an hour, it meant a long night for the carpenter. He had made many Suez Canal transits and was not in the least impressed.

By the time we reached the Bitter Lakes it was midnight and by then my watch was over, but my excitement exceeded my weariness and I remained on deck for the duration of the trip through the canal. The canal ended at Port Tewfik which seemed a pleasant town with its tree-lined streets and the lights of Suez twinkling in the distance. As we headed down the Gulf of Suez the temperature rose dramatically and another tedious job was added to my morning duties. The passenger decks were fitted with canvas shades which had to be lowered at daybreak and rolled up at dusk. As our general direction was southerly the morning sun was on our port side but by the afternoon, the starboard side was the hot side and the shades were lowered while the port ones were rolled up. The upper class, when booking passage to the East, would stipulate their preference by insisting that their cabins were "posh", i.e., Port Out, Starboard Home, hence the most likely origin of the word. By now, Chips had assembled the swimming pool on the after-well deck. It was no more than 10 feet wide and 6 feet deep but it was always popular with the passengers. We were not allowed to use it at all, but did so when none of the officers were looking. When on the 4-8 watch it became my job to fill the pool in the morning and drain it at night.

Port Sudan was the most important port in what was then the Anglo-Egypt Sudan. The pilot took us into the harbour where we dropped anchor to wait until a German ship had cleared the dock. The company's Greek agents were Cartimichaelos and Darke whose representative came aboard with mail. A cluster of white buildings under a fierce sun lined the water and in the background was a treeless plain with bluish-coloured mountains in the distance. When we were alongside the dock several officials came aboard but there were no bumboats or traders selling their wares. The Sudanese people had a very different appearance from the Egyptians, especially the workers who came aboard to unload the cargo. These were tribesmen from the plains, tall and dressed in tattered clothing, but their most striking characteristic was their long, bushy, matted hair which hung down to their shoulders. A bone skewer was stuck into this mass and was frequently used to probe and scratch. The British were to respect and fear these warriors who had a reputation for ferocity in battle and were the only men to break the British line during the siege of Khartoum. Because of their outlandish appearance, the British Tommies called them "Fuzzy Wuzzies". They were recruited to work aboard ship because of their ability to withstand the heat, and they relished the work, performing feats of strength which belied their scrawny physiques. I was fascinated by the "Fuzzy Wuzzies" and the way they handled the cargo with such apparent ease. They chanted as they worked. I went to get my camera for a picture but Greenall warned me against it; he'd had his camera smashed during the last trip when he snapped a picture of a group of them. They regarded the "magic box" as containing an evil spirit!

Wild tribesmen driving the winches on the "Burma" in Port Sudan in 1937. These men were recruited from the plains and were renowned for their strength and endurance. Men of this tribe broke the British line during the siege of Khartoun in 1885. The British Tommies called them "Fuzzy Wuzzies" because of their long hair.

During our time in port most of the passengers remained aboard and in an effort to remain cool, jumped into the ship's swimming pool, even though the water was a soup-like 95 degrees ! On leaving Port Sudan we headed down the Red Sea and in spite of the breeze, the heat was terrific. The electric fan in our cabin stirred up the torrid air and a chute was fitted into the port hole to catch any breeze. "It is worse up in the Gulf", said the 4th mate who had been in tankers. We passed the island of Perim, a lonely outpost of Empire with a few radio masts sticking above the sand. Apparently it was of strategic value to monitor the ocean traffic. On Sunday, March 17th, 1937, there was Divine Service conducted by one of the passengers and held in the saloon. I told the mate I could not go because I was a Catholic. He seemed taken aback at first, but then said that I must go to the fo'c'sle and toll the bell. This I did with some feelings of embarrassment when I saw two mates on the bridge laughing!

Sunday was also inspection day. We had to completely clear our cabin of everything moveable. Our mattress and bedding was placed on No. 3 hatch. The blue counterpane bore the company colours and had to be folded correctly. As soon as we saw the old man, the chief officer and chief engineer approaching, we would line up quickly and stand at attention. The captain gave us a stern glance in reply to our, "Good morning, Sir!" No pleasantries were exchanged. They would then walk inside our accommodation where we knew that fingers would be run along the edges looking for dirt or dust. On one of these inspections a very "un-nautical" magazine was discovered. The mate picked it up and flourished it like a trophy before consigning it to the deep! This was followed by a brief sermon on morals. But there were times we could have fun. When the officers and passengers were out of sight, we would sneak down to the afterdeck, discard our clothing and jump into the pool. A problem arose for me when I became careless about removing salt water from my skin. This was because our bathroom and toilet were some distance from our accommodation down on the main deck, and to bathe in fresh water was not always an easy operation. I contracted "prickly heat", a skin rash which caused acute itching. It was a common scourge of the East and the treatment was a liberal application of calamine lotion.

I was beginning to feel that in spite of a bad start, I was becoming more useful, pulling my weight, and able to perform in a more seaman-like manner. So when the mate ordered me to lower the outriggers I jumped to it with alacrity. The outriggers were made of heavy steel bars forming a triangle, which were lashed to the shrouds of the foremast when not in use. They were lowered for port use to support arc lights to illuminate the deck. I climbed the ratlines, (ladder), halfway to the cross trees and began to release the lashings. This was a situation where one had to use both hands, the trick being to lean back on the shrouds to maintain balance and not to take too many turns off the lashings, otherwise the rigger would take charge and fall. With sweat dripping from my chin, I gingerly began to slack on the line, and my heart thumped when the rig began to fall in jerks which shook the ratline on which I was standing. Just when I thought I had managed to lower it without mishap, the line jammed and the lift wire went slack. In desperation I took off another turn and the weight took control, the outrigger fell with a terrific jerk to its extremity but fortunately the lift wire held. The mate had watched this performance from the bridge and told me in colourful words to be more careful! After clearing the Gulf of Aden, we passed the islands called The Brothers and shortly afterwards sighted the rugged island of Socotra. I'd heard stories about this rather sinister place. The Indian Ocean pilot (guide book entitled "Indian Ocean Pilot") advised mariners to give it a wide berth as apparently the inhabitants were hostile.

The absence of toilet facilities in our deck house was inconvenient to say the least. The toilet allotted for our use was on the after main deck This meant walking aft along the boat deck, down two decks and into the steward's alleyway. Of course the officers' toilet was just a few feet away but was strictly out of bounds to us. When the need to relieve oneself became urgent and no passengers or officers were about, it seemed sensible to walk to the side of the ship and save ourselves a long journey. One afternoon I did precisely this and thought that I had got away with it, when I heard a cry of distress from two decks below. I looked down to see the upturned, angry face of the ship's nurse, a large, middle-aged woman. I felt guilty because I knew her to be a kindly, understanding person. She had given me a pill earlier in the trip when I was seasick, but now her compassion for me had ceased abruptly! This episode landed me in trouble again when the mate heard about it.

The old man noticed that my hair was too long and ordered me to go to the ship's barber. When he saw me he insisted that not enough had come off and sent me back again. The barber then proceeded to clip vigorously leaving my head shorn almost to the skin. I was so embarrassed by this that I wore my cap continuously whenever I came out on deck! Our course across the Indian Ocean took us 50 miles off the coast of Ceylon, (Sri Lanka). I was surprised to look out to sea and sight outrigger canoes far from shore — each manned by only one fisherman as they rose and fell in the long swells.

During our passage across the Bay of Bengal one of our firemen went berserk, attacking others in the stokehold with a slice bar, a heavy rod used for raking the clinker out of the boiler fire boxes.. He was overpowered but not before he had inflicted some damage to the head of the 5th engineer who had attempted to restore order. One hot afternoon Greenall and I were sent aft to work on the stern. We heard strange noises coming from the ship's hospital. The port holes were open and we peered inside. The fireman lay outstretched, half-naked and manacled to the four corners of a bed. With eyes rolling and contorted expression he was not a pleasant sight. When the ship reached Rangoon we heard that he would be sent to a penitentiary on the Andaman Islands.

Due to heavy rolling earlier in the trip some of the heavy beams blocking our deck cargo had worked loose. I was sent to assist Chips in securing them and was holding a block of wood so he could hit it with a heavy maul. It was his custom to take a nip or two of whisky when the mate was not around and this affected his aim. He swung the maul once and missed the block completely, and on his next attempt I caught a glancing blow on the arm. Painful as it was, no great damage was done, but Chips was far from apologetic and instead accused me of moving the block, which may have been true! I shouted in pain and told him he was a careless bastard. These were fighting words and I expected to receive a battering from this powerful man. To my surprise, he told me to go away (or words to that effect!), and I slunk away to nurse hurt feelings and a sore arm. The mate came to see what all the shouting was about but said little other than to send me to a job elsewhere.

Early on the 25th of February, 1937, we arrived off the mouth of the Rangoon River. We had taken thirty-four days to reach our destination. The pilot, dressed in spotless whites, climbed aboard and we proceeded up the winding, muddy river. I watched in fascinated awe as the spire of the Shwe Dagon Pagoda came into view. Sheathed in gold leaf and standing some 300 feet high, it was one of the most sacred temples in the East. We steamed silently up the river past ramshackle buildings on the water's edge. The river at Rangoon was crowded with ships big and small, including many passenger ships of the British India fleet. An elegant four-masted Bibby liner, the "Worcestershire", steamed past us homeward-bound. When the ship came alongside, an offshore breeze wafted the strange smell of an Oriental city. One of the first men to come aboard was Verraswami, the Dhobi Wallah, (laundry man), who told me that he had served the Henderson Line for over twenty years and wanted my business. He spread a sheet on the deck onto which we piled our soiled whites. His prices were very reasonable especially when he assured me that the grease stains on my white suits, which had resisted my best efforts, could easily be removed. The price was ten annas, (5 cents), for a shirt and twice that for a white suit. He did a roaring business. When my dhobi, (washing), came back two days later it was immaculate. Without proper laundry soap,and using water of dubious purity, the garments had been pounded vigorously against the rocks then left to bleach in the hot sun.

View of Rangoon, 1937, sampans in foreground. The Strand Hotel is in there somewhere - where I went with my ship-mates for an occasional shandy.

I stepped off the gangway onto foreign soil for the first time. Greenall had volunteered to show me the sights. We were immediately surrounded by rickshaw men eager for business. He had more experience at haggling, and the price was set at three annas each to take us to the Mayo Marine Club. This renowned watering-hole for white sahibs stood overlooking the harbour, but life in the city was more interesting and we soon found ourselves in the crowded streets. A number of our passengers had moved into the Strand Hotel which had been built in the late 1800's and was the most imposing building overlooking the harbour. The giraffe-necked women and their entourage made their way back to the Shan States. An article appeared in the Rangoon Times describing how they would make that journey by train and car, finally reaching their remote village by oxen cart.

As in all Oriental cities, there was a great press of people walking, on bicycles, squatting or lying on the pavement. Vendors with trays and carts shouted their business to all comers. Large numbers of dogs roamed the streets; these were pi-dogs and they looked like any other stray dogs. But they were considered dangerous as some of them were rabid and a bite could be fatal. Little was done to reduce their numbers as the Buddhist population believed in the sanctity of all life. The population of Rangoon was made up of four ethnic groups: the Burmese, the Chinese, the Indians — mostly Bengalis who together with the Chinese controlled most of the commerce — and the British of whom few could be seen on the streets. Indeed, most of the whites walking about were from the ships in port. We walked towards the glow of hundreds of lights on the Sule Pagoda, where saffron-robed monks stood accepting gifts from the faithful. Some of the monks appeared to be no more than ten years old.

There was considerable tension in Burma. The Burmese were becoming increasingly restless under British rule and sided with the Japanese in the following years. After Japanese occupation they realized that they were far worse off than they had been under the British. There was also resentment against the Chinese who controlled much of the economy and against the growing population of Bengalis who performed most of the labour.

Once the ship had been unloaded, a process which in those days took several days, she was moved and secured to buoys in mid-stream. Barges came alongside with about 5,000 tons of sacked rice bran which was to be loaded. About 100 Indian coolies swarmed aboard and there was much shouting and pushing to reach the best vantage spots to work. One figure stood out among them. Mr. Dashwood was a tall, angular Anglo-Indian, dressed in khaki and armed with a long bamboo cane. He seemed perpetually angry and his shouts rose above the rest as he let everyone know he was the labour foreman. When his charges did not move quickly enough for his liking, he stormed among them swinging his stick. He hit the men repeatedly on their backs and legs. It was considered a normal method for inducing the men to work and did not appear to cause physical damage. The sacks were stowed in neat rows in the holds. After one row was completed the beaters were called. For some reason most of these were muscular Burmese, whose bodies were almost completely covered with tattoos. Armed with heavy wooden pads at the end of a stick they pounded the sacks until they were flat. Five or six men pounding in unison while chanting a shanty added gusto to the work. This resulted in a more compact and heavier load. I was kept busy taking temperatures by sticking a long thermometer into sacks at random. If the sacks got too hot there was extreme danger of spontaneous combustion.

Now that the passenger decks were deserted, there was an opportunity to maintain the teak decks. Beautiful as these decks were they required constant upkeep. A section was roped-off and we boys were put to work removing the pitch and oakum from the planking, being very careful not to damage the wood in the process. Then we rolled strips of new oakum and hammered it into the seams with a caulking iron. Meanwhile, Chips had brought the pitch pot to a boil and began to fill the seams. The "Burma" had teak decks from stem to stern and these were kept clean in a novel way. When at sea the deck crew were up before dawn washing down the decks, sand was sprinkled over a section, and a gang of kallassees would squat down in Eastern fashion and scrub the deck with coconut husks. One day I incurred the mate's wrath when, painting the lifeboat station numbers on the bulkhead on the shade deck, I carelessly dropped a few spots of red paint onto the deck.

After ten days in port the ship was fully loaded. Besides bran, there were bales of wax, small sacks of very heavy wolfram, hundreds of tons of lead ingots and thousands of teak wedges for use on British rail lines. Several large teak logs floated alongside and these were stowed on deck. While we were loading, a smart white launch came alongside. A short man of advanced years stood on deck, wearing a white suit and an outsized topee which had been specially designed for him. He was Captain Rushall, the company superintendent in Rangoon, and he had come to see the master. He was the object of some ridicule because of his appearance, and it was said that though he was close to eighty years of age the company was reluctant to retire him. He had lived in Burma for many years and had no desire to return to Scotland.

I heard stories about men who had "gone native" in Burma. They had married local women and completely abandoned western ways. They were despised by their compatriots and for this reason lived in remote areas up in the hill country. Wearing lunghis, (native dress), bare-footed, bare-chested and very brown from sunburn, it was difficult to determine their origin until they spoke their native tongue, English. There were white sahibs who loved Burma and whose wives hated it. It was said that the climate was hard on white women. Often their lives were miserable with husbands away in the hinterland on long tours of duty. They had nothing to do and only those with strong characters could take it. Utterly demoralized and homesick, the memsahibs would have the servants pack up and they would board a homeward-bound steamer.

On the day of our departure, a large, steam river boat came alongside with our passengers. Most of them were government officials, tea traders, teak merchants and employees of the Irrawaddy Flotilla Company, accompanied by their families. There were children travelling alone; they were being sent to England to be educated. There were tearful good-byes as they stood on deck waving to their parents. Poor little beggars, they were off to the homeland which in most cases they had never seen, to be parted for months, perhaps years, from their parents.

One of the most stately ships in the harbour was the British India Company passenger liner, the "Sir Harvey Adamson". She was a small vessel of about 2,000 tons on the run between Rangoon, Mergui and the Tavoy Islands. She would sweep by majestically, flags fluttering in the breeze, her decks so crowded that some were standing on the rigging. She was a beautifully-proportioned ship, her masts and funnel raked back in the style of early yachts. She was popular with passengers because the atmosphere aboard was not as stuffy as on the bigger B. I.

boats. Shortly after the war the "Adamson" sailed with a full load of passengers for the Islands. She was never seen or heard from again.

The voyage home was relatively uneventful except for one commotion in the steward's department. The galley which prepared European food was located on the main deck at the after end of the accommodation. The process of delivering dishes from there to the passenger dining room was a lengthy one. They had to be taken up three decks and then carried the length of the midship accommodation. A procession of white-coated Indian stewards bearing silver dishes hurried along the alley ways under the watchful eye of the butler. He in turn was watched by the chief steward. Dinner aboard the Henderson Line ships was considered the social event of the day. The ladies appeared in their fashionable dresses and the burra sahibs, (V.I.P.s), trotted along in their evening wear complete with cummerbunds. They sat in order of their importance around two dozen tables with the stewards hovering over them. On this particular occasion, the chief steward was distressed because the soup had not yet arrived. He sent the 2nd steward to the galley to find out the cause of the delay. Meanwhile, the galley was in turmoil. The soup had been upset by some clumsy fellow and was washing about the deck. The bare-footed cooks and topazes did what to them was the only sensible thing to do. Gathering up mops and rags, they soaked up the soup and wrung it back into the pot. By the time the 2nd steward reached the galley, the soup had travelled along another route to the dining saloon, and before long was being served to the unsuspecting passengers! The fare aboard British ships was such that something amiss in the soup would not have been noticed.

Four days after leaving Rangoon, we arrived at Colombo, Ceylon. There was a strong south-westerly wind blowing and the seas crashed over the breakwater as we entered the harbour and dropped anchor as there was no jetty large enough to take vessels like the "Burma". Nearby was one of the beautiful, all-white P & O "Strath" boats, which was on the U.K. to Australia run. She was surrounded by bumboats. Her passengers lined the decks, haggling for souvenirs such as ebony elephants, pieces of ivory and wonderful woven mats. We loaded several chests of tea, and I went to my cabin to find some rupees as I fancied buying an ebony elephant. But the 4th mate caught me and quickly sent me down to the hold to watch the cargo.

Crossing the Gulf of Arabia the sea was as calm as a mill pond and while it was intensely hot during the day, the evenings were magical. Although the bows were strictly out-of-bounds at sea, I was in the habit of sneaking up there under cover of darkness to enjoy the breeze of 12 knots made by our progress. It was wonderful to lie flat on the deck and stick my head through the rail, gazing down at the bow waves as the ship thrust through the swell like a gigantic plough. The sea sparkled with phosphorescence and flying fish would dart away from our rude intrusion, skimming the surface to disappear into the night. It was at times like this that I began to realize that life at sea was not so bad after all. There always seemed to be something to look forward to, like the next port, and best of all, arriving home after a long absence.

On March the 14th, we reached Aden and found many other ships at anchor in the harbour. It was an unattractive place. A collection of white adobe houses lay at the foot of completely barren hills shimmering under a fierce sun. The garrison of British soldiers referred to Aden as "a hell on earth". They were there to protect this outpost of the Empire and to discourage war-like tribesmen who were likely to attack the outlying fort. It was rumoured to be a punishment station for Tommies — not surprising since the temperature often rose to 140 degrees with an over-abundance of flies, scorpions and sandstorms. It was not a place recommended by travel books. Bumboats came alongside and I purchased 250 Scissors cigarettes for 2 shillings and sixpence. I intended to give them to my father but was told by Greenall that they were virtually unsmokeable.

When we reached Port Said we were in need of coal bunkers. Coaling ship was a wretched business and the passengers were encouraged to go ashore while it was in progress. Large hatch tarpaulins were stretched out and hung over the side on which the coal was to be loaded in an effort to keep the dust from getting into the accommodation. Two large barges heaped high with coal came alongside. Standing on top of the coal were about 100 Arabs armed with shovels and wicker baskets. Rivulets of sweat and coal dust streaked their glistening bodies as they had already moved the mounds of coal from the stocks of Worms and Company on the shore. We rigged clusters of lights over the side as it was now dark. With much shouting and shoving, the workers lifted two long wooden planks which reached into our coaling port, the doors of which had been swung open. Coaling began. It was a scene which could be likened to a Goya painting. A line of barefooted men, each with a loaded basket on his head, walked up the plank. They formed a line so close together that it became a human conveyor belt. They shouted, pushed and jostled each other. A tallyman stood at the top to count the baskets as their contents were tipped into the bunker. A line of workers ran down the parallel plank to collect another load. About 1,000 tons were loaded in six hours. It was said that this method of coaling a ship was quicker than the mechanized ones employed in Europe. It was less messy too.

Among the most colourful characters to come aboard in Port Said was an Egyptian called "Jock MacKay". He wore a business suit with a red fez and boasted that he could provide anything we might need. A made-to-measure suit could be produced in one day, although it was said that if the wearer was caught in a rain shower the stitching was apt to fall apart. Carpets, leather pouffs and damascene jewelry were his main business. Other Egyptian entrepreneurs with the names "George Robey", "Angus Macleod" and "Tam O'Shanter" catered to the needs of the well-known shipping companies. All kinds of touts would manage to slip past the quartermaster on gangway watch, to perform sleight of hand tricks for any gullible passengers. The best known of these were the "gully gully boys". One of them would squat on deck and place three cups upside down before him and move them about to show that there was a chick beneath one cup. Onlookers were invited to guess which cup concealed a chick and to back this with a few piastres. They were always wrong.

Even pimps got aboard, soliciting business for peep shows and the "nicest girls in Port Said." Strange things happened in Egypt and I was told the story of a certain master of a ship about to transit the canal. He was standing on the bridge and waiting impatiently for a pilot. Finally, he blew the ship's whistle to vent his frustration. A pimp approached and called out, "Hey mister! You like a nice girl?" The furious master shouted, "No, I want a fucking pilot!" to which the pimp replied, " O.K. mister, take a little time, but can do!"

A white troopship arrived and anchored near us. She was the Italian "Leonardo da Vinci", her decks crowded with soldiers bound for Abyssinia where a very nasty war was going on. I was surprised that such a large vessel could take a considerable list due to most of the soldiers standing on one side. The run through the Meddy took us between Sicily and the coast of North Africa and past the Italian island of Pantelleria on which there was a large penitentiary.

Our first port in Britain was a spot near Tilbury at the entrance to the Thames where the Customs men came aboard and began to search the ship. I was woefully ignorant about any limits of such items as liquor and tobacco and became alarmed when, at this late hour, Greenall quite casually asked me whether I had anything to declare. I told him that I didn't know what he was talking about but said that I had 250 cigarettes. He told me to throw them over the side or hide them immediately. It seemed an awful waste but I had visions of being placed under arrest and broke into a cold sweat. I reached my cabin as the Custom Officers were searching the officers' quarters. Minutes later, one of them came in and began opening drawers and looking under bedding. When his back was turned, I deftly moved the box of 'Scissors' to a place he had already searched. He mustn't have noticed the sweat on my face and to my intense relief, made a chalk mark on my door to show that the search was complete.

I was not so lucky after my second trip on the Burma. My father asked me to bring back some Burmese cheroots which he had heard were of high quality. A packet of 100 cheroots could be bought for about five rupees. I picked up two. The day before our arrival in London I became apprehensive about this as I had exceeded my allowance.and had to find a good hiding place for them. The flag locker on the bridge seemed a safe place from prying eyes. I removed one of the code flags from its pigeon hole, inserted the packet, replaced the flag.and hoped for the best. But the customs men were a canny lot and were on to such tricks and one of the first places they searched was the flag locker. Because the bridge was the third officer's responsibility suspicion immediately fell upon him. Angrily protesting his innocence he came bounding into our cabin and demanded to know who the idiot was using his territory to evade the customs. The cheroots were confiscated and I only got off the hook because the customs man who found them struck a deal. He would not report my transgression if he could keep the cheroots! Smuggling was considered a sporting event among seamen. It was innocent enough and I never heard about anybody making a profit from the sale of tobacco or liquor. It was for our own use ashore or to pass on to family and friends. But the smuggling of drugs was another matter. I once watched zealous Customs Officers moving a heap of coal in the stokehold looking for opium!

I was anxious to try and get some shore leave. Nothing seemed certain but I was told that I might be given a few days off when the ship reached Liverpool. There was no such thing as entitlement. The granting of leave was entirely in the hands of the mate. If he thought a boy deserved it and the needs of the ship were not sufficiently pressing, then we would be told to go home for a few days. As we were close to Dover, Greenall was told to go home, and when we reached Liverpool I was allowed to leave for five or six days leave. I felt sure that the mate was relieved to see me go! I had received news earlier that my father had sold our house in the Midlands and moved to Buckfastleigh in Devon where he had friends. He was helping a lady friend run a large guest house. I enjoyed seeing my brother and sister again and catching up on the family news. After a few days I returned to the "Burma" to find that Turnbull, the senior cadet known as "Know-all" had left the ship to go up for his certificate.

August 6th, 1937, was my 17th birthday. I had made two trips aboard the "Burma" and we were in Antwerp discharging ore concentrates loaded in Rangoon. We lay in the oddly named Siberia Dock and to reach the city meant a long walk on a warm afternoon. But it was worth it. What a pleasant and interesting place it was. I visited the medieval cathedral, strolled along tree-lined boulevards and sat outside a cafe eating ice cream. I noticed that a crowd had gathered farther up the street and smoke was billowing from the upper storey of a building. I walked closer to the edge of the crowd. Flames were shooting out of the windows, glass crashed onto the pavement and there was shouting which seemed to indicate that people were trapped inside the building. I had no wish to stay any longer and made my way back to the ship.

My visit to Antwerp was memorable for another reason. Before we were allowed to steer the ship, we had to be able to "box the compass" which meant understanding the quarter points. The compass card was graduated that way and if, for example, the helmsman was ordered to steer north-west by west a quarter west, he had to know which way to turn the wheel. I had studied this and felt confident that I was competent to steer as I had taken the helm on several occasions in open waters. When the "Burma" steamed down the River Schelde bound for London, I was ordered to relieve the quartermaster at the wheel. I stood with my eyes glued to the compass and things appeared to be going well until we approached a bend in the river. The pilot ordered a change of course. I misunderstood him and began to turn the wheel in the wrong direction. This caused a commotion and I was hastily removed from the wheel. It took me some time to get over this blunder, and it wasn't until I was aboard the "Mandalay" that I was able to steer again.

After my first trip, when the "Burma" was in Glasgow, I saw a medium-sized passenger ship lying ahead of us. She looked interesting and I went aboard to take a closer look. She had just been completed and was the pride of the City

Line fleet of ships. Her name was the "City of Benares" and she was destined to become a war casualty and the centre of a bitter controversy. She was a cargo-passenger ship of about 10,000 tons and her twin funnels gave her a distinctive appearance. She was built for the India trade, and as I walked along her fine teak decks and peered into her luxurious accommodation, I envied the men who would be taking her to sea. During the blitz on British cities early in the war, the government decided to evacuate children to safety in Canada and the U.S.A. The "City of Benares" was among several ships chartered for this purpose. In the winter of 1941, she sailed from Liverpool with over 100 passengers most of whom were evacuee children. Being a medium-speed ship it was considered safe to send her across the North Atlantic without an escort. She was about a third of the way across when she was sighted by a U-boat and torpedoed. It was at night, the weather conditions were terrible, a heavy sea was running and the ship immediately took a heavy list. This resulted in some panic aboard. But there was great heroism among the children some of whom had been injured in the explosion. The crew had difficulty in launching the lifeboats because of the list and of the few passengers who did get away, many died of exposure. Almost 100 children lost their lives, and when news of this tragedy reached Britain there was an outcry of criticism as to why the ship had been sent to sea without a naval escort.

I made two more voyages on the "Burma". My third and last voyage was different from the previous two. For some reason she was withdrawn from the regular run to Rangoon and suffered the indignity reserved for a tramp ship. She was loaded with a full cargo of coal bound for Rangoon and Akyab. We felt sad as we watched coal dust settle on the beautiful teak decks which we had worked so hard to keep clean. Our regular crew of lascars were sent to other ships and Malays were sent in their place. They were a very different crew — having lived in Britain they spoke English well and dressed like any British seaman. In fact, they had taken part in a movie about the Orient in which extras were needed. They soon made it known that they were unhappy about their accommodation recently vacated by the lascars. They refused to sail unless certain changes were made. Faced with delay, the company agreed to make changes and avoid trouble. Filthy bedding and other material were thrown out and the fo'c'sle was repainted in record time before the Malays, who had meantime been accommodated in the Seamen's Club, agreed to come aboard.

Bob Greenall left and was replaced by John Myers who became my room-mate. He had been at sea for two years and although easy enough to get along with he was reluctant to stand up for what we thought was an injustice. The food which we were given was the left-overs from what the passengers had been served the previous day. It was usually unpalatable. I led a delegation of three apprentices and we picked up our plates and walked up to the captain's cabin. He came to the door and asked me what the problem was. "Please, Sir, we cannot eat this food!" He tasted it, made a face, and sent for the chief steward. The outcome of this was that for a few days the food did improve and then reverted to its previous state!

Akyab was a small port on the coast of Burma near India. It was a quiet and beautiful place. We lay at anchor and unloaded the coal onto barges. The shore was thickly-wooded and the roofs of a few buildings appeared among the trees. I was eager to get ashore after a few months at sea. I also had an infected finger due to handling an old rusty wire. Because we carried no passengers and thus had no doctor aboard, the mate agreed that my injury merited a trip ashore. The one and only launch owned by the Port took me to the landing stage and a short walk through town to the Port Building took me to the Burmese doctor who treated me.

As the launch went elsewhere, I took the opportunity to explore the town. If Akyab appeared to be a Garden of Eden when viewed from off shore, it became less so as I walked about the streets. I was fascinated by groups of Burmese women dressed in white blouses and lungis with their faces covered in a thick, chalky substance. Most surprisingly, all were smoking large cheroots. Any work being done in the streets or on buildings was by Indians and most of the shopkeepers were Hindus. The Burmese strolled about in groups but kept very much to themselves. I heard about savage rioting in Rangoon. The Burmese anger against foreigners in their midst was mainly aimed at the Indians, who they felt were exploiting them. The streets of Rangoon were littered with battered corpses. The Police were overwhelmed and order was only restored when the British Army was called in. The Burmese suffered colonial occupation with less tolerance than most British colonies. In later years, with the fall of Singapore and the swift advance of Japanese armies there was to be a general feeling of jubilation among the people who thought their freedom was imminent. They welcomed the Japanese with enthusiasm who told them they had come to free them from the yoke of British colonialism.

The discharge of our cargo of coal was a remarkable operation as most of the workers were women. In each of the five holds was a gang of about a dozen men who shovelled the coal into wicker baskets which were picked up by women and carried on their heads to be tipped into a large bin which was lifted up by the ship's gear and swung over to a barge alongside. There were about a hundred of these women aboard and it was astonishing how frail they appeared to be, most of them no more than five feet tall. They wore plate-sized cushions on their heads to protect them from the heavy load of coal. It was equally astonishing how quickly the coal was unloaded. While we were at Akyab, reports reached us that there was a cyclone in the area. The old man must have been watching the barometer because he decided to weigh the anchor and put to sea. A day later the edge of the storm passed over us and we experienced nothing worse than a strong gale, but the eye crossed the coast to the north near Chittagong, the sea surged over low-lying land and hundreds of people were drowned. We returned to anchor and watched the passenger ship, "Jalagopal", steaming by. She had lost a lifeboat and her awnings were in tatters.

From Akyab we steamed south to Rangoon to load the usual cargo for Britain, and it was here that I strayed "off the straight and narrow"! I sat in the sampan pondering whether to have a drink at the Mayo Marine club, or seek out something more exciting. I jumped onto the jetty to be met by a cluster of rickshaw men. "Ah, sahib, Mayo Club?" They may have detected some uncertainty on my part and read my mind. "Jigi-jig, sahib, memsahib munta?" This was a moment of decision — the Mayo club or the "way of all flesh"? "Mayo club," I said firmly. We set off at a good clip and I was congratulating myself when the rickshaw wallah interrupted my moment of rectitude with, "Sahib, memsahibs very beautiful." We turned around and headed for Phayre street where the so called "Bag Shanties" were located.

My heart was thumping as we entered a narrow lane between run-down buildings. "Plenty girls here, sahib," said the wallah. I got out and fumbled for some money to give him. As I did so I felt a tug at my sleeve. A seedy-looking fellow indicated that I should follow him along a passage until we arrived at a door. By now I had become nervous, wondering what I had got myself into. Before I could change my mind, he had knocked on the door, a peep-hole opened and I became conscious of being scrutinized from within. The door opened and I was ushered in by a large Indian woman whose saturnine gaze should have been sufficient to discourage me. But there was no turning back. The room had a rather squalid atmosphere; a few wicker chairs and a shabby couch lined the walls and a fan whirred overhead. The madam told me to sit down and asked whether I wanted a drink. "No, nothing," I replied, although a stiff whisky might have bolstered my sagging enthusiasm. The madam called and four girls came from behind a curtain at the end of the room. They were Anglo-Indian and quite attractive in a jaded sort of way. After the sordid business of payment had been settled, I indicated my choice and she led me into an antechamber where there was a bed with rumpled and grimy sheets. By this time my innocent notions of romance had become disillusioned, however the girl seemed determined to go through the motions. It was, after all, a business deal. I began to think that she was quite pretty, that she even liked me and that perhaps I was proving myself as adept as the stalwarts on the French postcards. Then I glanced at her half-turned face. Without my being aware of it, she had lit a cigarette and in a languid manner was blowing smoke towards the ceiling. It was time to leave, and this I did in a hurry, feeling like a man who had just learnt he had leprosy. I thought about the implications of what I had done and was stricken with remorse. Back aboard I met Myers who said, "I didn't see you at the Mayo club. Where did you go?" I tried to look noncommittal and answered with, "Oh, I went to the pictures." He looked at me knowingly and asked, "Was it good?" I smiled weakly and said, "Oh yes, very exciting."

I began to feel restless. Life aboard passenger ships was restrictive. One of the quartermasters, who had taken time to teach me some seamanship, told me, "You won't learn much here. Ask the old man for a transfer to a tramp ship." I waited for an inspection day, and when the old man came to look us over, I asked him for a transfer. He looked taken aback and asked, "Aren't you happy on the

'Burma'?" I replied that I was, but wanted experience on a tramp ship. He said that he would think about it, and he was as good as his word for early in 1938, I was sent to the Company's oldest ship, the "Mandalay".

Chapter 2. The "Mandalay"

I was excited about joining the "Mandalay". A year's sea experience surely prepared me well for a more rigorous life aboard a tramp. I carried my sea bag up the gangway on a warm summer's day in Liverpool. The old ship looked very untidy. Her decks were covered with a deposit of rice bran which was being unloaded. A sling of sacks was being lifted out of the holds, and some of them had burst, spewing bran across the decks. The "Mandalay" was a typical tramp steamer built in Scotland in 1911. She was approximately 400 feet long of a type known as a three-island ship with a raised fo'c's'le, two hatches forward, one amidships and two aft. The midships section accommodated the master whose quarters were a deck below the bridge. The mates and engineers were accommodated in small cabins beneath the boat deck. The "Mandalay" was several years old before the company was obliged to install a wireless set (after the "Titanic" disaster). Two rooms were built on the after end of the boat deck to house this equipment and the operator. We apprentices were accommodated in a cabin on the starboard side, two to a room in spartan conditions, one bunk above the other, a small settee and hardly enough room to stand up in. The door opened directly onto the outer deck, which was decidedly unpleasant if it happened to be the weather side, when seas would crash against the door which, being far from weather proof, would allow water in. Before long there would be several inches slopping about the floor. Being the junior boy, I was given the upper bunk.

The "Mandalay": Built by Dennys of Dunbarton, Scotland in 1911. A 7,000 ton tramp with a crew of 14 Europeans and 80 lascars. I was one of four apprentices and spent two and a half years of penal servitude aboard her. Housed, fed and paid poorly, yet we thought of her as a happy ship.

One particularly unpleasant night in the North Sea we were bound for Antwerp. The ship was labouring in a heavy sea whipped up by gale force winds. It was winter and bitterly cold. We boys were on day work which meant from dawn to dusk. Dog-tired, we were lying in our bunks when we were called to help Chips secure the lid covering the deep tank in No. 4 hold. It had been flooded to give the ship more stability but it had not been topped-up and a free-surface effect existed. The heavy steel lid was secured by many bolts and Chips was tightening them when we arrived. As we rolled, the water sloshed to one side and spurted out in torrents from under the lid. We worked feverishly to secure it. It was cold, wet work. Our course had been altered to ease the rolling and there was some concern until the tank was finally full.

My blue uniform could be stowed away and more or less forgotten as they were very seldom worn aboard tramps. My one and only white suit which I hated had been left aboard the "Burma". The rig of the day was a pair of dungarees and sea boots in cold weather and khaki shorts in the tropics. To enter the saloon we were required to don a shirt. There were four apprentices aboard; the senior boy was Bob Ashby-Todd. He was a tall lad from Glasgow who was the son of a chief engineer with the company. He had almost finished his time and had only one more trip to make before going ashore to take his ticket. He had an air of efficiency and authority without being obnoxious. George Sinclair, whose father was the Superintendent of Scottish Railway Steamers, was a brawny lad of 18 years. He was to distinguish himself during the war when, as an R.N.R. Lieutenant, he almost lost his life in a midget submarine attack on a German warship off the coast of Norway. My room-mate was Peter Gunn, a cheerful Londoner who took the trouble to teach me some seamanship and we became good friends. He, too, went on to what promised to be a distinguished career. After four years of apprenticeship and getting his ticket, he joined the Port Line and soon became 3rd officer. He lost his life in 1942 when his ship was sunk by bombs in the Meddy.

"Popeye" in the rig of the day for apprentices.

The "Mandalay" was a happy ship. The mate was a kindly man called Campbell who kept us busy, and although some of the work was unpleasant, we knew it was necessary and so didn't grumble much. Conditions aboard were spartan. Water was obtained from a pump located outside the galley. We could draw as much as we wanted while the ship was in port but once we were at sea, the pump was locked and the key was in charge of the carpenter, a foul-mouthed, muscular Glaswegian who never seemed to be around when we needed a bucketful. The fresh water tank held 8,000 gallons but, with a crew of 70 men on a long voyage mostly spent in hot weather, the tank soon became depleted. Chips would sound the tank daily and when it reached the danger level, he would report to the mate and from then on we were rationed to one bucket per day.

The lascars were accommodated in the fo'c'sle in the bows of the ships, and conditions were even more cramped and squalid than on the "Burma". Fifty-seven men endured a life which in port was bad enough, but when the ship was heaving and plunging, became abominable. They secured water from a pump on the foredeck. As the foredeck was frequently under water when the weather was bad, the process of pumping water became difficult and hazardous. The lascars had their own galleys in the mast house on the foredeck, the deck crew on one side and the firemen on the other. How the bandaries, (cooks), managed to feed eighty men from such a confined space was remarkable. In rough weather with seas breaking onto the well deck, the steel doors had to be kept shut but the water poured through the cracks anyway. The mates on the bridge would get a strong whiff of ghee (goat's butter), as smoke poured out of the galley when chapatis were cooked.

The master was Captain Roderick McInnes, a large, reclusive man with short, cropped, grey hair. He stood 6'4" tall and came from the Island of Skye. For a man with such large hands, he had beautiful, meticulous handwriting which my discharge book was later to attest to. He was also a man with eccentric habits who very seldom spoke to us. In fact, I was aboard for six weeks before he even acknowledged my existence. Yet I never heard him raise his voice in anger. He would go ashore in the sweltering heat of Calcutta wearing the same dark serge suit that he wore on a freezing day in Glasgow. Very little was known about him for chatty conversation was not his way. He would appear in the saloon for meals, but we apprentices were never allowed in at the same time except for Christmas Day dinner. On that occasion he would sit solemnly at the head of the table in silence. Afterwards, we boys were summoned to his room in a group; he would meet us at the door, shake hands with the words, "Merry Christmas, boy," and that was it for the year! It was not that he was unfriendly; he was a quiet man of few words, and we respected him because we knew that he was a fine seaman. So far as anyone knew the only relative he communicated with was a sister in Southern Rhodesia.

While the ship was still unloading and the weather was fine we were kept busy cleaning the outside decks and even polishing the brass which included the ship's whistle — a job I did not mind as it was not as awkward as the one on the "Burma". The "Mandalay" was no beauty with her large black funnel and generally nondescript appearance, but we took a certain pride in the ship. The mate, whose job it was to maintain the vessel, would allow us to knock off early if we completed our tasks to his satisfaction. Once the ship was unloaded we sailed for Swansea, South Wales, to load 6,000 tons of coal. All our efforts to keep the ship clean seemed in vain when the first load went thundering into the hold. This was accomplished by cranes lifting rail wagons from the dockside and swinging them over the hatch, while the hatchman armed with a long pole would knock out the pin holding the gate. This antiquated method was not only slow, but also did nothing to reduce the dust which enveloped the whole ship in a cloud. Nobody seemed to care except the ship's crew who had to live in the wretched mess. In the U.S.A., where more advanced coaling methods were employed, the coal was delivered through a pipe lowered into the hold and moved about as desired with much less dust as a result. But this was South Wales; the dockers were a tough breed accustomed to such work. When the coal had been heaped up into a pyramid, the trimmers came aboard. They were a sombre crowd with faces as black as their clothes and only the whites of their eyes shining through the dust. They carried candles and shovels. Most of them had cigarettes hanging from their lips and some were puffing clay pipes. No doubt the tobacco gave them a much needed lift during the long hours of hard work.

It was our job to rig clusters, (4 light bulbs set in a bowl-shaped cover), to provide more light for the trimmers. We tried to keep the coal dust from getting into the accommodation. All the ventilators were removed and canvas covers were put over the apertures and old newspapers were stuffed into every nook and cranny. A paste of flour and water was mixed to stick paper over the cracks. But this did not prevent dust from settling on everything. In the saloon I would look down on a plate of food and run my finger around the rim to remove the dust. It became a great relief to escape the mess by going ashore, but even that was not without some difficulties. By the end of the day we were filthy and if it had been raining, the dust turned into a black slime which was difficult to remove. We would strip off our loathsome clothing, and with towels around our waists, take our buckets to the pump and after filling them, place them on the galley stove to warm. But if the bandari was in a bad mood or there was no room on the stove, we would have to wait and there would be a lot of cursing. Sometimes we were able to draw hot water from the winches by simply opening a steam cock on the water jacket and this would usually produce rusty water which was good enough for a shave. When the water was lukewarm, we carried our buckets along coal-littered decks to the afterwell deck where the washhouse was located. With much shouting, cursing and good-natured jostling we put our buckets on a board which straddled the bathtub. Trying to remove a layer of coal dust from our bodies was not easy. The trick was to always leave enough water to tip over one's head and wash away the carbolic soap. Then we would run back to our rooms to put on what we called our "glad-rags" or shore-going clothes. It was a mark of respectability for us to wear a collar and tie. The collar was detachable, and in order to try and keep it clean it was put in a pocket until we got ashore. A nearby railway station cloakroom provided a mirror where we put the finishing touches to our collars, ties, hair and faces. A pub was never far away from the dock gates of any British port and the nearest provided a pint of beer to remove the coal dust from our throats.

Swansea, like most ports, was a dreary place. Rows of red-bricked houses and the occasional chapel or pub did little to break the monotony. But I always found the Welsh people to be friendly and cheerful. After a pint or two, we felt primed for feminine companionship and on one occasion we walked into a dance hall as we felt that the sort of girls who frequented pubs were not the sort we wanted to meet! Alcoholic beverages were not available in dance halls but in spite of this they could be quite lively. Sometimes, animosities sprang up when the local lads resented the invasion of boys from the ships in the dock, and as there were usually 15 or 20 ships in port they represented a formidable force. It was the blonde-haired Scandinavians who seemed to attract the best-looking girls, and occasional fights would break out, but in a crowded hall thick with tobacco smoke and the din of dance music supplied by some colliery band, nobody would take much notice. The males tended to gather in groups discussing the merits of the girls, who, if they were not dancing, stood apart, and who, no doubt, were making similar observations about the boys, and there was much giggling and laughter. I plucked up enough courage to ask a girl for a dance. To my surprise, she accepted. Her name was Doreen and we shuffled and stumbled about but she didn't seem to mind. She was pretty and spoke with a delightful sing-song accent. She asked me what ship I was on, what I thought of Wales and whether I would like to take her to the bioscope. I was elated at this prospect, but what was the "bioscope"? On my way out, I asked the doorman. "The bioscope is the pictures, man!" he replied with a grin.

The next day, as we worked in the grime and the clatter of coaling, we boys discussed the previous evening. "Winstanley, did you get a date with the little one in green?" "Yes, I did, and what's more, we are going to the bioscope!" They all laughed, and Ashby-Todd said, "That's too bad, Winn. You're out of luck. She promised to meet me, and I'm senior to you and have more experience!" I felt badly about this and went red in the face. I had been anticipating a romantic evening with relish. I vowed not to be put off by Ashby-Todd and I would go and meet my date at the time we agreed on.

But events decreed otherwise. Loading had reached a point where the ship was almost down to her marks. As each hold was filled, hundreds of hatch boards were placed across the beams. We laboured with the heavy canvas covers, three on each hatch. The cover in best condition went on first, followed by one with more wear, and on top of that was the tattered one. It was surprising how heavy these covers were. There was some boasting and competition amongst us to see who could carry one on his back and run down the deck with it. Peter Gunn was the strongest; he could carry the No. 2 hatch cover, which was the largest, and run without his legs buckling underneath him! Not to be outdone, I bent forward while a cover was lifted by two others and dropped suddenly on my back. This one had been out on deck and was wet, but I had no idea how heavy it would be. I dropped like a stone under it and lay squashed on the deck, much to the delight of the others! "You will have to eat your mush in the morning!" said Sinclair in his Scottish burr.

My eagerness to go ashore to claim my date, regardless of Ashby-Todd, was to no avail. The 3rd mate ordered, "There will be no shore leave. You must carry on covering the hatches as they finish loading. We expect to sail after midnight." So much for any ideas I had of a romantic evening. It was hard work. Once the covers were on, steel side battens were placed in the cleats to hold the canvas in place. Then with Chips in charge and shouting instructions, we banged in the hundreds of wooden wedges. Meanwhile, the lascars, under the supervision of the serang, were busy swinging the derricks inboard, and lowering them into their crutches. By midnight the ship was loaded — we had been on deck and hard at work since seven in the morning with only short breaks for meals. Tired and covered in muck from our exertions amidst the coal, we were eager to get to sea and away from the grime of the coal dock.

Because the "Mandalay" was a coal-burner, as much fuel as possible was taken aboard. No. 3 hatch lay between the officers' accommodation and the galley. This hold was the last to be filled and after it was covered up, several additional tons of coal were dumped on top of it. So much in fact, that it formed a pyramid in the middle, and covered the deck on both sides up to the bulwarks which were over four feet high. This meant that in order to reach the bridge or fore-end of the ship from the afterpart, we had to scramble over a mound of coal. It was bad enough during daylight, particularly when carrying something heavy, but we had reason to curse it on a pitch black night at sea.

It was my job to reconnect the wire which ran between the bridge and the whistle mounted high up the funnel. It had been disconnected to clear the hatch while loading. Dog-tired, I clambered up the ladder holding the end of the wire, and without much thought as to what I was doing, shackled the wire to a bracket and returned to the deck. Shortly after, the old man went to the bridge and grasped the wooden whistle-lever to blow a series of blasts to summon the pilot. As hard as he pulled, nothing happened. The mate was called and a few words were exchanged about the ship's readiness for sea. "Who is the silly bastard who connected up the whistle?" rang in my ears, and I ran up the ladder under a torrent of abuse to do the job properly. It took me a few days to live down that one. Apart from such occasional lapses, I had begun to feel a part of the crew and able to "pull my weight" aboard so that the word "useless" was no longer directed at me!

Once clear of the coast, we steamed south towards Lands End and into the Bay of Biscay. It was marvelous to hear the steady thump of the triple-expansion engine under my feet, each turn of the screw taking us into warmer waters. But the dirty work continued as we shovelled the coal from the holds and threw it into the side bunkers. We toiled on deck and the work became more unpleasant as the ship began to heave about in the swells sweeping in from the expanse of the

Atlantic to the west. In a loaded condition with the engine turning at near maximum revolutions, the "Mandalay" made about 9 knots. At a push in fair weather she had been known to reach 11 knots. Now with a heavy swell, she was making about 8 knots. But no matter; we were on our way and by the time the Rock of Gibraltar came into sight, the coal had been cleared from the deck and we began cleaning up the ship.

There were five engineers and they were housed on the port side; their small cabins had easy access to the engine room. The chief engineer was a portly, friendly man in his sixties, whose main passion seemed to be horse racing which he shared with the mate. During our lengthy stays in Calcutta they would go ashore to bet on the Australian-bred horses. We would be amused by their graphic accounts of how their favourites would invariably lose the race. The chief claimed to have a "secret system" which could beat the odds, but it never seemed to work!

The 1st mate, Mr Campbell, and chief engineer, Mr Whyte, at No. 3 hatch aboard "Mandalay". It was a rare occasion when any of the officers wore a white suit. The mate and the chief loved to bet on the horses in Calcutta. The chief had a fool-proof system but they never seemed to win!

The wireless officer was known as Sparks, a middle-aged man with a flabby face and a taste for whisky. He was frequently under the influence at sea, which was not uncommon for wireless officers whom we tended to dislike for not having enough to do. We resented the fact that once the ship was in port they were free to go ashore for as long as they pleased. Our Sparks took advantage of this and was in the habit of disappearing for days on end; where he went nobody knew, although it was suggested that he would always find a woman to look after him. Nobody seemed to care until the day we were about to sail from Saigon. No one had seen him for two or three days. The pilot was already aboard when someone said, "Where is Sparks?" At that point, a rotund figure was spotted sitting in a sampan as it was rowed towards the ship. He was so drunk he nearly fell off the ladder put over the side for his benefit. It was his last voyage on the "Mandalay".

The deck officers lived on the starboard side. The 2nd mate was a pleasant man called Marsh who spoke Hindustani fluently. I would watch him in earnest conversation with the kallassees; obviously he took a personal interest in their affairs. He had an interesting background having served as an apprentice aboard the "Olivebank", the last windjammer under the "Red Duster". The officers were expected to address the crew in their own language and a handbook was available for this. It was called "The Malim Sahib's Hindustani" and we were expected to acquaint ourselves with such phrases as "pani medallo", which translated as "throw it over the side"! Nobody liked the 5th engineer. He was a large, coarse Glaswegian, who liked to tell us how cruelly the company was exploiting us and that the day of reckoning was near when the oppressed masses would rise under the red banner. He was an ardent communist and we called him "the raggedy-arsed philosopher". None of us bothered to argue with him as he had a bad temper and was strong enough to demolish any of us. Eventually he would give up trying to provoke a fight and wander away singing, "Keep The Red Flag Flying High." He had an antipathy for all things English saying "There will always be an England so long as Scotland's there." He came from the Gorbals which was the worst slum in Europe so perhaps his views were to be expected. His ambition was to visit his comrades in Russia, and as far as we were concerned, the sooner he went the better.

By the time we reached Port Said, the ship was looking as clean and "ship-shape" as an old tramp could look. Our load of 6,000 tons of coal had been consigned to Worms & Co., whose business was the supply of ship's bunkers. We entered the busy harbour and when near the entrance to the canal, the pilot turned the ship skillfully, until we were at right angles to the channel with our stern to the shore. This was known as a "Mediterranean moor". Barges came alongside with a large crowd of "Gyppo" labourers armed with shovels. Unloading was a slow process as the derricks lifted large wicker baskets from each hold, but at least we had less dust to contend with. We were one of several ships discharging coal — our closest neighbour was a German ship of the Hansa line, registered in Bremen. With our increasing worries about imminent war, there was curiosity about the sort of people the Germans were. We looked across at the seamen working on the "Bahrenfels" decks — they looked harmless enough. It was hot working on deck in the blazing sun and when, at the end of the day, we saw the German seamen jumping overboard for a swim we decided that we would do the same. It seemed strange to be swimming among men who might soon become our enemies but we found that there was no animosity between us. There was always a certain bond between men of the sea; we shared a common interest. Several of the German seamen spoke English and we were soon exchanging information as we splashed about. "Where were we bound for?" "What is your Captain like?" Once the barriers had been broken down, we were asked to come aboard for a drink. This was an invitation we couldn't refuse, particularly as there was no beer aboard the "Mandalay"! The "Bahrenfels" was a much larger ship than ours, but it wasn't her size that was so impressive, it was the cleanliness and comfort of her accommodation. German, Dutch and Scandinavian seamen enjoyed far better conditions at sea than their British counterparts. We watched in wonder as our hosts produced bottles of the best German beer, but I was careful not to drink too much as I had to swim back to our ship. The hospitality was one-sided, however. We did not invite our new friends aboard the "Mandalay" as there was nothing to offer them.

As the coal slowly disappeared over the side, we laboured to clean up the ship once again. When the mate was satisfied with our efforts, he gave us a day off and we took the dinghy for a sail. This was an adventure for me, for although the older boys knew how to manage a boat under sail, I did not. We threaded our way through a maze of traffic in the harbour, past the big liners at anchor, until we reached the Eastern Exchange Hotel jetty where the bumboats, hawkers and pedlars surrounded us. We retreated to a more secluded spot where we found an Arab boy only too willing to guard our boat for a few piastres. How pleasant it felt to be away from the noise and dirt of the ship. We reached the sandy beach and jumped into the warm Mediterranean only to find ourselves amongst large numbers of jelly fish of the stinging variety! We decided to explore the town instead. A road lined with palm trees ran along the waterfront and it buzzed with the din of car horns and the noise of the hawkers of brass ware, carpets, spanish-fly, coffee and Turkish delight. Men in shapeless smocks and red fezzes vied with each other to catch the attention of groups of Europeans, most of them passengers from the P & O boat in the harbour. Members of the Egyptian Police in brass-studded, white uniforms and holding truncheons, stood ready to subdue the more aggressive traders. Horse-drawn gharries threaded their way through the crowds driven by wild-looking men swinging whips. When we wandered away from the waterfront the town became dirty and squalid. Groups of ragged children surrounded us with hands outstretched begging for money. The bolder ones, snatching at our clothing, cried, "No father, no mother. Hey mister, you want girl, very pretty girl, very clean?" It seemed funny at the time and we waved them away, but when a group of sinister-looking men came towards us, wanting to show us some of the lurid shows for which Port Said was well known, we beat a hasty retreat. We felt in need of a drink and headed for the exclusive Eastern Exchange Hotel but were refused entry because of our unsuitable attire. We'd had enough of Port Said and returned to the ship.

Once we had transited the canal and were heading down the Gulf of Suez, we only had five days to prepare the holds for a load of salt in Aden. The other boys told me that if I thought I knew what hard work was all about, I was about to learn otherwise. In the sweltering heat of the Red Sea it would be our job to limewash the holds. Once the kallassees had washed away all vestiges of the coal we lowered large drums of limewash into the hold. We rigged stages to reach the higher parts of the hull plating. Working with large brushes secured to the ends of long sticks, we sloshed the mix on as quickly as possible. The mate had promised us that if we completed the job in good time, he would give us a day off in Aden. Even though the "Mandalay" was not a large ship her holds were capacious enough to keep us busy from dawn to dusk and we were hard pressed to finish it on time. We only stopped for meals and because we were covered in limewash, were not allowed in the saloon so we sat on the hatch outside the galley. The only interruption to work was caused when a full drum caught on the coaming as it was about to be lowered. Peter Gunn, looking up from where he stood 40 feet below, received half the contents over him!

We entered Aden harbour and anchored among many other ships, including the "H.M.S. Emerald", a large cruiser. She was here to show the flag and lay close enough for us to observe the spit and polish of naval life. We watched and wondered at the meticulous way the slightest hint of rust was removed from her grey hull. The melodious strains of a bugle would be followed by increased activity on deck. and we wondered whether the Jack Tars had better grub than we got!

The town itself stood on the slope of an extinct volcano and was known as Crater. The hills surrounding it were desolate and barren. The buildings were adobe, bleached white by the sun. The people of Aden were of the Berber tribe who did not take kindly to the presence of foreigners in their midst. The mate gave us a day off, so we went sailing as there was little to entice us in going ashore. There was enough breeze to fill the mainsail and jib, but it was uncomfortably hot in the blazing sun. We were tempted to jump over the side for a swim to cool off but had been warned that there were a lot of sharks in the harbour. We sailed close to a large P & O liner which swept majestically into the harbour. No sooner had she dropped her anchor than a cluster of bumboats surrounded her. Lines were thrown up to the passengers lining her decks and a brisk business began. It amused us to hear the haggling over brass trays, sandals made from old car tires and the notorious "Scissors" cigarettes!

After one afternoon sail we felt the need for a walk ashore. We found a spot amongst the large sailing dhows, secured the dinghy and wandered up a dusty street. A bar of sorts offered lukewarm beer. We sat down amidst a cloud of flies to enjoy our drinks and were soon joined by two sad-faced Tommies. They told us about the miseries of army life and how fed-up and homesick they were. After hearing this we thought that perhaps life aboard a tramp ship wasn't so bad after all. There was an open-air theatre in Aden and as this was something of a novelty, we decided to go. The enjoyable part of the evening was the sheer magic of the warm tropical night as we sat high up on the slope, with the barren rocks at our backs and a myriad of stars twinkling overhead.

The salt was brought out on barges from large deposits where sea water had evaporated. The Arab labourers were a wild-looking bunch, dressed in rags with cloth wound around their heads in a sort of turban. They seemed to be constantly at war with each other, shouting, shoving and slapping until the foreman, armed with a long stick, would restore order. This clamour blended with the continual clatter of the steam winches and we longed to once again reach the peace and cool of the open sea. At last the holds were almost full, the ship was down to her tropical load limit and we steamed out into the Gulf of Aden bound for Calcutta. What a relief it was to put sweltering Aden behind us. A day later, we were off Cape Guardefui at the north east tip of Africa. There was a lighthouse on this point of land in Italian Somaliland and a troop of soldiers was required to protect the light and its keeper from hostile tribesmen. It was the monsoon season in the Indian Ocean and before long we were rolling heavily in a south-west sea and swell.

The only non-European who lived amidships was the butler. On ships with an all-white crew, he would have been known as the steward, but for some reason he was not accorded that rank. He was a high-caste Hindu and did not mix with the rest of the crew. He had never been seen to smile. He had his own cabin near the saloon where he could supervise the distribution of food and being as stingy with it as most stewards, he was always on the alert to make sure we didn't steal food that we were not entitled to. It was six weeks since we'd left Swansea and provisions were running low. The butler was strong on curries; it was a way of treating meat that was a bit "off". A curry once or twice a week might have been all right but when dished up daily, sometimes making its appearance for breakfast as well as dinner, there was cause for grumbling. The bandari made some effort to produce edible food but was thwarted by the butler, who certainly may have been handicapped by the fact that not enough was put aboard in the first place. There was a strong suspicion among us that the butler was "on the fiddle". While it may not have been easy to arrange "short supply" with merchants in British ports where the Board of Trade might query food supplies, elsewhere there was little control of such matters. It was accepted in places like Calcutta that ship chandlers would take their "cut" and pass on some of the profit to the steward. But they were not the only ones to blame for poor food. It was the practice of some ship owners to supply the bare minimum so their dictum became "adequate provisions", whatever that meant.

One day I was sent down to the dry food locker to investigate an unpleasant smell. The cause proved to be some tins of rancid butter which had burst open due to the heat. But what caught my attention were two chests of tea. One was marked "cabin tea", (officers only), and the other, "crew tea"which was little more than dust.! I also noticed several boxes of tinned fruit which was served to the officers, but we never saw it, not officially, anyway. It all served to heighten our dissatisfaction with the quality of the food given to us. One night after a particularly poor supper, the four of us sat on the hatch and talked about food and how we would make up for the lack of it when we got ashore. I mentioned the tins of fruit I had seen in the store. We hit on the idea of helping ourselves to it. On the deck outside the butler's room there was a cowl ventilator which led down to the store room. We waited until we knew the butler was asleep and the deck was deserted. As I was the smallest boy, I was the obvious choice to gain entry via the ventilator. A rope was secured around my waist and I was lowered as quietly as possible. I landed on what must have been sacks of rice. In complete darkness I fumbled about trying to remember the location of the fruit. Finding a large tin, I secured it to the line and tugged it as a signal to pull up our booty. When the tin banged against the side I was sure the butler would be alerted, but the only sound was cursing from the deck. "You idiot, it's lard, not peaches!" Finally, someone lowered a torch and before long we were in our room enjoying our ill-gotten gains.

Calcutta lies 200 miles from the open waters of the Bay of Bengal. It stands on the Hoogly River, one of the tributaries of the Ganges. Pilotage along the winding waterway was a tricky business with shifting sand bars and strong tidal currents, especially during the monsoon season. However, the men of the prestigious Bengal pilotage service were equal to the task. It was considered one of the top jobs in the maritime world and only those with the most impeccable credentials could belong to such an elite group. They were selected from the best shipping companies, and were, of course, European. It was our job to receive the pilot as he stepped aboard, and I looked forward to my first encounter with a renowned Bengal pilot. We couldn't even see the land when we approached the pilot boat and she appeared more like a luxury yacht, gleaming white and over a hundred feet long. A small boat left her side and was rowed across to us by smartly-dressed lascars. They were well-drilled and handled the boat superbly. The European pilot stood in the stern; he was dressed immaculately in whites and looked the very epitome of colonial correctness. The pilot looked up at me and with an air of superiority and disdain at having to board a dirty tramp ship, shouted that the ladder was not enough without proper pilot ropes. He would not come aboard until these ropes were available and I scrambled about to oblige him. He was accompanied by a leadsman, helmsmen, personal servant and a heap of baggage. The leadsman was skilled at casting a line while the ship was underway, and because this was a well-drilled exercise between him and the pilot, the ship's crew did not take offense even though it was seamanship that could have been performed by our crew. The pilot was fluent in Hindustani and in a very officious and efficient manner took command of the bridge. He wore a white topee during the daylight hours and when the sun went down, he called his servant, who appeared with a conventional naval cap worn during the hours of darkness. We thought that all this pompous behavior was amusing and I remembered the story about a dirty old tramp bound for Calcutta which had arrived off the pilot station. The pilot was disgusted by the condition of the ladder hanging over the side and decided to speak to the captain who was a hard-bitten "Geordie", (a man from the Newcastle area). He looked down from the bridge and made the sort of remark expected from a man who feels that his vessel is under criticism. The pilot, somewhat ruffled, shouted, "Do you realize you are speaking to a Bengal pilot?" to which the captain replied, "I don't give a fuck if you're 'Pontius Pilot'. Use that ladder or none at all!"

We proceeded up the river without any delay, passing a stream of traffic coming down river. The largest and finest ships on the coast of India were those of the British-India Company, known as B. I. Boats. They were impressive ships, especially the "Tilawa", a passenger ship of some 8,000 tons. She sported three funnels and because of this was very popular with the Chinese who thought "more funnels, better ship". She was sunk in 1942, torpedoed while en route from Bombay to Durban. 252 passengers and 28 crew were lost.

We passed the town of Budge-Budge and soon the buildings of India's most populous city came into view. Only passenger ships went alongside the wharf so with a cargo of salt we were relegated to lie midstream secured to buoys. We couldn't have gone further upstream as the Howrah Bridge lay ahead of us. The muddy waters of the Hoogly ran so strongly off Calcutta that ordinary mooring lines were not strong enough to hold the ship and the anchor cables were employed. This meant "catting" the anchors — lifting each one and securing them on either side of the ship's bows. The cables were then unshackled and lengths of them were lowered into a barge to be secured to the buoys ahead and astern. I was sent to help Chips on the foc'sle head. He was working feverishly with his special tools unshackling the cable while the lascars toiled dragging the heavy cable across the deck. Under a blazing sun it was uncomfortable work and I did what I could to assist without catching my fingers between the heavy links. The barge was moved to the stern where the second mate and his crew secured two lengths of cable to the buoy. This operation took over four hours to complete and was a good lesson in seamanship.

Once the hatches were uncovered it was surprising to see how much the level of the salt had gone down. This shrinkage was due to the water which ran off the salt and was pumped over the side on passage. The salt caused considerable corrosion and great sheets of rust would form on the hull plating. It was reasonable to think that 6,000 tons of salt could have been unloaded in two or three weeks even with the primitive methods in use. Such was not the case in Calcutta. The "Mandalay" lay in mid-river for seven weeks due to the customs duties levied on the import of salt. Shore labour came aboard, opened up one or two hatches, then large wicker baskets were filled with salt and lifted on deck where an Anglo-Indian customs officer sat at his desk beside a scale. Each load was carefully weighed and noted before being lowered onto a barge. A day's work amounted to only 40 or 50 tons being unloaded then the hatches were covered and work ceased for the day. This was a good opportunity for the mate to send us over the side to chip rust from the ship's side. Standing on wooden stages a few inches from the swirling, noxious waters, we chipped away at the rust for eight hours a day, often distracted by the sights and sounds around us. The river was like a highway during rush hour with hundreds of sampans and large river steamers so crowded with passengers that some stood on the roofs while others clung to the sides. Once, we watched what appeared to be a haystack floating on the water but was actually a barge obscured by its load. Two men stood on the top guiding this cumbersome cargo down the river. Other objects floating by were not so intriguing. The bloated carcass of a cow with several crows pecking at it was revolting enough but when a swollen, blue corpse went bobbing by we almost fell off the chipping stage. I asked the serang about it and was told that a certain sect of Hindus considered the waters sacred and threw their dead into the river. The crows in question were commonly known as "shite hawks". These voracious birds were forever on the look-out for scraps of food thrown overboard. If a seaman happened to be carrying a plate of food along the open deck between the galley and fo'c'sle, a shite hawk would swoop down and grab the food with its talons! On the shore close to where we lay there was a burning ghat, a temple-like building with steps leading down to the river. On occasion, smoke and flames could be seen rising from it when a funeral was in progress.

We were free to go ashore after a day's work but getting there was often quite an adventure. The ship's accommodation ladder took us down to a waiting sampan and after the price had been agreed on, we set off for the nearest landing place about a quarter mile off. The sampan-wallahs were skilled at maneuvering the boats. Standing in the mid-section facing the bow, they would propel the craft deftly through the traffic. The wash from the fast river boats could be dangerous. Once, with four passengers, two in the bow and two in the stern, we were midway between the ship and the shore and were passed by a fast river steamer whose three-foot wash came rushing towards us. The sampan-wallah cursed and frantically turned the bow into the wave. The craft was thrown heavily over and almost swamped but luckily righted itself again. At certain phases of the moon a tidal bore swept down the Hoogly River. One occurred during our stay and all cargo work ceased until it had passed. The harbour master came aboard to advise the old man about extra moorings. These were necessary because some time earlier a ship had been torn from her moorings by a bore which was higher than usual. We waited expectantly for the bore to arrive not realizing that the only sign of its arrival was the wave which ran along the banks of the river. As there were always thousands of people bathing or standing up to their waists in the water, the sudden arrival of a five-foot wave had a dramatic effect. It was not big enough to drown anyone but bowled people over by the hundreds.

I heard that the largest tree in the world stood in the park on the side of the river opposite the city. I walked across the Howrah Bridge to see it. It was a very old banyan tree, the branches of which had grown out to such an extent they had formed a kind of umbrella covering several acres.

If there was one impression that remained after visiting Calcutta it was the press of people. If one looked down any street, it was filled with swarming humanity and the progress of cars, trucks and rickshaws was very slow. I rode in a rickshaw and marvelled at the way the man running between the shafts weaved his way through the mass of people. The rickshaw-wallahs of Calcutta were among the poorest of the poor. They came from the impoverished countryside to the city to find work with companies owning the rickshaws. These undernourished, spindly-legged men had surprising endurance. As I travelled across the city under the heat of a fierce sun, I watched the sweat trickle down the back of the rickshaw man who maintained a steady speed, his bare feet slapping rhythmically on the hot pavement. Gaudily painted and overcrowded buses thundered down Chowringee, the main street. Cows were considered sacred by the Hindus and no effort was made to remove them from the sidewalks where they often lay so it was necessary to walk around them.

It was the beggars of Calcutta who invoked pity. Some of them were horribly disfigured by leprosy and elephantiasis which caused extreme enlargement of limbs. Some had no arms or legs and it was said that deliberate mutilation was practiced to improve their chances of attracting attention. One hot day, I was pushing my way through a dense throng of people when I saw a strange creature darting between people's feet. It was a legless man no more than two feet tall. He was sitting on a trolley which he propelled with his stumped arms. It was not uncommon to see raving lunatics roaming the streets and the populace showed no concern or fear. I wondered what the reddish-brown spots were that lay on the roads and pavements of the city. The chewing of betel nut was widespread; it produced a mild narcotic effect and, although it blackened the teeth, it helped prevent decay. The men working down the ship's hold would pause in their labour to prepare a chewing wad. In the folds of their lungis they carried small boxes containing pieces of betel nut, some arek-leaves and tins of lime. The lime was spread on the leaf, the betel added, the leaf folded into a wad and then stuffed into the mouth. After some chewing, juice dribbled out of the user's mouth and the excess was spat out.

Not far from the Chowringee was the Governor of Bengal's palace. It was not possible to walk beyond the ornamental iron gates but it was an impressive place viewed from that distance. The palace was guarded by men of the famed Bengal Lancers mounted on white horses. Recruits for the regiment had to be six feet tall. They made a splendid sight dressed in their red and gold braided jackets and red turbans their swords glistening in the sun. It could have been a scene from an Errol Flynn film.

Taxis were American Fords and Chevrolets driven with great speed and dexterity by bearded Sikhs. For a European looking for night-life the renowned Firpos Club catered to the pukka sahibs, which meant only those with money, the right dress and manner gained entry past the doorman. As we didn't meet these criteria, the Continental Bar provided a cool drink and perhaps the chance to meet some girls.

When we ran out of money, which was often, the Marine Club offered a swimming pool and a chance to mingle with men from the other ships in port. It was run by a church group. The Padre's wife felt sorry for ships' apprentices who were poorly fed and a long way from home. A few days before Christmas, the old man received a letter from the Marine Club inviting the apprentices to Christmas dinner. We were required to wear our company uniforms, and although we were anxious to partake of what promised to be a better meal than was available aboard, we begrudged having to resurrect a uniform which we seldom wore. About thirty apprentices turned up for dinner and it was easy to tell which boys came from the B. I. ships as they were smartly turned out and even carried their caps beneath their arms. The lads from hard-case ships appeared in rumpled, ill-fitting uniforms and some even wore brown shoes. We shuffled self-consciously into the church hall and sat down at a long table laden with Christmas fare. We were anxious to get started but were asked to stand and join the Padre in prayer, followed by a few words about men of the sea having a special place in his heart. After the meal, we were asked to stay and sing Christmas Carols which seemed quite inappropriate in the heat of Calcutta. Just as we were about to leave, the Padre called for silence and said, "I regret to have to tell you that one of you has seen fit to abuse this hospitality. But if the boy who took several spoons returns them immediately, nothing further will be said." There was a titter of embarrassed laughter and we looked around for the culprit. We would have felt some satisfaction had the thief turned out to be one of the haughty B. I. boys, but it was a lanky, unkempt apprentice from one of the old Baron Line tramps, a ship even more decrepit than the "Mandalay"!

Two ships owned by the Jardine Matheson Company of Hong Kong were regular callers in Calcutta. They were the small passenger ships, "Kutsang" and "Suisang". They were fitted with steel grills on the after end of the accommodation to prevent pirates from gaining access to the upper decks. Piracy had always been a problem off the coast of China and officers were forced to carry arms in an effort to prevent attack. As there were large numbers of Moslems who wanted to make the pilgrimage to Mecca, the ships "El Medina" and "El Hind" arrived in Calcutta to take them to Jeddah. Although they were no more than 5,000 gross tons, they had the distinction of holding a licence to carry 4,000 passengers, about twice the number carried aboard the 80,000 ton super-liner, "Queen Mary"!

After the last load of salt was gone, we slipped our moorings and proceeded down river to the dreaded Kidderpore Docks. It had been hot enough lying in the river but the docks were away from any breeze and like a furnace. Fortunately, loading pig iron for Japan did not take long and we were soon down to our marks. The mate was anxious to have the ship looking decent for our arrival in Japan and put us to work sanding and canvassing the wooden derricks. This meant sitting astride the derrick and removing the old varnish with a wad of canvas. The mate gave us a week to complete the work and since there were ten derricks to clean and re-varnish, we set to work with a will, knowing that if we did it before our arrival we'd be rewarded with shore leave. We competed with each other to be the first to finish a derrick. One afternoon, Peter Gunn and I were working at No. 3 hatch and I saw that he was almost finished, so I put on an extra spurt of energy. Sure enough, I became careless when shifting my position, lost my hold, and fell with my bucket onto the hatch. I had only fallen about six feet — no bones were broken, but I was unable to carry on which did not do my ego any good!

It was still winter in Japan when we arrived at Moji at the western entrance of the Sea of Japan and the surrounding hills were covered in snow. The pilot was smartly dressed in a dark suit and spoke good English. He had been a master in the famous N.Y.K. Line. He told the old man that when he was a N.Y.K. cadet, the captain and most of the senior officers had been British but that after the last war, they had been replaced by Japanese officers. Shortly after we dropped anchor, barges came alongside and gangs of stocky men began unloading. We were impressed by the efficient and energetic way they worked. They wore shapeless, baggy clothing and didn't seem very friendly. Any attempt to communicate was met with a blank expression. There was tension between Japan and the West, mainly due to the "China Incident", and certain unfriendly acts had occurred. We heard that there had been a collision between a Japanese and a Norwegian ship. The Norwegian master had been languishing in jail for eight months and any attempts by consular officials to free him were ignored. We were to experience harassment from officials ourselves when a number of us went ashore on the night of our arrival. As we stepped from the launch onto the dock, we were immediately confronted by customs officers. We were ordered curtly to stand in line and raise our hands above our heads. "How many cigarettes you got?" they asked. Their manner was such that any argument would have been futile. We did as ordered and they emptied our pockets. Those of us who had more than fifteen fags had them confiscated.

I had been looking forward to my first visit to Japan which I had been told was very different from India. The encounter with the customs officers was soon forgotten as we entered a tea house and were warmly welcomed by several charming ladies, dressed in kimonos, who motioned us to sit "Japanese style" around a fire which was recessed in the floor in the centre of the room. We were given hot towels, tea in small bowls and rice cakes. They giggled and smiled at us in a most beguiling way and I tried to tell one girl how much I liked her, but she didn't understand a word I said. It was nightfall by the time we stepped out on the street; a multitude of coloured lanterns gave us only enough light to see a few yards. The wooden buildings were various shapes and sizes. The whole population seemed to be out on the streets and there was a strange clicking sound, made by hundreds of sandal-clad feet. Everyone was wearing kimonos as western-style dress had not yet become popular. It was bitterly cold. People shuffled past with gauze pads covering their noses and mouths; the Japanese were very disease conscious.

Having unloaded part of our cargo, we weighed anchor and steamed into the narrow channel which led into the Inland Sea. The current was so strong that even at full speed, we were only making about five knots. We were bound for Osaka, a day's run at our speed. Our passage through this land-locked sea was a memorable experience. I was on good terms with the 3rd mate and he allowed me to stay on the bridge to look through the brass telescope — a wonderful old instrument, three feet long and made by Barr and Stroud of Glasgow. The ingenious Japanese had made use of every foot of arable land by a system of terracing and irrigation which reached to the top of the hills. Small villages dotted the landscape. When viewed through the telescope, the houses appeared to be so close together that only foot traffic could pass between them. We passed many fishing vessels and ferries. The pride of Japan's merchant marine, the "Asama Maru" hove in sight ahead, and our pilot altered course to get a better look at her. She was a passenger vessel of 18,000 gross tons, and she sped by at over twenty knots. A few years later, this splendid ship was thrown ashore in a typhoon which struck Hong Kong. She was refloated, repaired and put back in service only to be sunk during the war, torpedoed by a U.S. submarine in the China Sea.

Osaka was a large, bustling and prosperous city. As soon as we were secured to the dock, dealers in egg-shell china, silk paintings, ivory carvings and lacquer-ware had established themselves on deck to do business. Even with the few pounds at my disposal, it converted to what seemed a lot of yen and I promptly bought a set of egg-shell china. The main shopping centre was known as the "Dotum Bori". It was utterly fascinating and different from anything I had ever seen before. In the evening the thoroughfare was a blaze of coloured lights, not just ordinary light bulbs but coloured lanterns. This gave it an extraordinary air of unreality, like a dream city, so different from any western city. Very few people wore western dress. Some of the women wore exquisite kimonos, and these restricted them to a short, shuffling walk. The men also wore the traditional, plain kimono, and odd-looking sandals with wooden bars on the soles, which added two or more inches to their height. The clatter of hundreds of sandals hitting the pavement filled the air. People seemed to regard us as curiosities; they were neither friendly nor unfriendly. It was difficult to make ourselves understood as very few people understood English. They were too polite to stare, yet as we walked among them, we were aware that our presence caused a stir but their faces never revealed it. The inscrutable Orient! The port of Osaka was one of the busiest in Japan. I watched a ship leaving the dock, her decks lined with soldiers of the Imperial Japanese Army. They were bound for China where a dirty, unofficial war was going on. Someone remarked that our cargo of pig iron would probably be used to make armaments.

One of the enjoyable aspects of life on tramp ships was that we would often put to sea without knowing our destination. We sailed from Japan in ballast and there were rumours that we were going to Australia to load wheat, or to Hong Kong; either being preferable to a return to the Indian Coast where Henderson Line tramps seemed to spend most of their time. We had been at sea for several hours before Sparks received orders for us to proceed to Saigon, French Indo-China, to load paddy (husks of rice) for ports on the Indian coast. Saigon lay about thirty miles up a winding river and was sometimes referred to as "the Paris of the Orient" with its tree-lined boulevards and sidewalk cafes. But tramps like the "Mandalay" were not afforded a berth near the city, so we anchored about four miles down-river. French Indo-China was also known as Annam, now called Viet Nam. Captain McInnes, never a talkative man, surprised us boys by delivering a lecture about the "temptations of the flesh" to be found in Saigon. "I dunna want to hear about any of you boys getting V.D. No girls allowed aboard!" He asked the shore agent to provide a watchman for our gangway. He had been in Saigon before, but subsequent events showed that these precautions had little effect.

Barges came alongside and we began loading sacked paddy. We were down a hold moving stacks of dunnage wood, which was to be used to protect the sacks of paddy from contact with the steel sides of the holds. It was just getting dark when Chips put his head over the coaming and yelled, “Hey, come and look, the girls are coming!” We dashed up on deck, and in the fading light looked across the river to where he was pointing and shouting, “There they are, a sampan full of whores!” At the river bank, some 300 feet away, a sampan full of chattering girls was pulling out into the river with several others still on shore preparing to do the same. There were about five ships at anchor nearby and the sampans fanned out in their direction. While the sampan-man stood in the stern dipping his oars slowly into the murky water, the madam crouched in the bows watching her charges who could be seen holding mirrors, combs and lipsticks in preparation for business. Fascinated, we watched a sampan cross our bows and disappear from view. As we wondered how they intended to get aboard, several lascars ran up to the foc'sle-head and there was a lot of laughter and shouting. To our amazement, half a dozen, bare-footed, giggling girls clad in black trousers and white blouses, appeared at the bow. They climbed over the rail onto the deck. With incredible agility, they had walked up the anchor cable! We looked across the water and to our amazement saw girls climbing up the anchor cables of other ships. By this time, the mate had appeared wondering what all the commotion was about. He considered this invasion as no serious threat to anyone except us and cautioned us to get on with our work. But shortly after, I happened to be near Spark's cabin where he was standing in his ragged shorts watching the excitement, when two girls came running along the deck as if being chased by someone. As they reached his cabin, he grabbed one by the arm, pulled her inside, closed the door, and we didn't see him again for two days! It was no use pretending we didn't feel envious. Here was Sparks with nothing to do but keep a pretty girl company while we had to work. He was only responsible to the old man who never seemed to venture far from his cabin. However, as mentioned earlier, Sparks finally “shot his bolt” for arriving back aboard in a drunken state and was sacked.

One morning we stood at the rail and watched four warships coming up the river to “show the flags” of their respective countries. One of us ran back aft to dip the ensign. The U. S. cruiser, “Marblehead”, steamed proudly by, her crew, dressed in tropical whites, lining her decks. Shortly afterwards, she was followed by the British submarines “Otis”, “Odin” and “Grampus”. They looked like a school of whales going by. Those who knew about warships congregating in port said that it meant trouble!

Saigon was around a bend in the river and out of sight. One evening we climbed into a sampan which took us to the river bank where some rickshaws were waiting. These rickshaws were different from those in India, having two bars which curved up at the back. We heard the purpose of these was to eject an unwanted passenger. All the rickshaw-wallah had to do was let the shafts go and it tipped backwards on the bars and the occupant was thrown out! As our 5th engineer discovered when he drunkenly staggered out of a cafe, got into a rickshaw and lay back in a stupor. When the rickshaw-wallah reached a lonely stretch of road, he suddenly let go of the shafts and the engineer was thrown out.

He was relieved of his wallet and left bleeding beside the road. He managed to stagger into a village nearby and was taken back to the ship. Our own trip was exciting but luckily for us ended well. There were three of us, each in our own rickshaw, and as we entered the busy streets of the city our pullers began to race each other. The wheels of my rickshaw came within inches of the wheels of the other, threatening to spill us into the dust. These fellows were far more reckless than their counterparts in Calcutta and had a lot less respect; indeed they began to mock us with obscene gestures. I began to wonder whether we would reach our destination as we spun dangerously round the corners.

Finally, we arrived at a large cafe-bar which was popular with seamen as a group of pretty girls were attending the tables. As we sat enjoying cool drinks in the company of girls who wanted us to pay for drinks we couldn't afford, the cafe began to fill up with British "Tars" and American "Gobs". They stood around in groups and as soon as the beer began to take effect, voices grew louder, insults and threats were exchanged and the room echoed with cries of "Yankee bullshit!" and "Limey bastards!" Pushing and shoving soon escalated to punching and wrestling. Many sailors enjoyed a "bust-up" of this sort. Cooped-up for weeks on end aboard their ships, it was a way of venting their frustrations and proving their superiority over men serving under another flag. News of a "rumble" spread quickly and reinforcements from both camps arrived. It was time for us to leave. I was glad that we were not in uniform and thus able to slip away without being identified. Before getting into our rickshaws for a hasty exit, we glanced back to see over a hundred men fighting in what had now become a riot. Next day we heard that the French gendarmes had attempted to restore order and went in swinging their batons. This infuriated the sailors, who promptly stopped fighting each other, joined forces and attacked the French!

On our way to India we stopped at Singapore to put one of the firemen ashore. He was an opium addict and was so sick that he died a few days later. Our first port was Calicut on the Malabar coast. It was the place where Vasco da Gama, the discoverer of India, landed. There were no facilities ashore to handle our cargo and we lay at anchor some two miles off where large sailing dhows came out and lay alongside us. I had never seen these wonderful craft at close quarters before, but had watched them sailing into Aden their great lateen sails bulging to the wind. For centuries these vessels had traded between ports in Africa, like Zanzibar and Mombasa, and ports along the coast of India. The only navigational instrument they carried was a compass and it was said that their captains had an uncanny ability to know their way across the ocean. The discharge of our cargo was made difficult by a moderate ground swell, and as the ship rolled, our cargo gear came close to fouling the rigging on the dhows as they plunged and rolled alongside. It was our job to place fenders between the ships to prevent damage.

Our next port was Cochin, a beautiful place. We entered a bay surrounded by lush vegetation. Red-roofed houses sat amongst the coconut palms; it was a scene of tranquillity and I looked forward to going ashore. Any prejudices formed about India and Indians in Calcutta were countered by our experience of the Indians along the Malabar Coast where the people were friendly and helpful. One hot afternoon, the mate let us go ashore early after we had finished a particularly dirty job cleaning the bilges. We walked to the cafe and were sitting down enjoying cool drinks when a young Indian came to our table. He was dressed in casual European clothes and we thought that he was an official of some sort. He told us that he was an officer in the Indian merchant service, that he had a car, and asked if we would like a tour of Cochin. As there were four of us, it was a tight fit in his small Austin. We swayed about as the car ran over bumps and swerved to avoid deep holes in the dirt road leading to a country club on the outskirts of town. It was a splendid place facing the ocean. Here we were introduced to other Indians and sat down to enjoy drinks put before us. None of us were dressed properly for the circumstances in which we now found ourselves and we appeared to be the only non-Indians in sight. We were on our best behaviour, no one was rude enough to discuss Anglo-Indian relations and a good time was had by all. The remainder of our cargo was for Tuticorin on the south east tip of India. Here we were less exposed to the swell than at Calicut and we lay quietly at anchor while unloading into barges.

We sailed from Tuticorin in ballast and after clearing Ceylon, set a south-easterly course for the Straits of Sunda. We were bound for Surabaya to load a cargo of sugar. When we entered the straits I was on the bridge when the 2nd mate pointed to a group of islands on our port bow and said, "That is where Krakatoa blew up. It was once one island and now is three." He went on to tell me that the explosion was heard in Australia and the resulting wave wiped out hundreds of villages and towns on the coasts of Java and Sumatra. It was the greatest volcanic eruption in history.

We looked forward to our arrival in Surabaya as Sparks had told us that the girls there were very pretty. As we entered Tanjung Perak it appeared to be a clean and orderly place. The buildings were painted white with red roofs and the Dutch flag flew over the Harbour Master's building. The Dutch had given their colonial outpost the appearance of any town in Holland but in a tropical setting. It was very different from the chaos and dirt of Calcutta. The Javanese appeared to be a happy-go-lucky people and we were not besieged by beggars as we walked through the streets. Instead of rickshaws, we rode in small taxis to the city of Surabaya, which was about five miles inland. Instead of viewing the temples and bazaars, we squandered our time by drinking too much good Dutch beer. There was much laughter as we admired the girls and, for a time at least, forgot the discomforts of our lives aboard ship. I ended up in worse condition than the other boys for I didn't remember our return aboard except that it was at dawn of the following day. An unsympathetic mate roused us shortly after dawn to chip the rust from the afterdeck. It was not a pleasant job in the blazing sun with a hangover!

The loading of sacked sugar progressed quickly, and I realized I had purchased nothing with what little money I had to show for my visit to Java. But shortly before our departure, a man came aboard with three monkeys for sale. The 4th and the 5th engineers bought the two male monkeys which were apt to bite. They became known as Oscar and Kong. I paid two guilders for a female which I named Fuzzy and promptly hid in our cabin. This did not please Peter Gunn, my cabin-mate, after he discovered the mess she had made on his bunk. We were at sea before the mate knew that the ship's complement had increased by three, but he was a tolerant man and merely told us to be sure the monkeys were our sole responsibility. Peter, too, was tolerant and enjoyed the entertaining antics of the monkeys who seemed to settle down quickly to shipboard life. We fed them as well as our meagre fare would allow. They were Rhesus monkeys, common to Asian countries, with tails as long as their bodies. The bandari did not object to the presence of monkeys appearing at the galley door and would throw them scraps of fruit and vegetables. He gave me a small, wooden barrel which had contained pickled herring. This became a bath for Fuzzy, who would amuse us as she sat in soapy water, splashing like a baby. But Oscar and Kong were more troublesome than Fuzzy. For the first few days at sea, while their owners were busy down in the engine room, the monkeys were given the run of the ship. This was bound to cause trouble and it did. The officer's alleyway had been given a fresh coat of white paint and when the mate spotted both Kong and Oscar with white fur, he feared the worst. The alleyway had to be repainted and the two offenders were banished to the steering flat on the stern. I thought that Fuzzy's behaviour was beyond reproach until one day when Captain McInnes was having his lunch. It was his habit to eat alone and on this occasion he sat at the table with his back to the portholes, all of which were open. A solitary piece of cheese was on a plate in front of him. Always on the lookout for something to eat, Fuzzy had arrived unobserved in the port hole behind the old man. She quickly leapt onto his shoulder, from there onto the table, grabbed the cheese and jumped back to the port via the same route! This caused a furor, particularly as the cheese in question represented the ration for four men!

Surabaya, Java, 1938. I bought a monkey named "Fuzzy". She was one of three aboard which caused some disruption! She was aboard for almost a year but fell overboard in the Bay of Biscay.

Our times at sea were pleasant enough and we found it easy to keep ourselves amused during off-duty hours. We would sit on No. 3 hatch, swapping ribald stories and listening to those who had been at sea the longest telling their stories. Jimmy Sutherland, (who joined the ship at a later date), would tell us about life in the Orkney Islands and how he and his pals would take a boat out into Scapa Flow to look at the scuttled ships of the German fleet.

One night, I was woken from a deep sleep and ordered to take the wheel as the secunny (Indian quartermaster) had been taken ill. As I was on day work and had had little sleep, I was not pleased at this extra duty. It was hot and stuffy in the wheel house and after a few hours standing with my eyes glued to the compass, I became drowsy and nodded off to sleep. Sometime later I awoke with a start and saw that I was 60 degrees off course! The 2nd mate, standing out on the wing of the bridge, had not noticed this lapse of concentration. Perhaps he was as sleepy as I was. Sweating profusely, I eased the ship slowly back to the course. This took about 15 minutes. The 2nd mate must have been perplexed when he fixed the noon position as it showed a strange drift away from the expected one.

We were running low on coal as the furnaces burnt about 20 tons a day to produce enough steam to push us along at 10 knots. We steamed up the straits of Malacca and into Sabang, a small port on the northern tip of Sumatra. We entered a narrow channel past a wooded headland and into one of the most beautiful harbours I had ever seen. There was only enough room for one ship alongside the dock and an old tug pushed us under the coaling tip and we began to load. We were allowed to lower the dinghy over the side and we rowed out into the bay. It was an enchanting spot. The water was so clear we could see the submerged part of the ship's hull right down to her keel, a rare phenomenon. Later we walked along the beach, amusing ourselves by throwing stones at huge spiders which had woven webs between the wires and poles stretched along the edge of the jungle. Sabang was a brief and very pleasant interlude and we soon sailed after taking on enough coal to take us to Rotterdam.

Once we had transited the Suez Canal, it was our job to assist Chips in dismantling the searchlight on the bow. The most delicate component was the glass reflector, which the senior apprentice removed from the light and gingerly handed to me with instructions to place it carefully on a ventilator cover lying on the deck before all the pieces could be stowed safely in the carpenter's locker. All was going well until I stepped backwards to receive another piece and shattered the reflector into a thousand pieces! For a moment there was a stunned silence as the seriousness of what I had done sunk in. To be told that I was a clumsy bastard only served to make me feel worse, although someone was considerate enough to point out that at least we had gone through the canal and were homeward-bound. I was advised to report the calamity to the mate, whose usually benign expression turned to one of shock and disbelief. He recovered his composure and told me to go and inform the old man. Captain McInnes, a calm man in any circumstance, listened to what I had to say and remained unperturbed, merely saying. "Boy, this will go against you in the company." I thought that my service with the Henderson Line had come to an end but, oddly enough, I never heard any more about it. The chief engineer was not happy because we had taken on about a thousand tons of inferior coal. According to him it was more like pitch than coal and there would be difficulty producing enough steam. He was right, as our passage via Suez turned out to be a long one and we averaged little better than 8 knots all the way.

Pre-war Rotterdam rivalled Hamburg as the busiest port in all of Europe. We dropped anchor amongst ships of many flags. We had been away for seven months and my thoughts turned to home, a few hundred miles across the North Sea. Bob Ashby-Todd had finished his time and was leaving to go up for his ticket. He asked the mate whether some of us could take leave anyway. The mate estimated that our stay in port would be ten days, so two boys could go on leave for five days, then the other two could leave. We drew lots to see who would go first and George Sinclair and I had to wait for the others to return. After watching Peter and Bob leave for England we decided to go ashore. In Rotterdam there was an efficient system of summoning a launch. Pennant No. 3 was hoisted to the yard and the "Speedo" boat soon came alongside. As there were many other ships in the harbour, the launch had to made frequent stops to pick up passengers and it was a long time before we got ashore.

Rotterdam was an attractive city, much cleaner that Liverpool or Glasgow. Language was not a problem as it seemed everyone we spoke to understood English. There were many seamen ashore and the city catered to their needs. The district known as the "Schiedam Schiedyke" was where the well-known Cosmopolie dance hall was located. The girls outnumbered the men and, although I was already under the influence of too much to drink, I managed to find a dancing partner. She soon tired of my stumbling about and led me to a small room where the following encounter was far from satisfactory mainly because she spent the entire time talking about the wonderful Norwegian sailor whom she had entertained earlier. I left with a dreadful hang-over and a damaged ego. To make matters worse, I was sick in the taxi returning to the docks. All I could do was hand the furious taxi-driver my remaining guilders which did little to placate him. On the jetty I met George, who was in better condition than I was and he assisted me back to the "Speedo".

The next day, I had time to reflect on my errant behaviour. I had been foolish enough to spend all my money and was now facing the prospect of shore leave and returning home without a penny. The mate noticed my deep gloom and called me to his cabin. After delivering a brief lecture on basic economics and the need to exercise common sense, he asked me how much money I had. Receiving the reply he'd expected, he reached into his pocket and produced enough money to pay for my return fare. Shamefaced, yet grateful, I promised to repay it. As my wages at the time were one pound, ten shillings a month, it took me a long time.

George and I took the train to Zeebrugge, then the ferry to Harwich where he left for Scotland. I went on and spent five happy days with old friends in the Midlands.

Upon my return I learnt that Captain McInnes had left and the new master was Captain Beaton. A new senior cadet had also arrived who needed only a few months to complete his sea-time before going for his ticket. His name was Peter Batten and he had an air of authority about him due to his height and strength. He did not like me and the feeling was mutual. I also had a new room-mate, Jimmy Sutherland, a tall, blonde boy from the Orkney Islands. His knowledge of the sea and navigation far outstripped mine and we were to become good friends. He had won a sextant for high marks when he was a cadet aboard the "Worcester". Jimmy had the rather odd ability to sleep so heavily that it was difficult to wake him up. Sometimes, when the master saw fit, we were required to stand bridge watches with the mates and it was then that I had trouble getting Jimmy to relieve me. I would leave the bridge at 3:30 a.m. to call the 4 to 8 watch. Most seamen hated to be shaken awake, and once a mate struck an apprentice for shaking his arm. It was usually sufficient to tell a man that it was seven bells, and on British ships it was customary to bring a cup of tea to one's relief. Some men refused to go on watch without first having it. I would call Jimmy four or five times, then leave the cabin after being told each time, "O.K. I'm awake!" only to return and find him sound asleep again! As a final resort, I would thrust a cigarette in his mouth, light it and leave him. He would fall back asleep and only when the cigarette fell from his lips and burnt him, would he get up!

The ship was enveloped in coal dust once more and long barges had come down from the Rhine, bearing coal destined for Port Said. These barges were family owned and were usually spotless. I leant over the rail watching as the barge-master, his wife and children, made vain efforts to keep their beautiful vessels clean from the dust. They must have hated the stuff more than we did. My attention was caught by a splendid liner sailing past. She was the flagship of the Holland American fleet, the Niew Amsterdam. 36,000 tons leaving on her maiden voyage to New York. I was to see her later during the war years painted drab grey and far from the waters she was designed to sail in.

We sailed for Suez. It was spring 1939 and war clouds were looming over Europe, although we cadets were not aware of them. War clouds of another kind appeared one day when Peter Batten and I were working on the rigging. I still harboured something of an "attitude". This, coupled with a quick temper, resulted in a tendency to get into fights in which I invariably got the worst of it. Whenever scores had to be settled aboard ship, the combatants would "battle it out" on No. 3 hatch . The threat was usually expressed as "I will knock seven kinds of shit out of you!" I once watched Chips give the 5th engineer an awful thrashing on this hatch, with half the crew egging him on because the 5th was not liked. By the time it was over the engineer had a black eye and a bloody nose. Bare fists could inflict a lot of damage but at least it was clean fighting — no kicking or gouging. Peter and I were replacing the seizings which held the ratlines to the shrouds. I was working below him and as he moved down he put his foot on my face. I called him a "clumsy bastard" and with apprehension noticed the anger on his face. He scrambled down onto the deck and I followed knowing that there was trouble ahead. "What did you say?" he demanded. Foolishly, I repeated myself. His fist shot out, connected with my mouth and I crashed to the deck. Later the old man noticed my battered appearance and asked me what had happened. He laughed when I told him that I had walked into a stanchion! Many years later when I was in Canada and a junior officer on the C.P.R. Coastal ships, I was told that the Assistant Marine Superintendent wanted to speak to me. To my surprise, he was none other than my old nemesis, Peter Batten, who wanted to point out something I had neglected to do. This time I held my tongue.

Our passage down the Spanish coast was not without excitement. We heard the rumble of gunfire in the distance and before long, two French battleships and several destroyers passed by. They were preparing for war which was just a few months away. We discharged our coal at Port Said and steamed down to Aden to load salt for Calcutta as before. On September 3rd, 1939, we were off Cape Guardefui when Sparks received the message telling us that we were at war. When we reached Calcutta, a naval officer came aboard and told the master that we were now under the jurisdiction of the Admiralty. For good measure the master was given two First World War rifles and told to barricade the bridge with sandbags. A load of sand was dumped on the deck and we spent several days filling bags and placing them above and around the wheel house. We were told that this was protection against aircraft strafing. It was hot work.

As on the previous trip, the salt was unloaded in six weeks, and war, or no war, we enjoyed what pleasures Calcutta had to offer. The engineers who owned "Oscar" and "Kong", the monkeys, had been told to get rid of them as they had become more than a nuisance aboard. The "City of Dieppe" was anchored nearby and her crew seemed interested and invited us to bring the monkeys aboard. One of the engineers and I, each with a monkey on our shoulders, crossed over in the small boat. We talked with an apprentice who had a mongoose which he told us was the ideal pet. I walked into one cabin where there was a chameleon, and into another where there was a mynah bird which could swear with some fluency. They did not think that "Oscar" and "Kong" would be any trouble!

When news came that we were to load a cargo of jute and gunny for Glasgow, it was received with mixed feelings because although Glasgow meant home, there was apprehension that Hitler might land in Britain before we got there. This was our second visit to Calcutta and as before, our stay was a lengthy one.

We had become friends with the apprentices on the "City of Dieppe" who told us that our stay in Calcutta would not be complete unless we went to Acre Lane. It was in a "semi-respectable" area of the city and was a row of white stucco villas which had once been occupied by the Europeans but were now rather run-down. The residents did not like the term "red light district" although that was what it was, albeit a "better class" one. Although the terms of business were quite out of our reach, we joined the boys from the "City of Dieppe" for an evening of fun. The rickshaw-wallahs were waiting outside the dock gates. We got in our respective vehicles and someone shouted "Acre Lane, 'boat geldie'!", (very quickly), and we were off. The madam answered the doorbell and we were shown into a large room with silk curtains and cushions, a fine carpet, pictures of Indian beauties lining the walls and a fan whirring overhead. It was definitely "better class"! We were asked what we wanted to drink. As we sat on the cushions sipping our beer, the madam showed signs of impatience at the flippant way we were beginning to treat the affair. She clapped her hands and several girls came from behind a curtain at the end of the room. They varied in size and age and some were quite beautiful. We pretended to haggle about the price and there was a good deal of vulgar chatter, but as time wore on, the madam realized we had no money. She became furious and demanded the money for the drinks we had consumed. We did manage to find that between the lot of us and left feeling that we had spent an entertaining evening.

About this time a book appeared which caused a lot of resentment among Indians against foreigners. It was called "Mother India" and was written by Catherine Mayo, the American after whom the club in Rangoon was named. The book was an exposé of social conditions, Hindu religious practices and the caste system. The 3rd mate had a copy in his room and was half-way through it when it mysteriously disappeared. It was only after he remembered that the Officers' "Boy" was a Hindu that he knew what had probably happened to it.

The voyage home took over a month. When we reached Gibraltar, we were ordered to anchor off the "Rock", and await convoy orders. We left in a thirty ship convoy, escorted by two French destroyers, the "Tigre" and the "Panther", which were as big as cruisers. Trying to maintain station in convoy was a novel but frustrating experience for the master and mates. Sailing in convoy was nerve-wracking for masters, who found themselves having to manoeuvre their ships clear of other vessels which had difficulty controlling their speeds and keeping their correct distances. For us, it meant a trying and challenging two weeks when, even at our low speed of 9 knots, we had to reduce to 6 or 7 knots — the speed of the slowest ship. We spent most of our time on the bridge, ankle-deep in flags as we wrestled with the flag hoists trying to read the signals made by the commodore who was aboard a ship close on our starboard side. We were woefully lacking in ability to read the Morse signals flashed in our direction by the expert naval signalman. When this happened to me, I made a feverish attempt to try and brush up my skills at Morse code only to have the mate take the lamp out of my hands. He wasn't much better and Sparks was called to take over. But what really irked the old man was when smoke belched from our funnel and resulted in a flag hoist appearing on the commodore's ship. Below the convoy number were flags which we did not understand until we hurriedly consulted the code book. It read, "You are making too much smoke, and thus endangering the convoy." The chief engineer was called and asked what could be done about it. He was frustrated as there was little he could do as the "Mandalay" was a natural draft ship, and there were no blowers to disperse smoke. Poor steaming coal produced volumes of black smoke. It was worse at the end of each watch when the tubes had to be blown with steam to clear them, causing the engines revs to drop. It was a common problem in steamships.

We plodded on and as the weather turned colder, bridge watches became more uncomfortable. We had become accustomed to tropical weather, and now had to rummage through our kit bags to unearth what cold-weather gear we possessed. My monkey had been aboard for over ten months and was wearing a red woolen outfit made from a sock with the toes cut off. Fuzzy had become accustomed to shipboard life and was now accepted as a member of the crew. How I expected to take her ashore I did not know, yet that was my intention. We were in the Bay of Biscay and the seamen were busy covering the forward well-decks with Stockholm tar to prevent corrosion. I had to tie up Fuzzy to prevent her from getting into this black mess. But she got free and ran on to the tar. I ran down the deck to capture her, but she became frightened and darted to the ship's side where she hung briefly. Before I could reach her, she fell into the water and was lost.

It was mid-December 1939 when we approached the south coast of Ireland in a howling south-westerly gale. We picked up the pilot off Gourock and entered the River Clyde. It was a bitterly cold, sunny day. At a point where the river narrowed two tugs appeared. They were ancient, steam paddle-driven tugs. Each took a line, one from the bow and one from the stern. At noon, I was sent to the stern to relieve the 2nd mate so he could have lunch. I stood watching the tug as it struggled to keep a strain on the line, her paddles thrashing the muddy water. It was a wonderful feeling to be back in home waters after so many months away. It all seemed worthwhile putting up with the discomforts of life, and with any luck, I would soon be on a train on my way home, and sleeping in a comfortable bed with no watches to keep and good food to eat.

I was shaken out of my reverie by a series of blasts on our whistle. This was followed by whistles in reply from another ship approaching us from up river. There was an unexpected thump as our propeller began to thrash astern. Being on the stern I was unable to see the reason for all the noise. Suddenly, a shattering crash knocked me off my feet. I jumped up, hesitated, then ran along the deck which had suddenly taken an ominous incline forward. The focsle head was a mass of tangled wreckage; the anchor windlass up-ended and a cloud of steam was rising from broken pipes. The mate, carpenter and entire fo'c's'le crew, plus others who had been fortunate to escape, stood surveying the wreckage. We had collided with the 8,000 ton "Gregalia", a Donaldson liner outward-bound for Montreal. She lay stopped in mid-river with her bows crumpled and a large rent in her hull. A crowd had gathered on the banks of the river. They had poured out of the factory on shore at the sound of the rending crash. Some of them thought a land mine had gone off. The forward tug, seeing that a collision was inevitable, had quickly cast off the towing line, and run clear. Now both tugs were busy pushing us towards the bank before the fore-end of the ship touched bottom and we blocked the river. Two men died in the collision, crushed by the impact.

December, 1939. Bows of the "Mandalay" after collision with the cargo ship, "Gregalia", in the River Clyde. Two of the lascar firemen were asleep in their bunks and were killed. The fore-end of the ship rested on the mud for two weeks and conditions aboard were very uncomfortable.

The "Mandalay" lay close to the bank, her fore-end resting on the mud. We ran a line to the shore, secured it, and this was used to pull a lifeboat back and forth to ferry people and supplies. This became our duty for several days while a salvage crew worked to raise the ship, before taking her up-river to discharge our cargo. Our mate, Mr. Campbell, left to attend the inquiry and then took home leave. Our new chief officer was Mr. Hughes, who we'd heard was very strict and it wasn't long before I ran afoul of him. As the lascars' galley on the foredeck was untenable, their food had to be prepared ashore and delivered to a spot on the river bank where we took our lifeboat. Several pots of curry and rice were taken across but during the course of handling, some of it fell into the bottom of the boat. The mate ordered me to clean up the mess. In a bloody state of mind, I refused, saying that the men who'd made the mess should clean it up. Insubordination, particularly from an apprentice, was not tolerated and the consequences were usually dire. The mate was enraged and ordered me on deck. He told me that the head office would be notified that I had refused an order. I was in deep trouble and worried about my uncertain future.

A salvage crew raised the ship from the mud of the Clyde and we were towed up-river to unload our cargo. The dockers working in No. 1 hold, struggling to remove the sodden bales of hemp, uncovered the remains of one of the lascars killed in the collision. They immediately came on deck refusing to touch the cargo until his corpse had been removed. The body of the other casualty had already been taken off.

One morning, I was ordered to put on my uniform and go to Glasgow to be interviewed by a legal counsel about events leading up to the collision. Meanwhile, Mr. Hughes left the “Mandalay”. He had been promoted to master of the “Empire Citizen”, a captured German ship which was being operated by the company. On returning from Glasgow, I was handed an envelope which bore the company name and I knew immediately what it was likely to contain. I opened it with trepidation. To my surprise, it was nothing more than a reprimand from the marine superintendent and a warning against further lapses in discipline. It ended with an order that I was to go aboard the “Empire Citizen” and apologize to Captain Hughes.

I walked up the gangway of the “Empire Citizen” wondering what reception I would receive. A cadet by the name of Peebles led me into the officers’ accommodation. I knocked on the master’s door, and on entering his room found him sitting at his desk. I told him I had come aboard to apologize. He said a few words about my needing a change of attitude; then, to my surprise, he extended his hand and wished me good luck. I should have expressed the same sentiments to him, for less than two weeks later, the “Empire Citizen” was torpedoed during the night off the west coast of Ireland. Two lifeboats got away in rough seas but were never seen again. Three days later, six survivors were picked up from a raft but one died later. They had survived bitter weather and mountainous seas. Captain Hughes was not among them. Peebles, the young cadet who had greeted me aboard the “Empire Citizen” was one of the six survivors. During his signing-on, his mother, had spoken to Captain Hughes, expressing concern for the safety of her son as it was his first trip to sea. After the loss of the “Empire Citizen”, he was transferred to another company ship. Several months later, it, too, was torpedoed. This time, Peebles did not survive.

After a few days leave I returned to find the “Mandalay” in dry dock. Conditions aboard were worse than when she had been afloat. Toilets were not useable and calls of nature meant a walk ashore to facilities which were primitive and filthy. It wasn’t surprising that some of us became ill. George Sinclair and I, the only cadets aboard, tried to keep out of the mate’s way, and we stayed warm by working down the holds of the ship. But George came down with the flu and was bedridden. A day later, I collapsed with pneumonia and was taken ashore on a stretcher. I found myself in a ward in Ruchill Hospital with about twelve other patients with respiratory problems. The first night I was kept awake by a man in the opposite bed who was delirious. His bony face was the colour of the sheets which he tugged at continually, all the while mumbling unintelligible words. This went on for hours. Eventually, I dropped off to sleep and was roused by a nurse wanting to take my temperature. The noise from the bed opposite had ceased and the curtains were drawn. I asked the nurse why and she replied, “He has gone.” Over the next few days the scene was repeated — as one bed became empty, another patient was wheeled in to fill it. At least five men died while I was there. As soon as the curtains were drawn, I knew the patient was "a goner". Over nine hundred people died that winter in Glasgow. Penicillin had not yet been discovered and M & B sulpha drug was the only medicine available for respiratory infections.

After I had passed the crisis and was expecting to see the outside world once again, a doctor asked me if I was willing to donate some blood to a patient who apparently needed it more than I did. My bed was pushed into another ward, and alongside another bed in which lay a boy of about 10 years. His face was deathly-white. Two pints of blood were taken from both my arms, and I watched as it flowed into a bottle suspended from a rack. Some powder was added to prevent coagulation, and it was then transferred into the boy, who lay silently some feet away. When the transfusion had been completed some colour had returned to his cheeks. Shortly after, I was given a memorable meal of bacon and eggs, and before I had finished eating it, I had some visitors. They were the boy's parents bearing a basket of fruit which was a rare treat.

Being over four hundred miles from home I did not expect visitors. When the nurse told me that a gentleman had come to see me, I had no idea who it could be. I was astonished to see the usually stern-faced marine superintendent looking down at me. He asked me how I felt and when I might expect to return to work! He brought me a book to read and after he left, I opened it expecting to find an adventure story of some kind. It was a copy of "Nicholls's Seamanship"! It was during the last few days in hospital that I began to sit up and take notice of the other patients in the ward. I felt well enough to read the newspaper and I passed it to the man in the bed next to me. The headline news reported a bomb thrown by a member of the I.R.A. into a crowd in Coventry. A woman had been killed. My neighbour and I agreed that it was an outrage, and I said what I thought should be done to people who threw bombs. To my astonishment this provoked a fiery response from a man in bed across the other side of the ward. In a strong Irish accent he called me every kind of English liar he could think of. His manner was so aggressive that had he not been a sick man he would surely have left his bed to follow up his threats. I sank back on my pillow wondering whether I would leave hospital in one piece.

By the time I was fit again, the "Mandalay" had sailed without me and the company generously gave me more time to recuperate. The parents of one of the apprentices on the "Yoma", a company ship in port, invited me to stay with them. The Russells lived in a comfortable house in Clarkston, a suburb of Glasgow. They were the kindest people imaginable. It was spring time and the countryside was at its best. I took long walks through the fields, chatted with the locals and returned to Mrs. Russell's delicious meals. An extra mouth to feed must have strained her ration book, but she was the soul of generosity and I was treated like a king. She must have thought that I was in need of feminine companionship as I was introduced to a charming lass called Jessie Craig. Mrs. Russell was right — to have company of this kind was the surest way to a quick recovery. Jessie was a blonde, vivacious girl whose ambition was to become a nurse and she certainly had the right qualities. We were out walking one afternoon and came across a group of people standing around a plane which had crashed in a field. It was a Hurricane fighter which was so badly damaged we wondered whether the pilot had got out alive. After three weeks with the Russells it was time to go back to sea. The company had repeatedly enquired after my well-being and I got the distinct impression they thought that I had taken enough leave.

Chapter 3. The "Salween"

In March 1940, I was sent to the newest ship in the fleet. The "Salween" was a luxury ship compared to the "Mandalay" and she carried nearly a hundred passengers with a crew of about one hundred. She was a handsome vessel of 7,000 tons and her modern turbine engines drove her at 15 knots. There were five of us apprentices accommodated in two cabins next to the quartermaster's room. The Q.M.s (Quarter Masters) on the passenger ships were able seamen who had been at sea for thirty years or more and most of them came from the western isles of Scotland. They wore a uniform similar to a naval rating and a sailor's cap with a band round it which bore the title "Henderson Line". Their main duties were steering, maintenance of the bridge, canvas work and gangway watches in port. There were one or two great characters among them. Ian McCaskell was one, and came from a long line of seafarers. He grew up on the island of Harris in the Hebrides, and went to sea in fishing smacks at the age of fourteen. His parents tried to persuade him to go to the mainland and look for a job with a future in a factory. He went to Glasgow and found work in a tanning factory. After a week, he could stand it no longer and left. He was about to buy a ticket to go home when, in a pub drowning his sorrows, he heard about a job on the ferries which ran across to Ireland. He signed on as an ordinary seaman after telling the shipping clerk that he was seventeen years old. When I met him, he had been with the Henderson Line for thirty-five years and had saved enough to buy a small holding back home on Harris. He had seen enough of the world and never went ashore, except in Glasgow. I used to sit on the hatch and watch him stitching. He was skilled at making things such as a golf bag or a suitcase for the old man.

The other apprentices were a good bunch but the mates seemed aloof and remote. The "Salween" was not as happy a ship as the old "Mandalay". For some reason tramp ships were better to serve on, perhaps because there were fewer restrictions on dress and behavior.

We made an uneventful voyage to Rangoon but called in at Alexandria on the way. The mate was in a good mood and allowed all five of us ashore together. An insistent gharry-cart driver wanted to show us where the Nile flowed into the Meddy. We had a few drinks before setting out to view this wonder of the world. Some of us wore red fezzes, which were being peddled by touts and we lay back in the gharry in a semi-stupor as it clattered along the rough streets of the city. The gharry stopped and the driver turned his head and said, "Take look-see at Nile." We piled out and looked in the direction he was pointing. We expected to see a great expanse of river flowing past. Instead, a stream of filthy water trickled by, no wider than our carriage. When we began to laugh, the gharry driver became angry and demanded more money than the price we had agreed to pay. But Moran, a pugnacious Scot, became just as angry. It was time to leave before a crowd gathered and things turned ugly. We drifted off and spent the rest of the day walking around the Botanical Gardens. Alexandria was an attractive place and a major base for the Royal Navy. Across the harbour from where we lay, the enormous palace, Ras el Tin, stood glimmering in the sun. It was one of King

Five apprentices from the "Salween" in the Botanical Gardens, Alexandria, Egypt, April 1940.

Farouk's royal palaces. Relations between him and the British had soured while we were there. He had hoped for a German victory as he wanted an end to British occupation. There was a good deal of tension ashore, and we were warned to be careful about not straying off the main streets as several British Tommies (soldiers) had recently been murdered.

The "Salween" was armed with a 4.7 inch gun mounted on the stern. It was an ancient piece, dating from pre-First World War days. A Royal Navy gunner was in charge, and he selected and trained members of the crew. I found myself part of the gun crew, and it was my job to carry the shells from their rack and place them in a tray along with the cartridge, which in this case, was separate. The tray swung in line with the barrel of the gun, and the load was pushed in, and the gun was ready to fire. Our first gun practice was unforgettable. Chips had built a large target from odd pieces of dunnage and a piece of old canvas was stretched across two uprights. This was thrown over the side. We were sailing independently, so we did not have to worry about the possibility of hitting another ship. The mate gave us wads of cotton wool to stick in our ears. I had never been in close proximity to any gun before, and was quite unprepared for what happened next. Guns (the gun-layer) was at the controls, elevating or depressing the barrel as required. I placed the heavy shell on the tray. The breech slammed shut within inches of my fingers, and someone shouted, "Fire!" There was an ear-splitting roar, a sheet of flames shot out, the barrel recoiled with incredible force, and we were completely enveloped in a cloud of smoke. I was momentarily in a state of shock, but recovered quickly enough to see the splash as the shot landed short of the target, which by now was a mile or two astern. The fourth shot demolished the target, and the old man was pleased and gave the gunners a drink. But we apprentices did not get one!

After loading in Rangoon, we sailed for the United Kingdom. As the Meddy was considered too risky, we headed for the Cape of Good Hope. Our next port was to be Durban for coal bunkers. We were approaching the Mozambique Channel when a message was received telling us that an Italian surface raider was in the area. It had already sunk one ship, so any ship we sighted would be regarded with suspicion if it failed to identify itself. We were immediately put on double watches, which meant working four hours on and four hours off, most of the time being spent on lookout on the bridge. Much as we hated this, we knew the vital necessity of keeping a vigilant lookout.The ship was blacked out, meaning no lights of any kind, and we were warned that anyone caught smoking on deck would be in serious trouble. A match light could be seen at quite a distance at sea. I was on the bridge one night when, suddenly, we were illuminated by a bright searchlight from a ship close at hand whose presence we were not aware of. The mate quickly recovered from the shock and rang the general alarm. We fully expected to be blown out of the water at any second. The old man and the other mates rushed to the bridge as we stood blinded by the light. Someone said, "It looks like a war ship!" Fortunately, it proved to be a British cruiser looking for the Italian raider. The "Salween's" profile with her long, black funnel soon convinced the cruiser otherwise, the searchlight went out and her dim, grey shape disappeared into the night. This incident shook up everyone, and the mate reminded us of the importance of keeping a good lookout, which we thought was quite uncalled for.

Our stay in Durban was all too brief. We tied up at the coaling dock adjacent to the whaling station. It was hot and the stench from rotting whale carcasses was overpowering. The mate gave us a day off and when two cars appeared on the dock and we were invited to go for a tour of the city, we jumped at the chance. A kind couple, who must have felt the need to boost the morale of merchant seaman, took us out into the splendid country of a thousand hills where we saw monkeys crossing the road ahead of the car. They insisted on stopping for drinks at the Athlone Gardens and we were only too glad to do so. After weeks at sea, it was a pleasant interlude.

Durban Harbour was protected from the sea by a long breakwater and once clear of this, we were pitching into a heavy swell with the occasional green one crashing onto the focsle head. It was tough to take after a late night ashore and, as usual, a bout of seasickness stayed with me for awhile. However, there was no slackening of work and we continued with double watches. The waters off the Cape of Good Hope were amongst the roughest and dangerous anywhere and this was particularly true for vessels heading in a westerly direction, as we were. The towering seas were caused by the Agulhas Current which flowed against the prevailing westerly winds across the Continental Shelf. By the time we reached the Cape of Good Hope, we were down to less than 5 knots and battling a gale and high seas. The incredible phenomena of seas in the Roaring Forties were the lengths of the swells and the distances between them. As much as a quarter of a mile between crests was not unusual. I looked ahead in awe as one particularly high sea appeared in the distance, rearing its foamy crest over the others. As it got closer and the ship's bows fell steeply into the trough, I wondered how much water would come thundering aboard. By then, we were hove to with only enough speed to maintain steerage. Uncomfortable as it was amidships, it was sheer hell for the men whose accommodation was located in the bows. How the Indian cook managed to produce meals in the galley on the well-deck, which was constantly awash, I did not know.

Two weeks later, we reached Freetown, Sierra Leone, to find many ships at anchor waiting to form a convoy. This British colony was known as the "White Man's Grave" because of the prevalence of malaria. This I was to learn at my cost on a later visit. For this reason shore leave was forbidden, not that there was any enticement. We lay two miles off the shore and every morning a steaming mist could be seen rising from the densely forested shore. The heat and humidity were bad enough off shore. It would have been unbearable on land. We left in a convoy of over forty ships, the largest being the P & O Liner, the "Mooltan", which had been converted to an armed merchant cruiser with 6 inch guns. She was a tempting target for any U boat, so she was stationed right in the middle of the convoy. Her presence was required should an attack come from a surface raider. We hated sailing in convoy as we were back on double watches and it meant long hours on the bridge. We were only a few days out when news of the fall of France and Dunkirk reached us. A rumour went around the ship that if Britain fell, we would be diverted to North America. It was a gloomy prospect.

As we approached the British coast we ran into fog and this made station-keeping very difficult. A fog buoy was put over the stern to enable the ship astern to keep her distance, but it was a nerve-wracking time as the buoy ahead would disappear and we would have to increase speed to catch up with it. Although the course of the convoy was the same for all ships, quite often we would find ourselves running alongside the ship which was supposed to be ahead of us. In such conditions, collisions sometimes occurred. One night, I heard one happening — the grinding crunch of two ships I could not see as they connected. One day, the chief engineer ran up to the bridge shouting, "U boat! U boat!" He pointed to a line of foam in the water between us and the ship abeam of us. It proved to be the fog buoy of the ship ahead of us!

We reached Liverpool intact and heard that one of the company's passenger ships had come to grief outside Liverpool. The "Pegu" had sailed with a full cargo bound for Rangoon. She was proceeding out through the buoyed channel when a mechanical breakdown occurred and she drifted on to the rocks off Bootle and was a total loss. She had a large consignment of whisky aboard and many cases of it floated free. The Customs and Excise men had to maintain a 24 hour watch on the wreck.

I went home on ten days leave. The train left Lime Street Station just as the air raid sirens heralded another raid on Liverpool.

Chapter 4. Turkey Via The Cape

A letter from the head office told me to report aboard the "Mandalay" in Liverpool. I was glad to be back as by now I had a sentimental attachment for her. George Sinclair had left to go for his ticket and a new boy called Stevenson was the junior apprentice. We were loading a military cargo for Turkey which was a neutral but friendly country. Apparently there was a possibility that the Turks would be drawn into the war as our cargo included such items as light tanks, ambulances, khaki uniforms, thousands of cases of boots and other things to equip an army. Two large crates were loaded on the after-deck; their contents were unknown. Our convoy of forty ships included two neutral ships, one Swedish and the other, Hungarian. We were two days out and I was standing, dressed in oilskins, on the open wing of the bridge in a south-westerly gale with spray whipping across our decks. Our station was third ship in the third column so that the bulk of the convoy was astern of us. The commodore ship was the newly completed "City of Calcutta". It wasn't long before our presence became known to the enemy and our escort of two destroyers and three corvettes began dropping depth charges.

North Atlantic Convoy, 1940. Bound for Turkey on board the "Mandalay". Tanker in ballast on our beam.

I was with Jimmy Sutherland making up flag hoists when there was a loud thump. The ship shuddered but, to our surprise, nothing appeared to be amiss. We reported this to the commodore. A destroyer came charging up to ask about the nature of the thump we had felt and there was speculation that we had struck a submerged object. Action stations were called and while I was standing by the gun, I glanced astern to see a column of water rising above a Swedish ship called the "Hedron". This was followed by a loud bang and almost at once she took a list. We put on our tin hats and stuffed cotton wool in our ears. We could see a boat being lowered into the water. Suddenly, the "Hedron" lifted her stern in the air and plunged beneath the waves. Few men had time to escape and the lifeboat was soon out of sight. There was a lull and we thought that the attack was over when the "Alcinous", a Blue Funnel ship in the column next to us, was torpedoed. Water raised by the explosion poured from her decks. Someone shouted, "U boat on the port quarter! Open fire!" We peered into the spaces between the ships. The 3rd mate, the gunnery officer, looked through his binoculars and saw something resembling a U boat and shouted, "There it is!" Guns looked into the sights and moved the barrel. The signal to open fire was given. After the first round blasted off, I ran to pick up another shell and looked astern to see the shell ricochet off the top of a sea and fall uncomfortably close to another ship. A cry of "Cease fire!" came from the bridge. After this embarrassing episode, the commodore raised the signal ordering the convoy to scatter and proceed at full speed to our respective destinations. We were anxious to get away on our own as it seemed the convoy was in for a severe mauling.

Jimmy Sutherland, Steve Stevenson, Me after a gun drill on 4" Gun. The shell and cartridge were separate for this gun dated 1910!

In a gale with driving rain and poor visibility, it wasn't long before we were alone. In the next few hours, Sparks received three distress calls from ships in the area which had been torpedoed. We heard later that a small passenger ship had gone down with a heavy loss of life. The "Mandalay's" old engine thumped madly as it was driven at maximum speed to take us south as quickly as possible. We were ordered to wear lifejackets and keep a sharp look-out. Nobody got any rest and when told to go below for a spell, we lay down fully-clothed with our "panic bags" handy. These bags contained necessary articles if we had to abandon ship in a hurry. We were surprised when a ship suddenly appeared on our quarter heading across our stern. She was the "Clan McPhail" and had been running alongside us in convoy. We had exchanged friendly signals by lamp before the attack. Now there was no inclination to communicate and she soon disappeared into the murk. From her course, it was evident she was bound for the Meddy. About an hour later, another distress signal was received. It was from the "Clan McPhail". She too, had been torpedoed and sunk, taking her crew with her. Nightfall came as a relief as we thought it was less likely we would be spotted. We began zig-zagging, hoping to throw off any pursuit. Further messages came through from the Hungarian ship requesting assistance in rescue work. The following hours were tense ones. The engineers had screwed down the safety valve in order to use the last ounce of steam, and the ship was galloping along at 11 knots but it seemed insufficient to take us clear of disaster. Peter Gunn received a blast from the mate for slamming a cabin door and even the usually cheerful Guns was silent and sober-faced.

Our varied courses took us about a thousand miles to the west of the Azores and a week after we'd left the convoy, we were in fine, balmy weather. The old man thought that we were now out of danger and allowed us to return to our normal watches. However, due to our less than inspiring performance in action, he ordered more gun drills. For a week it became a daily event. We would fire a few rounds using practice shells at a target which Chips had made. On the third day we finally hit it after firing ten rounds!

On the 1st of September 1940, we had been at sea for three weeks and were several hundred miles to the west of French West Africa. As we were bound for Turkey, the most direct route would have been through the Mediterranean but that was considered too hazardous and the Admiralty had routed us via the Cape of Good Hope. Thus, instead of a mere 3,000 miles, we would have to sail over three times that distance.

It was pleasant to be back in tropical waters. We discarded our cold weather gear for khaki shorts and the tension and strain of being in convoy among U boats seemed far away. We rigged a deep-sea fishing line. A stout bamboo pole projected horizontally out from the afterdeck and from it ran several fathoms of sounding wire and a large hook fashioned by the engineers. Someone's old shirt collar served as bait. We hoped to catch a sailfish or shark!

Late one afternoon, three of us were working at no. 3 hatch, when I looked up at the bridge to see the old man with the telescope and the mate with binoculars looking at the horizon on our starboard quarter. From where we stood, we could only see the masts and superstructure of a ship about ten miles away. As we debated its identity, our course was altered to put her directly astern. The Admiralty had cautioned masters to be wary of any vessel unless she could identify herself with the code signal, which changed every day and formed part of the confidential sailing orders. The stranger began to signal with a much brighter lamp than normally carried aboard merchant ships. The 2nd mate held our Aldis lamp which was not working very well. The flashing continued and we read, "What ship? What ship?" We did not reply and the flashing became more insistent — "What ship!" — followed by the order, "Stop!" Meanwhile, the chief hurried below to open up the throttle once again. The other ship had altered course towards us and was "hull up" above the horizon. Sparks was ordered to break radio silence and send out a distress message. It was now obvious that the ship astern had hostile intentions and was catching up rapidly.

German surface raiders were modern cargo liners, converted for naval use to prey upon shipping. They were capable of 18 or 19 knots and armed with 5.9" guns so were able to outrun, and outgun, most merchant ships. The mate ordered us to check the lifeboats thoroughly. Special provisions included a bottle of whisky in each boat. This was usually "in safe keeping" elsewhere and we found that one was missing. The culprit, however, was never found and the old man had to replace it with one from his own stock which caused him some consternation. We were now running for our lives but, as before, the "Hand of Providence" held in our favour. It came in the form of a tropical rain squall which soon enveloped us. This, together with the approach of nightfall which came quickly in Equatorial waters, meant that we did not see our pursuer again. We did not have radar, and neither did the enemy, and he must have been as frustrated as we were relieved; not that we slackened speed or lessened our vigilance. Extra look-outs were posted and we maintained our zig-zagging in an effort to throw off the raider. At dawn, after a long and tense night, we cast anxious eyes around and found ourselves alone.

On the 14th of September,1940 we were in Lat. 30 South and Long. 14 East, making 8 knots. I wrote in my diary the following: "We have discarded our tropical gear for warm clothing. Running into bad weather, wind force 7, sea — rough and a heavy swell. Temp. 68. We are being followed by a host of sea birds. Stormy petrels, cape pigeons and the magnificent albatross whose swooping flight is wonderful to watch. They do not flap their mighty wings, unless in a calm, but use them as sails to glide and dive." As we neared the Cape the weather worsened. With the prevailing westerly winds in the vast expanse of the South Atlantic, the great swells, unimpeded by any land mass, made it a wild place for any ship. We were approaching the area known to sailing ship men as the "Roaring Forties". Two days later, we sighted the lights of Cape Town and a flashing light from the signal station asked us to identify ourselves. The Admiralty in London were notified and we were no longer listed as missing. This news was passed on to my father who had earlier received a letter from the company which said that the "Mandalay" had sent out a distress message.

On the 20th of September, 1940, we reached Durban after 40 days at sea. It was a welcome sight, but we were still only half-way to our destination. We looked forward to a good night's sleep and a chance to stretch our legs ashore. Once we had been given a "draw" from our meagre wages, our first thoughts turned to food; the sort of fare unobtainable in Britain or aboard ship. Our favourite dish was known as a "mixed grill", and after three of us apprentices had tucked into this, we went to a well-known dance hall to meet the girls. This wasn't difficult as there were many attractive ones among the large crowd of patrons. But there was stiff competition from a British aircraft carrier in port. Her sailors were in uniform and we were in civilian clothes, which was a distinct disadvantage. Nevertheless, I managed to strike up a conversation with a striking brunette called "Zoe". Her name alone intrigued me. She spoke English, Afrikaans and Zulu, laughed a lot and was a good dancer, which I was not. I tried to be nimble enough to avoid treading on her toes. It was a heady experience after weeks at sea and I thought I was in love. We sat out on a terrace overlooking the harbour, held hands and said things totally unconnected with reality. I was due to sail the next day and we promised to write to each other.

We docked in Durban to take on coal bunkers and once this was completed we prepared to sail. We had been little more than a day in port, and were disappointed, until told that our degaussing equipment needed adjustment. This meant an extra day in port.

To counter the threat of German magnetic mines, scientists had devised the means of neutralising the magnetic field in a ship by sending a current through wires which ran completely round the hull. This system had to be calibrated at the naval dock at Maydon wharf. But our spirits were dampened a little when the old man called us to the bridge and told us that he had noticed slackness in our work since entering port. Unless we improved, there would be no shore leave. With this threat in mind, we re-doubled our efforts to rid the ship of coal dust and were rewarded with a day off.

We called our girl friends and met them on the beach. It was one of the happiest days I ever spent in South Africa. To plunge into the warm waters of the Indian Ocean on a hot day was sheer pleasure. Both Jimmy and Steve had rather severe hangovers; they lay inert on the hot sand while the girls threw buckets of water over them. We finished the day in a bar-restaurant and were sitting at a table when I suddenly remembered that it was my evening watch aboard. I was about to make a hasty exit and return to the ship, when to my disgust, I spotted the old man and mate at a table across the room! Fortunately, they did not see me so I quickly jumped into a rickshaw and returned aboard. The rickshaws in Durban were pulled by muscular Zulus wearing a headdress of feathers. Oddly enough, in spite of their strong physiques, they were unable to pull a rickshaw as far, or as fast, as their counterparts in India.

An officer and two ratings from the South African Navy came aboard to check our 4" gun. They told of an incident that occurred after a mine had washed up on a lonely stretch of beach up the coast. A party was sent out to defuse it. As their car came within sight of the area they saw a group of Africans with a horse and cart. They were trying to push the heavy mine on to the cart. It was a horned mine and one man was pulling on a horn in an effort to move it. The horrified Naval party shouted at them to stop. In vain, as before their eyes the mine exploded and the men, horse and cart disappeared.

As we lay waiting to depart, I stood at the rail staring wistfully at the shore. A large white flying-boat of Imperial Airways called the "Canopus" came past in a shower of spray and hurtled into the air. The mate shouted, "Stand-by!" and we went to our stations. The pilot was aboard, the anchor was raised and we steamed out into the swells of the Indian Ocean.

Once we had settled down to normal watches, a gun-drill was ordered due to rumours of enemy submarines operating in the area. Chips built another target and we managed to straddle it with the third round, which was an improvement over the last drill. Someone suggested that a kite be built to discourage low-flying aircraft. The 2nd mate enlisted my help and scraps of dunnage were used to build a frame about 12 feet high. Old charts were glued to the sides. It was to be flown at the end of a sounding wire. A crowd gathered on the afterdeck to watch its maiden flight. With the ship's speed plus a good breeze, it lifted majestically over the stern to a cheer from the onlookers. The 2nd mate controlled the spinning reel and for a while, we thought we had added a significant addition to our arsenal of defence. Suddenly, the upward draft reversed and our pride and joy plunged into the sea! The old man was disgusted and we were mortified. He ordered us to abandon the project.

A day or two later the albatrosses and cape birds left us as we approached the Mozambique channel. The 18th of September 1940, was my room-mate, Steve's, 18th birthday, and the bandari made a cake for the occasion. The P & O cargo ship, "Somali", over-hauled us so closely we could hear the beat of her screw.

One night on the middle watch I had a falling out with the 2nd mate. At 2:00 a.m. he sent me down to the galley to boil an egg for him. Because of black-out restrictions no lights were allowed, and I stood in almost total darkness trying to locate some eggs. This done, I had to stoke up the coal fire to get sufficient heat to boil the water. By the time the egg was boiled, I had been below for over an hour and the 2nd mate was furious. He sent the helmsman down to search for me. No explanation satisfied him and I was banished to the wing of the bridge to keep a look out. He refused to speak to me for several days. And all over an egg! Still, four hours on the bridge in the tropics was always pleasant and it gave me time to ponder my future at sea.

We were 300 miles off Italian Somaliland when crew trouble erupted. Most of the deck and engine room crew were Indians from the Chittagong area, but for some reason three Burmese were included among the firemen. It should have been obvious that there would to be tension between the Burmese and the different-tempered Indians. The engine room tindal, coming on deck from below, took a gulp from his water can. He let out an agonised yell and clutched his throat. The serang and several kallassees went to see what the noise was all about, and it took three men to hold the tindal who was thrashing about in agony. Someone had put caustic soda in his water and he was violently sick. The Burmese were suspected of this, and the old man and chief engineer went into the focsle to make an inspection and hold an enquiry. One of the Burmese was a troublemaker and there had been several fights between him and the Indians.

We were making 12 knots with a strong current behind us and the sea changed colour to a greenish hue. Seabirds made their re-appearance as we approached the Gulf of Aden. The 2nd mate became his normal chatty self again, having recovered from the egg episode. He took the time to instruct me on the use of the sextant. On my watch below, I was learning how to splice wire, and while doing so, dropped the marlin spike point downwards onto my foot and it dug in deeply. It appeared I had a talent for self-mutilation! The 2nd mate, in charge of the medicine chest, was suitably sympathetic.

In spite of the old man's orders about kite making, the engineers were determined to produce one that would fly. Their kite rose 200 feet or more and would have gone higher had there been more wire. It was very hot as we entered the Red Sea and we put up a canvas screen abaft our house as the bulkhead was too hot to touch and the fan in our room was almost useless. The ports had to be closed at night unless we wanted to sit in darkness. Tension increased in the fo'c'sle between the Burmese and the Indians, exacerbated by the living conditions of sixty men crammed into the bows with little ventilation. The heat and stench were nearly unendurable, and I hated having to go there to call the watch when no one else could.

We soon arrived at Aden and followed a mine sweeper past Steamer Point, then entered the harbour which was crowded with ships waiting to form a convoy. The town of Crater shimmered under a merciless sun. No wonder it was considered a punishment station by the army. The mate allowed us to lower a boat and go sailing, and there was a strong urge to jump over the side to escape the heat. However, we had been warned about the risk of shark attack.

Two days later, the Italian Air Force paid us a visit, but at such a great height we could hardly see them. The alarms went off and the anti-aircraft cruiser Cairo" opened up with her pom-poms. The noise was deafening as she lay close by, and we put on our tin hats as the shrapnel began to fall around us. A few bombs fell harmlessly into the bay and others fell on the town. It was a mere foretaste of what was to come. When darkness came, the Italians had another go with more dramatic effects. The drone of aircraft high overhead was followed by heavy crumps as the bombs fell around us, and the sky lit up with bursts of anti-aircraft fire. It was like the blitz on London. Next morning, we counted the ships and were surprised to see that none of them had been hit. We watched a squadron of R.A.F. bombers fly over, bound for Somaliland to return the compliment.

The old man was concerned about the growth of weed on the hull which effected our speed and now we had the opportunity to remove it. We put the dinghy over the side and, armed with long-handled scrapers, went to work on the green grass as far below the waterline as we could reach. This seemed a puny effort and the mate came up with the idea that more could be accomplished by dragging a length of sounding wire under the hull. We started this using two boats, working from the bow and dragging the wire from side to side. It was hot work in the blazing sun and the results were disappointing so the project was abandoned.

The apprentices from the "King Arthur", lying nearby, came aboard and challenged us to a dinghy race. We were ready to take them on when orders came to prepare to sail. There were thirty ships in the convoy and our escorts were the destroyer, H.M.S "Kimberley", and three corvettes.

The island of Perim lay ahead as we entered the Straits of Bab el Mandeb. The commodore was the B. I. ship "Karagola" in the next column, her decks lined with Indian troops. Enemy planes were high overhead as one hoist after another appeared above the bridge on the "Karagola" telling us to keep our station in the convoy. A number of bombs fell around us sending up plumes of water. One dropped between us and the "Karagola", and I looked across and noticed that her troops had disappeared below deck. The cruiser, H.M.S. "Leander", had joined us, adding her fire power and the sky was dotted with white puffs of smoke. But no ships were hit and we steamed on unmolested, expecting a rough night as we passed through the narrow part of the strait. Mine sweepers cleared the channel ahead of us. We spent a restless night; it was so hot I took my mattress out of the cabin and lay out on deck. To our surprise, no attack came until daylight. I was standing outside the galley with a mug of tea in my hand when I heard a strange rushing sound, followed by the crash of bombs falling around us, two of which landed close to our port side. Again, the raids produced no hits and there was a lull until the next night.

At about 2:00 a.m., I was dozing in my cabin when several loud explosions brought me to my feet. I ran out on deck to see the sky lit up with flares and tracer bullets as our escorts let fly. A lot of flashes and explosions came from our port quarter as we came under attack from Italian bombers, destroyers and even shore batteries in Massawa in Somaliland. There was an ominous whooshing sound as shells passed over us. Our escorts sent up a terrific barrage of anti-aircraft fire which scared the planes off.

At daybreak, we were astonished to see that every merchant ship was intact. A corvette steamed through the convoy with flag signals telling us that an Italian destroyer had been sunk by the destroyer H.M.S."Kimberley", herself disabled in the action.

The convoy now split into two parts and we were ordered to proceed at full speed to our destination. H.M.S."Leander" launched her seaplane which flew off in the direction of land but once again, there was no action and no damage to any of the ships. All the ships raised flags to congratulate the "Kimberley" now being towed by her sister ship, the "Kingston". The next day, we heard the BBC News report of the action. We also picked up an Italian broadcast which claimed a victory and the sinking of a cruiser and destroyer. In the afternoon, we met a south-bound convoy made up entirely of large troop ships, returning to Australia to pick up more men to fight in the western desert.

We reached Suez intact and several large vessels were in the bay, including the White Star liner, "Georgic", which a few days later was bombed by German planes, caught fire and was gutted. She was eventually towed to Bombay for repairs. Our transit of the canal was delayed by several other vessels heading south so we anchored in the Bitter Lakes and some of us went for a swim. The water was so salty it was not refreshing.

It was now two and a half months since we had left Liverpool and our cargo had still not reached its destination. We lay in Port Said for a week waiting for a convoy to take us on our last lap, which could prove to be the most dangerous. We were kept on sea watches because of the fear of sabotage from some Egyptians who would have welcomed a German victory. An Italian cargo ship had been seized and we loaded some of her cargo of rubber from Malaya which had been destined for Venice. A Bank Line ship lay nearby and her 3rd mate and senior apprentice paid us a visit. We sat on deck and they told us they had been aboard the "Myrtlebank" when she was torpedoed. The mate had been in the water for over an hour and was completely covered in fuel oil when he was picked up. He had swallowed a quantity of it and even now, months later, it would seep out through the pores of his skin The senior apprentice had been at sea for almost four years without returning home.

On November 5th 1940, we left Port Said in a convoy of only five ships. We were the commodore ship, which pleased the old man immensely as he liked to feel important. He called the three of us to the bridge and gave us a lecture on matters concerning prompt signalling. Our course took us past the Island of Rhodes and, once again, we drew the attention of the Italian Air force but without any losses although there were several near-misses. One bomb landed so close the spray fell on our decks and the explosion shook everyone up. Not long after this we had trouble of another kind. A Burmese fireman hit one of the lascars with a shovel with sufficient force to place him at death's door. Only the skillful attention given by the old man and 2nd mate prevented him from bleeding to death. Meanwhile, two of the engineers subdued the Burman; he was handcuffed and locked up in the ship's hospital on the poop deck.

On the following day, I was woken up early to hear shouting outside. I ran out on deck to see a kallassee dragging a hose towards the afterdeck. A smell of something burning was coming from the ventilators at No. 4 hold. We tore off the hatch covers and boards to discover that the general cargo at the top was undamaged but that the coal in the lower hold had caught fire. All we could do was cover up the hatches and put hoses down the ventilators in the hope that the fire would be put out. A fast convoy of troop ships bound for Greece came up from astern and overtook us as we were only making 8 knots. They were escorted by the cruiser, "H.M.S. York", which was later sunk by German bombers off the island of Crete.

As we passed the island of Ovo, our old friend, the cruiser H.M.S."Cairo" made her appearance. It was reassuring to see her and she congratulated us on our efficiency as commodore ship. That evening, we felt the ship shudder as several depth charges were dropped nearby. This was followed by flashes to starboard as gun batteries on the islands opened fire. No shells landed near us, and we concluded that they were directed at the fast convoy of troop ships now well ahead of us.

Our convoy split up, most of the ships leaving for Piraeus, Greece. We were on our own as we headed for the Zia Channel. The islands were a very pretty sight but we were too nervous to enjoy the scenery as reports came that a submarine had been sighted and we expected another air attack from the island of Rhodes. We were making a dash at full speed for the safety of neutral Turkish waters. After an anxious day spent on lookout, the mate told me to go up on top of the monkey island to watch for lights ahead, and sure enough, before long, I sighted the Dardanelles. We entered the straits with our navigational lights on for the first time in months. The old man was elated and appeared on the bridge in his uniform. Gold-braided cap and all! We stopped at the small town of Chanak to pick up the pilot who did not appear until dawn. Chanak was a quaint-looking place; some of the houses appeared ready to fall down. Quite a crowd gathered to watch us.

A launch came out with the pilot and I stood at the Jacob's ladder to meet him. As he stepped aboard, he looked exactly as one expected a Turk to look — thick-set, swarthy and dressed in shapeless, baggy trousers. Once we had reached the bridge and he had shaken hands with the old man, he became very agitated. As his English was poor it was not apparent what was bothering him. Eventually he was understood to say "Why no Turkey letter?" We then realized that we did not have the Turkish ensign at the yard — an unfortunate oversight as nobody had thought about ordering one. The old man was infuriated and vented his rage on the 3rd mate who in turn blamed us boys for not reminding him! The matter was cleared up when, on the pilot's instructions, a flag was brought out from shore. Once this crisis had been solved, the pilot immediately demanded something to eat. The cuisine aboard the "Mandalay" could not be described as gourmet but obviously the pilot liked what the steward managed to scrape up for him. He was a talkative fellow and it wasn't easy to understand all that he said, but his dislike for the Germans was evident as he described them as "dogs" and said what Turkey would do to them if they were attacked. He seemed to have forgotten that they had been allies not long before. I came on watch again as we steamed into the Sea of Marmora. On our port side was Gallipoli and we could see the rusting hulk of the troopship,"River Clyde", a reminder of the bitter struggle which had taken place on these shores twenty-five years earlier.

Steve warned me that I should keep the pilot happy by scrounging an almost continuous supply of food. This wasn't easy and I was obliged to get our lazy butler out of his bunk to search for whatever he could find. I took the pilot a mug of cocoa, which he didn't like and he demanded coffee. There was none aboard.

We were disappointed to hear that our destination was Ismid, the naval base some 50 miles from Istanbul. It was a bleak place; a few dilapidated buildings lay beyond the jetty where we tied up. At anchor out in the bay was the pride of the Turkish fleet, the battleship "Yavuz". Built in Germany in 1912 as the "Goeben", she was a major threat to the Allied forces during the Gallipoli campaign in the first war. She was considered invincible and pictures of her were displayed everywhere as a symbol of Turkey's naval might.

Our stay in Ismid was brief as there were no facilities on the jetty to take our cargo and it appeared that the only reason we went there was because the port of Istanbul was full. Three of us boys walked to the village nearby. The inhabitants regarded us with a mixture of suspicion and curiosity. They stood silent and unsmiling as we passed them. They were dressed in the heavy drab clothing of subsistence farmers. The great emancipator, Kemal Ataturk, had abolished the fez and the veil — the men wore cloth caps and the women wore shawls.

Next morning, the old man blew the ship's whistle to summon the pilot who had spent the night ashore. But he failed to appear, the old man ordered the lines to be let go, and we sailed without him.

On the 10th of November, 1940, we arrived in Istanbul. It was a splendid sight as we steamed into the Golden Horn. The dome of Saint Sophia, one of Islam's greatest mosques, gleamed in the morning sun. Ahead of us was the elegant bridge which crossed the harbour to the European section of the city known as Pera. Across the Bosporus lay Scutari in Asia Minor. The harbour was a crowded waterway and ferries, tugs and coastal vessels crossed in all directions. There were a number of deep-sea ships flying the flags of Russia, Rumania and Germany. After securing to buoys in the Golden Horn, we were put to work manning the ship's dinghy which was used to ferry people to and from the landing stage at Pera, the European side of the city. The constant weaving about among the heavy, water-borne traffic caused some anxious moments. Steve was at the tiller taking the old man ashore and passed too close to a speeding ferry whose wash almost capsized the dinghy, prematurely ageing the captain! By the time they reached the safety of the shore, he had recovered his composure and released a torrent of abuse at Steve for his carelessness.

After many weeks of working sea watches, it was good to be on day work with the prospect of a normal sleep in a bunk. Our thoughts turned to the attractions of life ashore and we discovered that Istanbul did indeed offer plenty of diversions to amuse weary seamen. It was a cosmopolitan city with a large Greek population and many refugees from Hungary and Rumania. We were moored to buoys in the harbour and launches called infrequently to take us ashore. There was a steep climb up "Step Street" to reach Pera where the shops, cafes and bars were. The most popular place was the "Krystal", its main attraction the orchestra of beautiful Hungarian gypsy girls who played seductive, haunting music. The place was always packed with seamen of many nationalities who tended to keep to themselves in groups at separate tables. We were warned to be careful about the company we kept. The city was a nest of intrigue and suspicion; one could never be certain that the friendly stranger was not a German agent and merchant seamen were considered easy prey.

One evening, a party of us were enjoying the music and drinks when the crew from the British ship, "Jhelum", walked in and sat at a table across the room. But the men that caught our attention were the crew from the German ship, "Hanover". It seemed strange to be sitting just a few feet from the enemy. As the evening wore on, the men became more boisterous and taunts and threats were exchanged between the crews of the "Hanover" and the "Jhelum" until the situation took an ugly turn. Someone called the police and we decided it was time to leave. Earlier, we had met a well-dressed man in civilian clothes who claimed to be a "King's Messenger" attached to the British Consulate. He was in an aggressive mood and spoiling for a fight. Before leaving I glanced back to see him pushing a tall German against a table. The police arrived and order was restored. The Turks were a tough lot and not adverse to using heavy sticks and gun-butts on heads.

Later that night, we heard that a group of British seamen had torn down the swastika flying over the doors of the German Embassy. When this news reached the Germans they did the same thing to the union jack over the British Embassy a few doors away! It seemed ridiculous that such things could happen in a neutral country and not long afterwards the company agent came aboard to warn the crew about taking part in such vandalism. He also told us that enemy agents were very active in Istanbul and to be wary about talking to strangers in the bars and cafes. It was a capital offence to give information which could be useful to the enemy. A British seaman had been paid ten pounds by a German agent he met in a bar in exchange for information about convoys. For this act of treachery he was tried, found guilty and hanged.

One evening, three of us apprentices were sitting in a bar drinking wine when a Turk sidled up and asked us in broken English what we thought of Istanbul. He volunteered to show us the "real" Istanbul! We knew that there would be a charge for such a service but agreed that it might prove interesting so didn't give our usual reply of "Muck off!" Sensing some excitement ahead, we followed him into the street where he hailed a taxi. It was dark as we drove along the narrow, dimly-lit, side streets and I got the impression that we were now entering the "Forbidden City". We stopped at gates where an armed guard peered at us and spoke to the driver. Our guide joined in, some deal was struck and there was much laughter. We began to wonder what we were getting ourselves into. On both sides of the dark street stood ramshackle, two-storied, wooden buildings. Groups of women stood posturing in the doorways. By now, I was feeling apprehensive. Was this the "red light district" the other boys had talked about? Peter Gunn, more worldly-wise, assured us that it was indeed. Giggling girls at one doorway told us of the varied delights available within. We were shown into a large room which reeked of garlic and incense. The madam, a heavy, severe-looking woman, offered us drinks, then called out and five or six girls appeared from behind curtains for our inspection. The drinks were strong enough to remove whatever inhibitions we had. One girl was much prettier than the rest and was the object of our attention, but Peter bolder than the rest of us, took her by the hand and disappeared behind the curtains. Her name was "Najlus". The others made their choices while I wrestled with uncertainty, doubt and guilt. The last girl had a countenance which was quite unremarkable and as she led me through the curtains, told me her name was "Gannou", and that she was very good value for the money.

On our way back to the ship we compared notes. Peter wore a satisfied smirk on his face, Steve gave a lurid description of events and Jimmy was all for going back. As for myself, I was stricken with remorse and remained silent. I was in dread of someone from home finding out. These visits went on for some time until one day Peter appeared on deck with a pronounced limp and a glum expression on his face. We wondered why. A lump had appeared in his groin and the mate (after consulting the old man who looked at the "Shipmasters Medical Guide) had solemnly told him he had a dose of the clap. This dramatic news had a salutary effect upon the rest of us and visits to the red light district came to an abrupt end. I thought of the not-so-delectable "Najlus" and soberly reflected upon my good fortune.

Considerably chastened I decided to pursue more respectable activities ashore. Sight-seeing seemed appropriate. To my surprise, Peter and Jimmy thought so too, and one afternoon we took a ferry up the Bosporus. The ferry was so crowded it was difficult to find room to stand, let alone sit. Most of the passengers were country folk who had brought their produce to the market and were now going home. Empty crates, unsold goats, chickens and even a few pigs vied for room on the decks. The master of the heavily-laden ferry must have been nerveless as other vessels came within feet of our bows and collision seemed imminent until, at the last moment, one would alter course. The ferry made frequent stops, crossing the straits from side to side; a port in Europe, then one in

Asia until we finally reached the Black Sea. We marvelled at houses perched so precariously on the edge of cliffs they appeared ready to fall into the sea.

By the time the ferry had begun her return run back to Istanbul, we began to think of food and pushed our way through the crowd to what was grandly called the "Dining Saloon". It consisted of rough wooden tables piled high with bundles and sacks with passengers perched where ever they could find space. The air was thick with a blend of smells from animals, tobacco and whatever was being cooked on the stoves at the end of the room. It was enough to discourage even the heartiest appetite. Several cooks stood behind steaming pots. One contained some kind of stew. A bowl was filled and offered to us but we declined after spotting something floating which could not be identified. A large, fierce-looking cook said, "You no like?" which we took to be more of a challenge than a question. We assured him that we were not hungry and only wanted a loaf of good, crusty Turkish bread.

Back aboard our own ship, we spent a lot of time down the hold watching the cargo to prevent pilferage. The dockers were an exceedingly tough-looking crowd and I wondered what reaction I would face if I caught one of them stealing. One day, a docker was stopped as he walked down the gangway. He had wrapped several boot laces around his legs and I felt pleased that it wasn't me who had caught him for such a trivial offence. A woman judge thought differently and he was sentenced to three months hard labour plus several lashes. It was a tough world for the Turks.

The fire in No. 2 hold, discovered two weeks before, had been smouldering ever since and we were kept busy directing a hose on it. While we were doing this I heard music coming from across the water. It was coming from large speakers aboard a Russian passenger ship as she entered the harbour. She was celebrating the fact that there had been a Russian success on the Eastern Front. Another German ship arrived. She was the "Salzburg" of Hamburg, so we were now outnumbered.

I was sent over the side in a bosun's chair to paint the ship's name and port of registry on our stern. This was a tricky job due to our having a counter stern, and a bowsing line had to be used to bring me within reach of the letters. When this was done, I started painting the draught marks near the water line. I was so intent on getting the paint on without spilling it that I did not notice the swell caused by a passing ferry boat. The fact that I got soaked did not matter as much as the loss of half of the black and white paint!

There was excitement on deck one day when lifting the first of two heavy steam rollers out of No. 2 hold with our 30 ton jumbo derrick. The steam winch jumped out of gear and the derrick came slowly down to the deck. The engineers took all day to fix it. This was followed by the arrival of the police to arrest one of our secunnies, (Indian quarter-masters). He'd been seen talking and drinking with a Nazi agent who had plied him with liquor in order to get information.

To make room for other ships in Istanbul we were sent back to Ismid where the farmers seemed anxious to do business with us. The old man went ashore and bought a turkey and several chickens for Christmas and we wondered if he had paid for it out of his own pocket. Shortly after, a Turk appeared at the gangway with a goose under his arm and I paid the equivalent of 4 shillings for it. The farmers ashore heard of this and, before long, several appeared with turkeys and chickens for sale. Before the day was out, the afterdeck looked like a farmyard. Pens had been hastily constructed from dunnage wood and housed several chickens, turkeys and my goose. The old man drew the line and would not allow any goats aboard, much to the annoyance of the lascars who were Muslims.

A few of us went ashore to take a look at Asian Turkey. We were regarded as curiosities and some of the inhabitants came to take a look at us, a few of them muttering, "Inglese, Inglese", as we walked by. Soldiers, riding sturdy little horses, passed us. These men looked exceedingly drab but we didn't doubt their toughness, having heard about the Gallipoli campaign during the last war. When we returned aboard, we were warned not to be seen near the railway line at night as strangers were likely to be shot.

I was standing on deck watching the old battleship, "Yavuz", put to sea, when the bandari rushed up to tell me that my goose had got out of its pen, had taken flight from the boat deck and was last seen heading for the farm yard! I dashed down the gangway and made for the farm some hundred yards away. When I reached it, I found several geese and unable to recognise mine, hastily grabbed the fattest and made off with it, hoping that the loud squawking wouldn't bring the farmer out!

On one filthy wet day, we were on deck mixing cement which we lowered into the hold where it was poured into the bilges. I found that carrying 100 lb. bags of cement was a back-breaking job. While we were doing this, the ship's cat fell forty feet down the hold. The unfortunate creature was in poor shape and we considered putting her out of her misery by throwing her overboard but none of us had the heart to do so. We wrapped her up in a cloth and let her lie in the cabin.

On the 10th of December 1940 we moved the ship to Scutari and went alongside a wharf crowded with refugees. It was an extraordinary sight of abject misery. We learnt that they were peasants from Rumania, driven from their land by the Germans to find refuge in Turkey. They wore their national costumes and stood around their worldly possessions in the rain, waiting for a vessel which at that moment was docking and presumably would take them elsewhere to be resettled.

The bitterly cold weather caused a strike among the Indian crew who refused to work on the grounds that they had insufficient warm clothing. We didn't blame them for their living conditions were miserable, however it meant that we had to take over some of their work. The mate told us boys that we had to work in the galley and the pantry as well as doing deck work. I laughed when Peter and Jimmy began peeling potatoes but wasn't amused when I found a mountain of dirty dishes and pans to wash! The strike continued, although the cook decided to return to work which was a pity as the gunner had produced good meals while the cook was on strike. Added to this, we had to assist the engineers who were stoking the furnaces in place of the firemen who were also on strike. After shovelling a few tons of coal, I was told to make tea for the Old Man and the British Consul who had come aboard to talk about the crew's strike. He must have wondered about life aboard a British tramp when I appeared, covered in coal dust, carrying a tea-pot and cups! The Chief of Police was with them and we later learnt that they had decided not to put the crew in jail as they'd committed no crime on Turkish soil. The only thing the old man could do was log each man a day's pay for every day of the strike. Meanwhile, the cook had his life threatened by the crew for continuing to work and he wisely decided to pack up.

I was kept busy one morning running between the galley and the saloon with hot dishes and, on one trip, slipped on the icy deck and deposited curry and rice all over the deck!

A Royal Navy sailor arrived aboard as a passenger. His name was Marshall Sault and he had a story to tell. He had been aboard the destroyer "H.M.S. Hunter" which took part in a raid on Narvik on the coast of Norway. In company with two other destroyers, the "Hunter" entered the Vest fjord and attacked several German naval ships, sinking two destroyers with gun fire and torpedoes. When attempting to make their escape, they ran into several more German ships and a fierce running battle took place. The "Hunter" was torpedoed and Marshall found himself in the icy water with depth charges exploding around him. Marshall told us the explosions felt like a giant clamp squeezing him and those swimmers whose heads were below the surface were killed. He was picked up by a German destroyer and held prisoner ashore for a few days. The Germans had no proper facilities for prisoners and eventually he and a few other men were pushed across the border into neutral Sweden after being forced to sign a declaration not to fight against the Germans. Suffering from cold and hunger, they walked in deep snow for twenty miles until they reached a small town and were interned in friendly

Sweden. Internment in Sweden was far from being a hardship compared with war-time England and life in the Royal Navy. The kindly Swedes allowed them almost complete freedom as long as they behaved themselves. Marshall showed us a photo of the beautiful blonde he had met and fallen in love with. He had been quite content to stay in Sweden but the British Government had other ideas and, after eight months internment, he was flown from Stockholm to Moscow, via Riga, and then by train to Odessa where he boarded a Russian ship for Istanbul. He stayed with us until we reached Alexandria where he rejoined the Navy. I often wondered whether he returned to Sweden after the war.

Our stay in Istanbul was coming to an end. We had loaded boxwood and dried fruit and had made our last foray ashore to our favourite cafe, the "Krystal". Earlier, it had been the scene of unpleasantness with the Germans but we had made friends with the members of the orchestra. They played some rousing music to wish us "Bon voyage" and the management gave us free drinks.

We were homeward-bound at last and after twelve hours steaming, were in international waters when we sighted a strange craft astern which we immediately regarded with suspicion. I rushed aft to put up our ensign even though it was still dark, but before I could do so, a powerful light was directed on us, then the vessel turned away and disappeared into the darkness.

On New Year's Day 1941,we arrived in Izmir, the old town of Smyrna. It was warm and sunny as we dropped anchor and secured the stern to the shore Mediterranean-style. The British Consul and his wife came down to the gangway and invited us to a New Year's Eve party. We thought that it would be a stuffy affair but as there was likely to be a lot of good food some of us went anyway. It turned out to be far from boring as there were several Greek and Turkish girls to dance with and we did not return aboard until the early hours. Ours had been an orderly night's outing but the 3nd mate, Chips, and Jimmy had looked for something more exciting. They had taken the ship's dinghy and rowed it along the shoreline towards the town in order to save themselves a long walk. The police were waiting for them when they stepped ashore and refused to let them pass. Chips was a reasonable fellow when sober but he became pugnacious when drunk. It was bad enough to hit a policeman in Glasgow, but far worse to hit one in Turkey. A melee ensued and strangely enough they were not arrested, but returned aboard badly beaten up. While I was helping the 2nd mate patch them up, the old man came to see what all the commotion was about. After hearing the story, he went red in the face and told the 3rd mate he was unfit to be an officer and the lot of them were lucky not to be in a grim Turkish jail.

Later that day another fight broke out. I was standing on deck talking to the butler when we heard a lot of shouting on the foredeck. Three of the Burmese firemen were pushing each other and two of them were holding knives! The butler and I managed to quiet them and take away the knives. So much for our prospects in the New Year! Those who had been involved in the fight with the police had their shore leave stopped and had to pay fines. There was more trouble with the three Burmese firemen. They started fighting in the fo'c'sle and one was badly injured when struck over the head with an iron bar and knifed in the side. The mate and chief engineer went forward and put the two assailants in handcuffs and locked them up in separate storerooms. Two days later the Turkish police took them ashore to jail.

Izmir was almost a resort town with rows of white, stucco villas overlooking the sea, tree-lined streets and a promenade as imposing as the one at Brighton. But further away from the sea the houses and streets became squalid and untidy. The ship's agent told the old man that it would be unwise for any of us to stray very far from the centre of town. Two weeks before our arrival a murderer had been hanged in the main square.

We must have made a fairly good impression at the New Year's party at the Consul's house, although the ship's presence in Izmir had caused him a lot of trouble as he tried to sort out our crew problems. We were invited for dinner and wild boar was on the menu, which we agreed was better than the tough old pork aboard.

By the 9th of January, 1941, we were almost down to our marks and ready to sail. We had loaded sultanas, figs, tobacco, aniseed and valona. Just before we were about to let our lines go, the police appeared on the dock with the two Burmese. The Turkish authorities wanted no part of them and we were forced to take them back aboard. My diary noted that "We now have a rough lot in the fo'c'sle, a murderer, a few thieves, pickpockets and a man who was about to give information to the enemy!" The Burman who was attacked by the other two was himself a murderer. During the riots in Rangoon he had killed a Mohammedan priest. His nickname was "Jo Beef" because of his strength. He had plunged a long knife into the priest's back.

A crowd of friends stood on the dock. They were mostly British servicemen and their wives stationed in Turkey. We blew a blast on the whistle and sailed away. It was a lovely sunny day and Izmir looked picturesque with white-topped mountains in the background but we were glad to see the last of Turkey.

It was a short run down the Aegean Sea to Piraeus, Greece. The ancient Acropolis with Athens in the distance came into view and we dropped anchor in the bay. We dressed the ship with flags from stem to stern to celebrate a Greek victory over the Italians — their troops had captured a town in Albania. The old man was the only person allowed ashore and when he returned he said he had watched crowds rejoicing in the streets of Athens. The victory was short-lived, however, as not long afterwards German troops occupied Greece.

We boys, accompanied by Sparks and an engineer, went sailing in the harbour. When we got back aboard we received a terrific blast from the old man who had been watching us with binoculars. He was angered because we had gone too close to the shore where there were some military defences. The cruiser H.M.S. "Calcutta" entered the harbour — she had had a hot time coming up from Port Said when she had been attacked and damaged by Stuka dive bombers.

We left Piraeus in a convoy of ten ships bound for Port Said; again we were the commodore ship. What a motley collection we were. Two Greeks, an Egyptian, a Chinese coaster and a Free French tanker were among the ships and problems of communication soon began to crop up. The old man became very frustrated when signals, such as "No. 23 — You are not keeping the correct distance from the ship ahead of you," or "No. 16 — Cease making too much smoke," were completely ignored. "They have no bloody savvy," said the mate. When one of the old Greek ships continued to send forth clouds of black smoke, the senior officer of the escort had had enough and directed a powerful searchlight in its direction. This eventually brought a response and a signal appeared on the Greek ship. It read "Cease flashing!" Despite the lack of discipline, we reached Port Said safely and anchored near the entrance to the Suez Canal.

We had room for more cargo and loaded 200 tons of potash, bromide and over 100 tons of sacked onions which were stowed on top of the hatches and caused problems later. The Egyptian police came aboard at the old man's request as he wanted to get rid of our trouble-makers. He was successful and the two Burmese and two secunnies were hand-cuffed and taken ashore. A new Indian secunnie came aboard — he had spent a year in jail in Port Said for smuggling hashish. We entered the Suez Canal and before long were in the middle of a sandstorm. Visibility was so poor that we almost collided with another ship which appeared out of the haze and we were forced to secure to the bank and wait until it cleared. The whole ship was covered with a layer of sand. It got into our eyes and mouths. We had to assist in removing it from the gun mechanism. Eventually it cleared and we reached Suez and anchored close to the troop ship "Monarch of Bermuda" loaded with Australians bound for the Western Desert.

I was on the bridge at 4 a.m. with the mate when air raid sirens went off and several low-flying planes passed overhead. Bombs dropped and every one of them missed. At daybreak, we saw a Panamanian ship with her flag at half-mast. One of her seamen had been killed by shrapnel. Several ships nearby had Italian prisoners aboard who were bound for camps in India. On our way down the Red Sea, poor Peter's venereal affliction became worse and the mate judged him unfit for duty. I took his place on day work which was better than standing bridge watches as I got a bit more sleep. He was put in isolation in the hospital back aft and was living by himself. We felt sorry for him.

Off the north coast of Africa and bound for Mombasa, we had another encounter with what was probably a German raider. It was February 14th, 1941, and I wrote the following in my diary: "We had another close shave today. During the afternoon watch a ship was sighted ahead, about 11 miles away. We turned immediately and headed in the opposite direction. On the bridge, the old man and the mate took turns looking through the telescope. It was their opinion that the stranger was one of the Nordeutscher Lloyd ships. Her movements then became very suspicious. As we altered course, she appeared to turn towards us. We increased to maximum speed in a moderate head sea. It was suggested that perhaps she was a submarine depot ship with a speed of about 15 knots as she was gaining on us."

Sparks was ordered to contact the nearest naval station but said that as our wireless set was obsolete he could only transmit a message for 150 miles. We began to prepare for the possibility that we might have to abandon ship. We carried about a dozen smoke floats and these were made ready to throw overboard. Just before darkness, we saw that the other ship had turned on her navigation lights. This was thought to be a cunning bluff to make us think that she was a harmless neutral. Once again, darkness was our salvation — we could see her but she could not see us. We returned slowly to our original course and by 2100 hours her lights had disappeared.

Two days later, the W/T station at Mombasa repeatedly asked us for our position but our transmitter had "packed up" and we were unable to answer. We entered the fine natural harbour of Kilindini to find it full of ships, both naval and merchant. We wondered why the destroyers and cruisers were not at sea chasing enemy ships until we heard that some of them had just returned after bombarding the Italian forces in Somaliland. One afternoon we were sailing the dinghy and came close to the stern of a cruiser. Several tars were standing on stages on her side, painting her hull. They told us that they had been "Wop" shooting. We headed for the nearest beach and after having a swim, I wandered around the beach and up to the trees until I realized I was standing amidst a swarm of inch-long ants.

Barges came alongside and we took on about 600 tons of bunker coal. There was coal dust everywhere, blown by a stiff breeze. Four large troopships steamed into the harbour. It was a splendid sight. The "Empress of Japan",

"Empress of Australia", Warwick Castle" and the old Orient liner "Ormonde". They sought refuge in Mombasa because the pocket battleship, "Admiral Von Scheer", was operating in the area and two British cruisers, "Raleigh" and "Hawkins", were out looking for her. Four seamen from the American ship "Charles S. Crump" came aboard and gave us some magazines hoping to get some in exchange but the only ones we had to offer were a few copies of the "Signal", a Nazi propaganda magazine we had bought in Istanbul. They asked us where we came from and how much money we made. Our reply to the second question seemed to baffle them!

On our way south past Zanzibar, we rigged up our deep-sea fishing gear again and this time we caught a large fish which the chief said was a "wahou". It weighed 48 pounds. Someone had devised a clever signal. A fender was secured at the top of a stanchion post and when an extra strain suddenly came on the line, the fender dropped to the deck and we knew that we had caught a fish. Our next catch was a 10 pound barracuda which was better eating than the wahou.

On the 3rd of March, 1941 we were greeted by a bomber of the South African Air Force — it came out to check us as we approached Durban. It had been five months since we were there and my thoughts were on seeing Zoe again. I crossed the harbour on the Springbok ferry and reached the centre of the city to find that over a thousand sailors from H.M.S. "Illustrious" had taken over Durban. When I called to renew my acquaintance with Zoe, I was told that she had taken the day off and was in the company of one of the sailors. This news was excuse enough for me to search for the closest bistro in order to drown my sorrows. However all was not lost as I met the other apprentices and we spent an enjoyable day walking about and keeping out of trouble.

It was about this time that we heard about an incident in Cape Town that must have put a strain on relations between South Africa and Australia. Several large troopships, which included the "Queen Mary" and the "Nieuw Amsterdam", loaded with Australians bound for the Middle East had anchored in Table Bay. Attempts to restrict shore leave had been in vain. The Aussies, noted for their disdain of discipline and no doubt with a fatalistic attitude about going into battle, got ashore in force for one last fling. Several hundred intoxicated Diggers, bent on raising hell, were more than the police could cope with and a riot ensued. Shop windows were smashed, monuments were scaled and horse-drawn carriages commandeered. The sight of these vehicles, with wild-eyed Aussies holding the reins and charging along the streets, must have caused more than raised eye-brows. Another group of Diggers was reported to have taken a traffic policeman and dressed him in ladies' underwear taken from a shop nearby. The well-known cafe-bar, "Del Monico" was reduced to a shambles. It came to an end when the Aussies ran out of steam and most of them returned to their ships .

But not all, for some soldiers took the opportunity to desert, heading north into Rhodesia and simply disappearing.

The stench of rotting onions pervaded the ship. The intense heat over the past weeks had produced a mass of steaming rot which dripped through the tarpaulins and into the holds. We spent hours dumping the sacks overboard. A Hotchkiss machine gun was brought aboard to supplement our armament. This ancient piece dated from the previous war and was considered worse than useless by our disgusted gun-layer.

We left Cape Town and headed out into a heavy westerly swell. A few albatrosses kept us company until we reached warmer waters and they deserted us. By now, almost all the onions had gone rotten and, worse still, their acid-like juice had dripped on to bales of tobacco. It was heavy work as we stood ankle-deep in the stinking mess, throwing what was left over the side. Our nights were spent restlessly, constantly swatting cockroaches brought out in force by the increasing heat. One night, we had to alter course suddenly to avoid hitting two whales which surfaced ahead of us. The day before we reached Freetown, quinine tablets were issued to counteract malaria.

In Freetown, the old man was convinced that another attempt to clear the hull of weed would be successful. This time we put two boats down to work on each side of the ship and did manage to remove some weed. It was exhausting work pulling the wire back and forth and we were not sorry when the wire broke and put an end to it! The old man and Sparks looked very important as they stood in the launch which came to take them to the convoy conference. It was held aboard the old Union Castle liner "Edinburgh Castle". She was an impressive ship with two funnels but was in a run-down condition and reputedly alive with rats. When the launch returned several hours later, its operator made a bad approach towards our accommodation ladder and clumsily took the launch under one of the ship's scupper discharges, which at that moment was emptying the contents of the galley sink. Both the old man and Sparks received a good drenching from the dirty, greasy water and the fact that we watched their discomfort added to the old man's fury.

On the 29th of March, 1941, we sailed on the last leg of our journey. We were in a convoy of thirty ships and the old man was pleased to be vice-commodore. We boys expected another lecture about bridge efficiency and we were not disappointed. He followed that up by immediately putting us on double watches, which we felt was his revenge for laughing at him in the launch incident. The cruiser H.M.S. "Dragon" and the armed merchant ship "Bulolo" were among our escorts and the cruiser ordered us to test our A/A guns on a kite she was flying. The 2nd mate, anxious to show his skill, fired off a few bursts with the old Hotchkiss but his aim was bad and the bullets went nowhere near the kite but almost hit a ship. The kite was shot down by another ship.

On the 2nd of April, 1941, I again wrote in my diary — "Message from the commodore was read this morning. It said that the convoy had passed over a U boat last night and urged us to keep closed-up or we will be torpedoed! A Sunderland flying-boat is patrolling over us and evidently detected a submarine. The 3rd mate said that he saw the track of a torpedo last night; it passed astern and one of the lascars reported seeing a periscope. The last convoy which passed this way a few days ago lost four ships."

Over the next few weeks I continued almost daily in my diary — 4th April, 1941 — "A steering break-down. A pipe leading to the telemotor in the wheel house burst and we stopped and drifted astern of the convoy. The old man is both furious and worried. Efforts to make temporary repairs were in vain. We changed over to our emergency steering gear on the stern. We now feel like a "sitting duck"; there is a heavy swell running and we roll heavily which makes steering on the stern very difficult. But we did manage to catch up with the convoy. A rumour circulates that we may have to put in to Gibraltar for repairs."

5th April, 1941 — "The engineers fixed the steering and we are glad to be back in the wheel house. We heard that two ships in the area had been torpedoed and one of our escorts left the convoy to pick up survivors and take them to Freetown. The cruiser "Dragon" left us and now we only have one escort! Later in the afternoon, a large Dutch troop ship joined us and took its station in the middle of the convoy."

7th April, 1941 — We are now well out into the Atlantic — our speed a modest 8 knots. The "Para", a Norwegian ship in the next column, has signaled to say that a seaman aboard is seriously ill and we have passed this message on to the cruiser "Birmingham" which joined us earlier. There is a heavy sea running but the cruiser has sent a doctor in her launch which runs between the ships and is lost to view in a cloud of spray."

8th April, 1941 — "The "Bulolo" crossed ahead of the convoy flying a large black flag which meant "I am hunting enemy vessel." Smoke was reported rising above the horizon and she dashed off in that direction. Shortly after, the "Birmingham" put on full steam and left us at high speed and we are now left without any escort."

9th April, 1941 — "I went on watch at midnight and saw a ship ahead of the convoy. She was ablaze with lights like peace time. When first sighted, she acted suspiciously by turning on lights and hoping to pass as a neutral. We heard later that the navy put a prize crew aboard and took her into Gibraltar. The old man was upset when we received a message from the commodore telling us that we were making too much smoke! This has happened before and the chief engineer has been ordered to do something about it but has told the old man that very little can be done. This time I was given a chit to deliver to the chief. I read it on my way to the engine room. It said "Reduce smoke at once. Master." The chief, to his credit, merely shrugged his shoulders and threw the chit into a bucket. The speed of the convoy is now down to six knots and there is lots of cursing as the date of our arrival in Liverpool is put back."

17th April, 1941 — "We are now doing little more than five knots and have been ordered to follow a series of course alterations which at one point had the convoy heading south! Some ships almost collided during this exercise and we still have no escort."

19th April, 1941 — "Very dirty weather. Strong south-west gale. Real Western Ocean stuff! We were rolling so heavily that getting about the decks was difficult. The temperature dropped to 38 degrees and even two woollen sweaters wasn't enough when keeping watch on the open bridge. I would duck down below the dodger as a sea crashed aboard, sending icy spray across the bridge. The saloon was a shambles. Broken plates, sugar and jam mixed with sea water sloshed about the deck. The butler was too sea-sick to care and remained in his bunk. The convoy became so scattered that keeping our correct position in it became impossible. Some ships could cope with the seas better than others. The smaller ones dropped astern and disappeared in the murk. The old man looked anxiously at the barometer which read 29.04 inches. A big sea carried away our accommodation ladder and a second one came aboard with a terrific thump and bent the rails around the old man's deck. I was in our cabin when this one hit us and I thought that the door would give way. It held, but the deck was flooded."

20th April, 1941 — "It was difficult to write my diary today as the sea was still very high and although the rolling was not as violent, the clinometer showed rolls of twenty degrees. In these conditions, sit-down meals become next to impossible. Even with the fiddles up, (wooden baffles), and the table cloth dampened, the dishes slide off. I took a plate to the lee side of the galley and felt grateful to get whatever the beleaguered cook had managed to produce, which wasn't much, not that anyone blamed him."

Later in the afternoon the weather moderated and the convoy formed up again. An old destroyer, the "Winchelsea", made her appearance. She told us that other escorts were on their way. Sure enough, before the day was finished we had four destroyers and four corvettes, one of which was an ex-Yankee with four funnels. A wag suggested that the first two were for smoke and the others were spare! I was sent on deck to secure any gear that had worked loose. I found Chips, who needed help knocking in hatch wedges. When we had finished and were standing in the galley warming up, he was not in a happy mood and said, "That's good enough for the money I get." He always said that after completing a job of work no matter how slap-dash. "They can stuff their bonus — it's not worth it." He was referring to the war bonus or danger money paid to seamen. Officers received ten pounds a month but lower deckmen such as Chips and us were worth less and got five pounds a month. "Going to sea is bullshit. When the war is over I will get a shore job in the shipyard," he complained. We seldom talked about money as there was very little of it anyway. I had now completed four years at sea and was being paid the grand sum of four pounds a month plus the war bonus.

Merchant seamen had always been poorly paid and as Britain imported over 80% of her food requirements, the nation had come to take them for granted. But long-suffering as they were, one ship's crew had had enough when their pay ceased the day they abandoned ship after being torpedoed. They were adrift in a life boat for several days before being rescued. When they went to the shipping office to sign off and receive their money, they found that they were off pay after the ship sank! The Ministry of War Transport hastily rectified this oversight before it reached the newspapers.

April 21st, 1941, was a very dark night and the old man was anxious as many of the ships were in the wrong position; there had not been time to form them up properly. At day-break, we were disgusted to find once again that all of the escorts had left us. This was probably due to our evasive steering done without informing the naval commander. A large bomber circled the convoy at long range and was identified as a Heinkel. We expected to be attacked but, to our great relief, allied planes drove him off and we knew we were in home waters once more. This was the time when most of us showed symptoms of the affliction known as the "channels", feverish excitement caused by proximity to home!

On April 24th 1941, we approached the mine-swept channel leading to Liverpool. The old man was in high spirits when he recognized the ships ahead of us as being part of a "fast" convoy. We had been designated as a "slow" one, yet we arrived at the same time! He ordered more steam to reach the pilot station first. But it did us little good as there was an air raid on Liverpool, the port was closed and we had to anchor. When the all clear was given we got going again. The old man began jumping up and down in fury when an Elder Dempster ship got ahead of us. His language was most colourful. We were about to enter the Mersey docks when the sirens went off and another air raid began; bombs dropped on the city but little damage was done. We had been away for nine and a half months. I had finished my apprenticeship and all I wanted was a good rest at home.

Before I went ashore, Peter asked me whether I wanted to buy his sextant. He was short of money and wanted a pound for it. It later became one of my most prized possessions and worth considerably more than one pound. It was the last time I ever saw any of the boys with whom I had served my time. Many years later, I met a man from Stromness in the Orkney Islands who knew the Sutherland family. Jimmy gained his Masters ticket before he was 27 years old and had a brilliant career ahead of him, and was soon in command of his own ship, but sadly his health deteriorated and he died in his early forties. He had been a good friend. I don't know what became of Steve. As mentioned earlier, Peter Gunn lost his life in 1942 when his ship was torpedoed. They were all good ship-mates and friends.

Chapter 5. Problems with the Board of Trade!

After a few week's leave it was time to prepare for my 2nd mate's ticket. I had been told that it was a difficult exam but I was not unduly worried. A few weeks of swotting and before the summer was over, I would be standing on the bridge of a fine, modern ship, with a stripe on each sleeve and in charge of the 8-12 watch. Unfortunately, I was in for a rude awakening.

"Jack's Palace" was known throughout the maritime world as the best place in London to stay while attending the Nautical School in the same building. It was situated in the seedy East End near the West India docks and the "Great Eastern" pub stood conveniently across the road where Commercial Road joined Burdett road. It was a great meeting place for seamen and distractions were abundant. I arrived to find that the "Palace" had no room — it was full of men up for tickets and I was advised to enquire further up the road at the " Memorial Hostel for Seamen" . This building was as grim as its name and was not so fondly called the " Stack of Bricks"! It was not a welcoming place. At the desk a scruffy clerk rudely demanded, "What's yer noime and whers yer book?" He was referring to my Seaman's Discharge Book, a record of time spent at sea. Mine showed four years of sweated labour as a cadet and this bothered the clerk because this was a hostel for men of the fo'c'sle and potential officers were regarded with suspicion and even hostility.

But I had no other choice, the rates were low and I found myself in a tiny room, several floors up. The communal washroom and toilets were at the end of a long corridor which gave off a strong odour of carbolic soap, tobacco smoke and urine. It was usually a noisy place — not surprising as the building was full of men either on leave or waiting for a ship and many of them spent their money on booze. So at any given time, half the residents of the "Stack of Bricks" were in an alcoholic stupor and some of them in a belligerent mood. Fights in the main entrance hall and in the corridors were a common occurrence. Indeed, nobody seemed to take much notice of them or bothered to try and break them up .

These then, were the circumstances in which I had to prepare for my ticket and coupled with my reluctance to study complex questions, it all became a recipe for disaster. My room overlooked the entrance to a pub on Salmon Lane. There was always a crowd waiting for opening time and a chorus of curses, threats and highly-explicit language made serious study difficult. I used to watch ragged urchins, some no more than four or five years old, waiting outside the doors of the pub for their parents to come out at closing time.

One warm evening, I decided that I needed a drink and wanted to see what the pub looked like inside. Once I entered I realized that I might be in hostile territory. The room was crowded and noisy and I saw that I was dressed differently from the other patrons and was the object of scrutiny. Lounging against the bar were tough-looking men and women in various stages of intoxication. A red-faced woman in a dirty apron, with a cigarette dangling from her lips, stood behind the bar. She looked at me aggressively and said, "What yer want?" Trying not to appear intimidated, I asked for a glass of wine. There was an ominous silence. Someone tittered and mimicking my accent, said, "Oh, 'e wants a glass of wine, 'e does. Oh, I say!"

As was often the case in Britain, one's accent betrayed one's caste and now I was "one of them". "We don't serve wine 'ere," she cried. I managed to recover some composure and said weakly, "Some beer, please," silently cursing my folly for entering the place. But it was not an entire disaster. As I made my way uneasily across the room to a dark corner to drink my beer, I caught the not-unfriendly eye of a pretty girl sitting alone, and before long we were talking. I asked her what her name was and why she was by herself. She was called April, she lived with her parents in Stepney and had "broken off" with her boyfriend. She was pleasant company but I was facing serious studies and felt that I surely did not want the complications which can occur when taking on a girlfriend. I decided to take a non-committal sort of attitude in spite of the strong need for companionship. I would use the need to study as an excuse to limit time spent with April but at the same time take care not to show any lack of interest.

The Nautical School was run by Captain Jeffries, a seaman of the old school. His lectures on seamanship were particularly entertaining. He would talk about cargoes, rigging, handling a ship in bad weather and the myriad problems facing a seaman. Someone would ask a question and this always led to a diversion which Captain Jeffries obviously enjoyed. He would sit on the edge of the table and carry us away with his adventures. He was an excellent story teller and always had an audience eager to hear about life in sail as he had spent his early years at sea in windjammers. As the weeks wore on, I began to encounter difficulties with certain subjects. My knowledge of the theory of navigation was hazy and as for stability and ship's construction I was woefully ignorant. My poor performance at school began to tell. Geometry and trigonometry were subjects which produced a sweat. I realized how little I knew. Nevertheless, with twenty other candidates I made application to sit for the exam. I "put in my papers" as it was called.

The examination for masters and mates was held in a dreary building in the heart of London's dockland. The area had a strong odour about it — a sweet smell of malt and barley. There must have been a brewery nearby. Air raids had damaged the roof of the building. It rained on the day I sat for the first two papers and our desks had to be moved about to avoid the drips. There was a time limit of three hours for each paper and we were advised by the teachers to tackle first the questions we could answer, leaving time to ponder over the awkward ones. It did not work that way for me as I found myself hard-pressed to answer what I knew in the time limit. It was frustrating to observe the clever fellows who finished well within the time limit, confidently handing in their sheets of foolscap while I watched the hands of the clock approach the deadline when the clerk would say, "Time's up!" The paper which most candidates feared was the K.O.P.

(Knowledge of Principles) exam for which there was reputed to be a fund of over 900 questions. But for me, the real ordeal was yet to come — the orals.

It was the accepted dictum that if a candidate did well in the written exams, the examiner would go easier on him in the orals. So by this rule I was in for a very rough time. I had heard of the fearsome reputation of Captain Hopwood, one of three examiners. He was the scourge of masters and mates. Any man whom he passed in orals had good reason to believe that he was competent to serve in the capacity for which he was being examined. I prayed that I would not be unlucky enough to be sent to him. The seven written exams were completed by Thursday, leaving the rest of the week for orals and signals. A notice appeared telling us when we would be examined.

On the dreaded day, I stood with a silent group waiting to be summoned for the third degree. The hall of examinations was a cheerless place, made more so by the gloomy expressions on the faces of candidates emerging from the seamanship room after a thorough going-over. A uniformed man announced in a solemn tone the name of the next candidate. I stood in a sweat and soon heard him say, "Winstanley to Captain Hopwood". With a heavy heart I entered a large room furnished with an assortment of equipment one would expect to find on the bridge and decks of a merchant ship: barometers, compasses, logs, sounding gear, lead lines, lengths of rope, wire, blocks and tackle, small boat anchors, sextants and charts. There was even a model of the deck of a cargo ship with derricks that could be moved about. On a large table stood small models of steam and sailing vessels, tugs, fishing vessels, buoys and all the other things that a mate would see from the bridge of a ship. But my attention was fixed upon a man of average height dressed in an ill-fitting dark suit. He was in his sixties with short grey hair and piercing eyes. He was the sort of man one could imagine standing on the deck of a square-rigger, barking orders at the crew. Indeed, he had served in sail and in all probability held a poor opinion of most of the men who came before him.

Captain Hopwood handed me a length of rope and asked me what I knew about knots and splices. Fortunately, I knew how to make the simple knots and bends and hoped that he wouldn't tell me to make a wall knot. He didn't. I was then asked about barometers, barographs, specific gravity and the like. But when I was unable to tell him how much a hand lead weighed and how it was armed, he became irritable. I had been there for over an hour before he began to find out what I knew about the important "Rules of the Road" .

They were 32 rules known as "Articles" — the longest and most difficult to commit to memory was Article 9. This dealt in detail with the many different types of fishing vessels and the signs, signals and lights they exhibited. The rules were couched in such a way that there could be no ambiguity or doubts as to their meaning and consequently they were difficult to memorize. Captain Hopwood moved the models and arrows, (to denote wind and current directions), like chess pieces. Knowing how to "box" the compass was absolutely imperative for this exercise in mental gymnastics. One had to be able to determine, on seeing a green or red light, whether it was a sailing ship and if it was, what tack she was on and between what points of the compass she was sailing. To come up with an answer quickly tested sharper intellects than mine; it reduced me to a state of sweating anxiety.

At noon I was told to go for lunch at the Ensign Club across the street. It was noisy and crowded with dockers, resident seamen on leave and men up for their tickets, all exchanging information about whether they thought they had passed or failed. At 1 p.m., I returned to face Captain Hopwood once again but by 2 p.m. he had had enough and said, "You do not seem to know much. I am failing you. You need more sea time. Come back in 6 months." He sounded like a judge pronouncing a sentence. I left with a heavy heart and pondered my future at sea.

I knew that without a ticket the Henderson Line would not give me a 3rd mate's job. Besides I did not fancy the likelihood of meeting former ship-mates after failing my exam, so I went to the shipping pool which was organized to find suitable men for an increasing fleet of ships. To my surprise it did not matter that I didn't have a ticket. Four years of sea experience was enough. I was sent to join the tanker "Macuba" as 4th mate. She was under the Dutch flag, was registered in Willemstad, Curacao, and was owned by the Royal Dutch Shell.

Chapter 6. Under the Dutch Flag

I arrived in Swansea to be told that the "Macuba" was still at sea and that I was to spend the night in the "Mackworth" hotel which was the best in town. It was a rare treat to luxuriate in such surroundings and enjoy the best food available, all at company expense. That didn't include drinks of course, but as I was wearing my uniform the barman in the hotel pub didn't think I should have to pay. He was an old seaman who had spent most of his working life on Welsh-owned tramp ships. When I told him I was joining a Dutch tanker the next day he said that conditions would be better than aboard British cargo ships. He added, "But if you are hit when loaded with petrol, you won't need a lifejacket, you will need a parachute!" I was in a deep sleep the following morning when I was awakened by a knock at the door. I could not think who had come to see me so early and with a feeling of apprehension said, "Come in." To my astonishment, a pretty young maid came in with a tray of tea and toast! This was Welsh hospitality at its very best. It was the first and the last time I ever had tea served to me in bed in a hotel room. Pity!

On the 2nd of December, 1941, I walked up the gangway of the "Macuba". She had arrived from the West Indies with 14,000 tons of aviation spirit to help keep the Allied planes in the air. It did not take me long to settle aboard as the Dutch officers were helpful and spoke good English. The master, Captain Koops, could have passed for English as he spoke without any accent. The mate, Schoemaker, was seldom without a cigar in his mouth when he was inside the accommodation. With such a volatile cargo, smoking on deck was strictly forbidden. He was apt to preface each sentence with, "Gott fordammer", but then he had a lot to worry about — he was responsible for the cargo and Chinese deck crew. The 2nd mate was Peter Gruen and the 3rd mate a cheerful fellow from Hilversum called Oscar Heilder. He and I became good friends and I was his best man when he married a girl from Scotland later that year. I was the only British officer aboard. The deck and engine crew were Chinese from Singapore.

The "Macuba" was a vessel of 14,000 dead weight tons driven by two propellers powered by Werkspoor diesels which gave her a speed of about 11 knots. Her cargo was carried in nine main tanks, each of which was divided into three sections, (port, centre and starboard tanks). The master, mates, Sparks and the Chinese steward were all accommodated in the amidships section of the ship. The Dutch engineers lived in the stern section in close proximity to the engine room. A bridge known as the catwalk connected the amidships house with the stern. The eating arrangements were rather odd. The ship's saloon was amidships in our accommodation yet it was only occupied at meal times by the master, chief engineer and mate. So while the chief engineer walked forward along the catwalk for his meals he was often met by the other mates walking aft for theirs! This was a minor inconvenience except in heavy weather when one had to make a dash along the catwalk to avoid getting soaked. The food was better and more plentiful than what I had received on previous voyages.

The ship's cargo pumping system was complicated. A series of coloured valves on the main deck controlled the flow of oil when loading or discharging. A mistake in closing or opening a valve could prove disastrous, particularly as the cargo was a highly-volatile liquid. It was very important to understand this system and the man who knew it better than anyone was the Chinese pumpman who seemed pleased to explain it to me. He spent his working hours in or around the pump room which he kept spotlessly clean.

Like the other Chinese crewmen, the pumpman was fond of gambling and as the Chinese steward's room was next to mine, I was often kept awake at night by the clatter of the mahjong pieces and the frequent shouts of excitement as bets were made and large sums of money changed hands. Sometimes the pumpman would win or lose a month's wages in one session. Most of the gambling went on in the crew's fo'c'sle in the bow. The mate and I were on the bridge one evening when we heard a lot of shouting coming from the fo'c'sle. Although neither of us understood Chinese, it was obvious that a serious fight had started. The mate knew how to deal with it. He walked into the wheelhouse and threw a switch on the bulkhead. This had the magical effect of producing immediate silence in the fo'c'sle because in complete darkness no man would make an attack on another. Shortly after, one of them came up to the bridge and asked politely for the lights to be turned on again. The Chinese did not have faith in paper currency and banks, so after being paid they were anxious to convert it into something tangible like gold or precious stones. It was believed that there was great wealth hidden in the cupboards and closets in their accommodation.

There was another commodity aboard treated with secrecy and that was opium. Once a month, I had to collect each man's wage book so his pay could be entered. The firemen lived back aft in the stern and I sometimes had trouble getting these books as they were reluctant to show me where they had hidden them, nor did they want me to know they were smoking opium although the sweet, sickly smell of it was overpowering. I would knock on the door repeatedly until a weak voice within asked what I wanted. My request for the wage book would be answered with a long pause. Then I would hear drawers being opened, keys being turned and eventually the door would be opened only wide enough to push the book through.

A few days before we left Swansea the mate told me that as 4th mate I would be in charge of the gun crew. This came as a surprise as I knew next to nothing about guns, besides there were five naval gunners aboard, surely they did not need me. "You have to attend the gunnery school" said the mate, "There must be an officer in the crew even if you don't do anything". My anxiety about this was partly allayed by Oscar the 3rd mate who accompanied me. "Nothing to worry about" he said "All you have to do is watch the gunlayer and when he gives the signal, you shout "Open fire!" Our first day at school was spent in a classroom learning the theory of firing guns and films were shown of ships in action. A cartoon entitled "Aim Off" depicted a boy throwing a snowball at a passing cyclist. In order to score a hit, the snowball had to be aimed at a point ahead of the target.

Next day we were taken out to the practice site to put theory into action. Firing Oerlikon machine guns at imaginary targets in the sky was good fun, but "Guns" the petty officer in charge was showing impatience at those of us who showed little aptitude for handling deadly weapons. He reminded us that our lives could very well depend on our paying attention to him. It was a bitterly cold day and we shuffled about uncomfortably hoping that the exercise would soon come to an end but "Guns", hadn't finished with us. "I am going to demonstrate the use of the Holman Projector," a devilish device and very effective against low flying aircraft. He pointed at a cyclinder mounted on a tripod. "This is a very simple weapon to operate," he said as he elevated it skyward. "All you have to do, is pick up one of these ére grenades, pull out this ére pin and drop this ére grenade down this ére barrel." There was a loud pop, it shot skyward and exploded high above us. We began to laugh at this, and someone was bold enough to say the Holman Projector was useless. "Guns" was not amused.

Before we sailed, the "Sky Pilot" came aboard. This was the name for the Padres from the Missions to Seamen. Like most of his brethren he was a jolly, well-meaning fellow and he was invited to join the party in the mate's room. He had brought religious pamphlets for our edification and was ready to give counsel to any who might want it. He was anxious to be regarded as one of us and accepted a glass of Bols gin. After we had been in conversation for some time, he said to me, "You speak very good English for a Dutchman!"

On January 17th, 1942, we sailed down the Bristol Channel in fine weather. A compass adjuster was aboard and I was kept busy taking shore bearings. When finished we set off to join the convoy. The ship was "in ballast", which meant that she had about 4,000 tons of sea water in her tanks. We had not gone far before a report was received that a ship further along the coast had hit an acoustic mine and we were ordered to anchor in Milford Haven. While the old man was ashore attending the convoy conference, some naval ratings came aboard to rig a balloon to the main mast which was supposed to be sent aloft to discourage low-flying aircraft. No one had much faith in this arrangement. We watched in disbelief as the ratings tried to get the balloon airborne. A moderate wind carried it up from the mast and for a short while it looked as though it might be a success, but then the wire came off the reel and twisted into a thousand turns. There was much cursing in good naval parlance and eventually the officer in charge decided he had had enough and they packed up and left. They were replaced by six D.E.M.S. gunners who would man our armament. When the old man returned, I managed to sneak a look at our sailing orders and was disgusted to see that instead of going to New York as rumoured, we were bound for Aruba in the Dutch West Indies.

Before heading out into the Atlantic we sailed up the Irish Sea to rendezvous with ships from Liverpool and Glasgow. For some reason they did not show up and we anchored for the night off Oban. The next day we went to Gourock at the mouth of the Clyde and anchored near two impressive ships — the new battleship "Duke of York" and the massive liner "Queen Elizabeth" now painted grey with a 6" gun on her stern. This unexpected diversion was a happy one for me. Some months earlier when aboard the "Mandalay" some "parcels of comfort" had come aboard. In the early days of the war when pictures appeared in newspapers of survivors in a pitiable state after being rescued at sea, a wave of sympathy and gratitude swept the nation. An appeal was made for warm clothing for men at sea. I opened my parcel and along with a woollen scarf and balaclava there was a note from the person who had knitted them. I replied with a note of thanks and promptly forgot about it. To my surprise, I received a letter telling me that if I should ever come to Glasgow I was to contact a Miss Helen Ferguson. The train from Gourock took an hour to get there, but it was well worth it as the lass in question was attractive and we spent a congenial evening together. I missed the last train back to Gourock and had to put up in a hotel for the night. I returned aboard to find that the Chinese bosun had been knocked unconscious when a heavy steel skylight fell on his head. He eventually came to and, after treatment, returned to work. A tough old bird!

On January 31st, 1942, we sailed in a convoy of thirty ships and headed out across the north coast of Ireland and into the swells of the Atlantic. I was on the 4-8 watch with the mate. At first I felt very much the junior man with little more to do than keep a look-out and write in the log book. But as time went on I was given much more responsibility due to the mate's insobriety.

In the past, aboard British ships, I had seen very little drinking at sea — that was done ashore. But aboard the "Macuba", drinking parties were a frequent occurrence. The chief engineer would hold a party in his room one night and the mate would do the same in his room the following night. The master was never present at these gatherings although he must have known it was going on. The two heaviest drinkers were the mate and the 2nd engineer. As they were both on the same watch, they would carouse until the early hours — their favourite drink was Bols Geneva gin. I would get up at 3:30 a.m. to go on watch at 4:00 a.m. and see the 2nd engineer stagger out of our accommodation and make his way along the catwalk to go on watch! Once he was so drunk he was unable to walk and crawled aft on all fours!

In different circumstances it might have been comical but in convoy, in dangerous waters, it was not. The mate was often in a similar state. I would stand in the dark wheelhouse listening to him talk to the 2nd mate who was about to go off watch. Then the mate would stumble into the chart room, flop on to the settee and fall asleep. The 2nd mate was used to this and would then tell me to take over the watch explaining the need to keep our correct station in the convoy, then he would go below. At first, I felt overwhelmed by this unexpected responsibility. To be left alone on the bridge of a large ship at night surrounded by many other ships at close quarters was daunting and I was very nervous. In order not to run into the ship ahead, I had to phone the engine room to ask them to reduce the engine revs and later would have to call again to increase speed. I would wonder who was in charge of the engine room but fortunately nothing went wrong. I would look into the chart room to see the mate stretched out, "dead to the world" with the hood of his duffle coat on and only his ruddy face showing. But the remarkable thing was that by 7:00 a.m., just before the old man came up to the bridge, the mate was always on his feet though bleary-eyed and dishevelled! The result of all this for me was a much-needed boost in confidence as a watch officer.

I was beginning to feel quite comfortable with my shipmates, not only with the Dutch but the Chinese also, until an incident occurred in the centre-castle store room. Under the mate's instructions it was my job to look after the ship's stores. Once a week, the cooks and stewards would come to the door requesting utensils, rice, flour, cans of vegetables and so on. On British ships the chief steward did this job but the old man did not trust the Chinese steward. On this occasion the 2nd cook asked me for a pot of some kind which I refused to give him on orders from the mate. The cook began to shout in a menacing manner, then went away. Shortly after, he re-appeared, and this time he meant business for he held a long knife and came towards me. Fortunately, I had enough time to slam the door shut and prevent his entry. As I sat sweating and listening to the commotion outside, someone called the bridge and Captain Koops came down with a gun in his hand. Order was restored and the 2nd cook never bothered me again but I was always wary of him.

We had been at sea a week before the enemy made any move to attack the convoy. Our escort was not a strong one as we only had three sloops and a corvette. Early one morning they picked up a contact and began dropping depth charges. But no attack came and the commodore decided to disperse us before it did. So we sailed off at full speed, glad to be on our own.

Once again, I started writing in my diary. 12th February, 1942 — "Things are going badly for us in Singapore and the old man instructed us not to tell any of the Chinese crew about the probable loss of the city. Most of them have families there and when they hear that their allotments will no longer be sent home there may be trouble. Although they will find out when we reach Aruba."

15th February, 1942 — "News came that Singapore has fallen to the Japanese. The mate put me to work typing a crew list, although whether this has anything to do with the above I do not know. At any rate I found that typing when the ship is rolling heavily is an exercise in concentration and balance. I lashed the typewriter to the table, wedged my chair with as many lifejackets as I could find and produced a page of Chinese names in an hour!"

16th February, 1942 — "The gun drill was a fiasco. I was in the crew and my job was to supply the ammunition, but some of the others did not seem to know what they were supposed to do. Everyone began shouting at once — suggestions, commands and advice. I felt sorry for the poor little gun-layer who was quite beside himself but eventually some semblance of order was established and we fired a number of rounds. As usual, I stuffed my ears with cotton wool but the gun went off with a terrific crash and I got a blast of hot smoke in my face. We received the news that Aruba, (our destination), has been bombarded by a U boat, one of the oil installations has been set on fire and three tankers have been torpedoed off Willemstad."

I had boarded the "Macuba" equipped for Arctic conditions in North America, and now found myself "schooner rigged" for the tropics and compelled to wear my one and only thick, black pair of trousers and heavy shirt. The mate must have noticed my discomfort as I stood in the blazing sun checking lifeboat gear and handed me a pair of his shorts. He had twice my girth but I was both grateful and comfortable, using a tie to hold up the outsized shorts.

On the 18th of February, 1942, the island of Puerto Rico came into view and a U.S. patrol buzzed over us at mast height. That afternoon we passed through the Mona Passage and entered the Caribbean. I was reading in my cabin when the engines came to a sudden stop. Thinking that there was an emergency of some kind, I put on my life jacket and ran out on deck only to be told by Oscar, the 3rd mate, that sudden stoppages were quite common on the "Macuba". This time, it was intentional in order to test the gears as the Werkspoor diesels had a tendency to refuse to go astern when they had been running ahead for a long period. Hendriks, the 5th engineer was emphatic about his opinion of the engines — "Dees machines no focking good, Werkspoor good name for them!"

We arrived in Aruba to find the people in a state of shock. They had been attacked four days earlier by a U boat which had sunk a ship outside the harbour, and had also lobbed a few shells on to the oil refinery. The damage ashore had been minimal, but the psychological effect was considerable as it was the first time enemy shells had landed in the Western Hemisphere. The Dutch pilot stood on the bridge puffing on a large cigar and telling the old man that now the United States was in the war it would be all over in a few weeks. Shortly after tying up in the port of San Nicolas, we were told that because of the danger of another attack on Aruba, we would not load there but would sail for a secret destination. There was time for me to see a doctor about treatment for a crushed thumb which had turned septic. A few hours before our departure, we were ordered to move the ship ahead to make room alongside the jetty for a Norwegian tanker. She never arrived, having been torpedoed off the coast of Venezuela a few hours' steaming away.

Two days later, we anchored off Cristobal at the entrance of the Panama Canal, one of the greatest engineering feats of the 20th century. Because of the danger of sabotage, the Americans were taking no chances and strict security measures were taken. Before we entered the Gatun locks, a contingent of U.S. soldiers came aboard. Some were stationed on the bridge, others went below into the engine room. They set up their own communication system to monitor every helm and engine movement given by the pilot as we moved through the canal. Crew members were warned not to take any pictures of the canal and nothing was to be thrown over the side. I watched in wonderment as the electric tractors (mules), pulled us through the locks. The ship had risen 80 feet from the salt water of the Atlantic into the fresh water of Gatun Lake, which was clean enough to be pumped aboard for the ship's use. By dusk, we had reached the San Miguel Locks at the Pacific end and an hour later the pilot left and we headed out into the Pacific. The canal transit of 45 miles had taken about 15 hours. Sparks received a coded message giving our destination as San Pedro, California.

On the 11th of March, 1942, the oil derricks of Los Angeles were visible on the horizon fifteen miles off and a squad of fighter planes came out to take a look at us. The Americans had not been at war for long and our arrival in such a glamorous place as California seemed to offer unlimited possibilities. Immigration officials came aboard and announced that the Chinese crew members would only be permitted ashore in a group under escort. This caused anger among them and an interpreter was called to explain the regulations, which were designed to prevent desertions.

The oil dock was miles from any visible habitation. The land was flat for a great distance with the San Bernardino mountains amid a bluish haze in the background. Scattered at intervals among scrub bushes were sheds where oil pumps worked away silently and unattended. No wonder we had come here for fuel — there was an abundance of it. There was little of interest within miles of the dock and there seemed to be no easy way of getting to the nearest town. But a highway ran past the gates of the terminal and, although I had no clear idea where I intended to go or what I expected to find, I stood at the side of the road in the hope that perhaps a bus would come along. Before long a car pulled up and a friendly fellow leaned out of the window and asked me where I wanted to go. When I said that Los Angeles might be an interesting place to see, he laughed and said that it was more than forty miles away. Then he said, "Get in. I will take you to the Southern Pacific Station. It's an hour on the train from there."

The train carriage was crowded and dirty but I found a window seat and looked out on depressing slums as the train lumbered slowly through the suburbs of the city. We had almost reached the terminal when a smiling, middle-aged man came up and asked me where I was from. He had recognized me as English and was pleased that we were now in the fight together. He had been in England with the army during the first war and asked how could he help me now. I told him that this was my first visit to the States and I was looking for some entertainment. "Hey buddy, we've got the best in the world here. What kind of fun do you have in mind?" We walked along what he called the "main drag" and he pointed at places of interest. Time was running short; he had a meeting to attend and apologized for being unable to take me home to meet his family and give me a "real American dinner". Before we parted, he told me that his son was in the Marine Corps stationed in the Panama Canal Zone and the next time I was there, to be sure to give him a call and say "Hello".

There was a brightly-lit building nearby which offered live entertainment and "the most gorgeous girls in the world". I spotted two men in R.A.F. uniforms standing in the foyer. Feeling that perhaps it would be worthwhile to capitalize on our popularity as allies, I walked in. The place was packed to bursting point. My shore-going clothes may not have been quite up to accepted standards for they aroused enough curiosity for someone to say, "Hey fella. What do you do?" When I replied that I worked aboard a tanker, I was invited to join a group of people who insisted that I have dinner with them. My host was a well-known band leader who handed me a menu and said, "Order what you like; it's on the house." While I tucked in to the best food I had eaten in years, I was bombarded with questions about how the war was going on in Europe. "Was there much left of London after the blitz?" and "When would the Allies invade Europe?"

While all this was going on, the floor show started and a bevy of dazzling, scantily-clad beauties began dancing to the latest craze in music. This was interrupted when the master of ceremonies called for attention and said that he wanted to introduce some of "our gallant Allies". The R.A.F. chaps were hustled up to the stage along with a few merchant seamen who, like me, were in civilian clothes. My kind hosts urged me to join my fellow gallants on the stage. I protested that being a slow eater I had not finished my meal. But they insisted and as they were paying the bill, it would have been ungrateful of me to refuse. I was glad that I did because after each one of us had identified ourselves and described what we did for the war effort, we were invited to dance with the chorus girls. This was an unexpected bonus but on closer inspection, the "world's most beautiful girls" looked far less glamourous than when viewed from a distance. The band leader and his wife invited me to spend the weekend at their house in Beverly Hills, an invitation I was loth to turn down but I was due to sail within 24 hours.

Before the club closed I met the R.A.F. chaps at the bar. They told me that they were in the States for flight training. I insisted on paying for their drinks, which was an act of folly as I soon realized that I had seriously depleted my cash reserves. I had missed the last train to San Pedro by several hours and to catch the first one in the morning meant a long wait so I looked about for somewhere to sleep. On enquiring at the desk of the Hollywood Plaza Hotel, I discovered that I had enough money for the cheapest room and the rail fare back. As the bell boy showed me to my room he put his hand out for a tip. I wondered if he would accept 25 cents and whether I might find that I didn't have enough for the rail fare after all. To my relief, he seemed well-satisfied and said, "Thank you, Sir. What sort of girl would you like — blonde or brunette?" I declined this extra service saying that I was far too tired and closed the door. I arrived back aboard to find the mate unhappy about my absence ashore so I hastened out on deck to assist him with the loading. I did not feel too guilty about this having taken some of his responsibilities on the bridge during our passage out.

Loaded with 14,000 tons of high-octane benzene we headed south believing that our destination was Britain although it was still a secret. I had been aboard the "Macuba" for three months now and felt that I had settled down well with my

Dutch shipmates. I had learned to write the log book in Dutch and to express the usual courtesies in that language. I even knew a few swear words. But I still suffered agonies from sea-sickness when the weather was bad and being the only British officer aboard, I was anxious to conceal this fact not only from my Dutch shipmates but also from the Royal Naval gunners aboard.

Our mess room on the "Macuba" was like a furnace in the tropics. As the butter was too runny to be lifted with a knife, a sash-tool paint brush was used to spread it on bread. The heat and smell of oil from the diesels pounding away immediately below us made meal times a matter of deciding whether I was hungry enough to endure the discomfort. When I felt seasick I tried hard not to show it, particularly as most of the naval gunners seemed to be immune. The ship would heave over heavily to one side and with a show of bravado I would shout, "Hold on lads, here she goes again, just grin and bear it!"

The Dutch were big eaters and some consumed more than others. I sat opposite Hendriks, the 5th engineer, a thin, pale-faced man who seldom said a word as he came to the mess room to eat, not to socialize. I would watch in fascination as he heaped up the food on his plate to form a pyramid, then, positioning his mouth level with the pile and with fork in hand, he would shovel in the food with great dexterity and speed until it disappeared. The food tended to be greasy and for my uneasy stomach it proved disastrous. One night, when the weather was rough, I sat down for supper with the engineers and naval gunners. The combination of heat and violent motion, plus a mouthful of food — the contents of which I was not sure of, produced a sudden onslaught of nausea which I was unable to control. I spluttered, gasped and put my hands over my mouth too late to prevent a stream of vomit shooting across the table towards Hendriks and his plate of food. This time Hendriks expressed himself with remarkable fluency and little restraint. "This is focking no good. I go engine room." I couldn't blame him. I, too, made a hasty departure to stand out on deck and ponder the folly of false pride.

Our diesel engines may have been more economical than steam power but they were not as reliable and a lot noisier. They also had the tendency to belch balls of burning fuel out of the funnel. One of these landed on a lifeboat and set the canvas cover alight. Before the crew were able to put the fire out, the paint on the boat was scorched and some of the equipment slightly damaged. Excessive build-up of carbon in the cylinders of the main engines meant having to stop the ship in mid-ocean. The ship would wallow about in the swell as the engineers laboured in extreme heat to complete the job as soon as possible. For the chief, the completion of this work was a good excuse for a party. Most of the officers had families in Holland and they had not been in contact with them since the German occupation, so it was not surprising that they felt the need to relax with a glass of Bols Geneva. I became friendly with 3rd engineer Haulsman. He had a good collection of classical music and would invite me to his room to have a beer and listen to his gramophone. We would sit under a whirling fan and he would tell me about his family back in Hilversum. His voice broke when he described how he left home to rejoin the ship. He told his mother that he only expected to be away for a few months. A month after the ship left Rotterdam, the Germans overran the country and he had not heard any news of his parents for almost two years and wondered whether they were still alive.

The run south to Panama was not without incident. On the 21st of March, 1942, I wrote again in my diary. "This morning, the port tank top at No. 2 was seen to be overflowing with benzene! The mate and I dashed up the foredeck and began opening valves to drain the benzene into a centre tank. For the next hour I was busy opening and closing valves. Needless to say, the mate was agitated."

On March 27th, 1942, we reached Panama and anchored off Balboa. We expected to go through the canal en route to Britain. We had been away for four months and in another month we would be home. But our sailing orders read differently. We were to proceed to Cape Town via the Magellan Straits as the Caribbean was infested with U boats and too dangerous. I remembered the words of the man in the London office who had assured me, "You will only be gone for three, possibly four months — no longer."

Once I resigned myself to a protracted voyage, I realized this would give me more time to prepare for another attempt to get my ticket. It was also an opportunity to see a part of the world which I had not expected to visit. On the 31st of March 1942 we crossed the line. It wasn't the first time for me, but the rest of the crew would not believe it and I had no certificate to prove it. So I had to suffer the indignity of being covered in soap, shaved and ducked in water by Father Neptune's aides. One of them was Tou, a muscular Estonian engineer, who simply picked me up by my heels and lowered me head first into a bucket of soapy water! It all ended well when the old man assembled the participants in the saloon, issued certificates and gave us all a drink.

On the 14th of April, 1942, we were off the entrance of the Magellan Straits in 54 degrees south. I resumed writing my diary. "The old man has decided to go around the Horn which is a longer route but is less risky than going through the Straits without a pilot." Surely he had not contemplated attempting to enter the Straits without a pilot! Possibly one was not available. At any rate, we carried on towards the Horn.

15th April, 1942 — "Bitterly cold. Temp. 41 degrees. We sighted the rugged coast of Terra del Fuego with lofty snow-capped mountains in the background. A cold, forbidding landscape."

16th April, 1942 — "I came on watch at 0400 hours. Islands on our port side at ten miles distance. We tried to determine which one was Cape Horn but were unable to do so. At 0645 hours we made out the highest, southerly peak on a group of islands and I logged this as the Horn. It appeared to be a grim and lonely place and with its reputation for terrible weather it is no wonder that seamen speak of it with awe. Yet we are lucky to have no more than a moderately heavy westerly swell, light winds and low sea. Besides the mighty albatross there is a great variety of sea birds to keep us company as we turn on an easterly course. The old man has decided to take a great circle track to the Cape."

17th April, 1942 — "A flock of birds around us. I have never seen so many at sea. Pretty pure-white petrels and a black and white bird no bigger than a sparrow dart swiftly just above the surface of the sea. But the albatross dominates the scene. Our course is South 76 East but this may take us into the ice. We have been unable to take any sights so we are running on dead reckoning. Westerly breeze and moderate seas; the barometer is falling."

Two days later the skies were still overcast and we were still finding our position by guesswork! We were making over 10 knots, running before a rough sea and with an easterly set were about 120 miles north of South Georgia but thought we might be as much as 30 miles ahead of our estimated position. The barometer continued to fall and was at 745 millibars. The old man ordered extra look-outs in case we ran into ice.

20th April, 1942 — "Temp. 41 degrees. A rough, following sea and heavy swell, wind force 7 and shipping seas on the main decks. We managed to get sights when the sun appeared briefly and found that we were 15 miles ahead of our dead reckoning position."

21st April, 1942 — "The temp. dropped to 34 degrees and the wind shifted to the south, a fierce force 9 gale. We were rolling heavily. I was on the bridge at daybreak and sighted what I thought was smoke from a ship on the port bow. The old man came up and looked through the telescope. It proved to be an iceberg. This brought men out on deck. The berg was about 200 feet high and we passed it about 3 miles off; a splendid sight as the seas broke on it sending up clouds of spray. A few hours later a number of growlers came into view. These were pieces of ice small enough to be tossed about in the sea but big enough to cause us serious damage if we hit one."

22nd April, 1942 — "The gale continued unabated and we ran at slow speed to reduce the chances of hitting a berg. This is one of the loneliest stretches of water in the world and the chance of receiving any assistance, had we required it, is remote."

23rd April, 1942 — "When I staggered out on deck at 0400 hours to go on watch and put my head round the corner of the deck to take a look at sea conditions, I was met by an icy blast which had a different howl to it. The old man was on the bridge and he reckoned that it was blowing between force 10 and 11, (a storm on Beaufort wind scale), with a following sea which I logged as 'high, steep and breaking'. I stood on the wing of the bridge and looked astern to see gigantic 'greybeards' rearing up, their crests higher than the funnel. Just as it appeared that one would crash over the stern, we would rise steeply to meet it. There was tension on the bridge as we passed the occasional berg. The old man must have realized that our sailing on a Great Circle route had been a mistake. At dusk, he decided to heave to as the risk of meeting ice during the hours of darkness was too great. He used the engines to bring the ship about as easily as possible but when we came beam on to the sea there were a few very heavy rolls. We could hear objects crashing about below us but when conditions were like this, nobody cared much and only blamed others for not securing loose chairs, tables, books, etc."

I had been reading about sailing ships rounding the Horn and wondered how it was possible to beat against the westerlies. It was bad enough running before the wind in an engine-powered ship. How did the old sea-dogs manage a sailing ship in conditions like this? No wonder they talked about steamship seamen as "wooden men in iron ships"!

At 10 a.m. the log reading was 25, and 12 hours later it read the same. We began to have trouble keeping the ship on course. She would constantly fall away from her heading and the wheel would have to be put hard over to bring her back on course. Even though the ship was hove to, heavy seas came tumbling over the fo'c'sle head and the foredeck was constantly awash, which was not surprising as our loaded freeboard (the distance between the water line and deck line) was only about five feet. The rolling became so violent that movement about the decks was difficult. It was a matter of holding on to whatever was at hand. The old man said that he had been at sea for over thirty years and had never seen seas as high. He described them as "precipitous" and he hoped that the engines would not fail us. In spite of the maelstrom raging outside, the mate propped himself up against the compass binnacle, puffing on his cigar which must have been a source of discomfort for the quartermaster steering nearby. It was just getting dark when a small berg was spotted ahead with several growlers around it, one of which we almost hit. That was enough for the old man. He ordered an alteration of course to due north to clear the ice as soon as possible. As we turned, a great shower of sparks came out of the funnel. There was no party in the chief's cabin that night!

On April 27th, 1942, the weather moderated. We were well clear of danger and, with the current behind us, made good progress towards the Cape of Good Hope. Our noon position put us 120 miles to the south of Gough Island and 300 miles from Tristan da Cunha. There was a heated exchange between the mate and 2nd mate with much swearing in Dutch and English about the collie dog, "Jennie", who had run along a freshly-painted alleyway and made a mess of the paint and her coat. The mate threatened to shoot the dog and the 2nd mate countered by promising to throw the mate over the side if he did! Apart from occasional rows, the "Macuba" was a happy ship. The Dutch rarely showed much emotion and whatever their innermost feelings were, they kept them to themselves.

On May 2nd, 1942, we arrived at Cape Town after a passage of 46 days from San Pedro. The troop ships, "Nieuw Amsterdam" and "Duchess of York", lay at anchor and our pilot said that the shore authorities had taken every precaution to make sure the troops remained aboard, as they did not want Cape Town taken by storm, as it had been a year earlier when hundreds of Aussies got ashore. Our stay was brief as only 2,500 tons of cargo were discharged. I did manage to stretch my legs ashore and walked along a path leading from the oil jetty until I was suddenly confronted by an armed guard who challenged me. I quickly explained where I came from and was told that I was in a military area and could be shot. I returned to the ship to find that some provisions had arrived at the gangway and I went aboard to tell the steward. He refused to get out of his bunk saying that the stores were late in arriving and he had "knocked off". It was not the first time this had happened but as time was short one of the seamen and I began to carry the boxes aboard. The old man noticed this and asked where the steward was and I told him. He was enraged and ordered the steward to pack his bags and go ashore.

The old man was dissatisfied with our compasses; the deviations on some courses were too high. A compass adjuster came aboard and we moved out into Table Bay to swing the ship. He was a decent old boy from Aberdeen and as I worked with him he talked about his early years at sea. He had run away to sea when he was fifteen and for the next ten years had wandered all over the world in sailing ships but had become tired of the hard work and poor pay. He got a 3rd mate's job on an old tramp steamer but conditions were not much better. The master, a hard-case Geordie, was cheating the crew out of their food allowances, cutting corners by buying the cheapest "grub" he could find from unscrupulous ship chandlers. They would then split the profit. The 3rd mate led a delegation to the master's room to protest and told him that the crew were going on strike. The master denied any wrongdoing and became so angry that he punched the 3rd mate in the face. This caused a scuffle in which the master was beaten up. Now the crew was in serious trouble and the 3rd mate knew that as soon as the ship reached Cape Town he would be arrested. But it did not work out that way. The master knew that if he reported the matter to the authorities ashore, there would be an investigation and his "fiddling" of the food accounts would come to light. But the 3rd mate had had enough. He packed his bag and walked ashore for good. As he put it, it was "the best thing I ever did. I lay low until the ship sailed, then found a job with the police. They needed men and did not ask too many questions!"

Three days later, we were running up the east coast bound for Durban when an error of navigation was made due to the difficulty of recognizing points of land on a featureless coast. We were unable to get a fix from shore bearings as our chart showed nothing prominent. Before long, we were unsure of our position and it was not until noon sights that we found we had passed our destination! We turned round and proceeded shore-ward until the tall buildings on the beach front of Durban came into view. We entered the harbour and steamed past the grand old

French liner, "Ile de France", which, with other liners, was loaded with troops destined for the Western Desert.

One hot afternoon, I had been ashore and was about to board the ferry to take me to the oil jetty when I was told that a fire had broken out on a tanker lying there. By the time I reached the ship, the fire had been put out by the shore fire brigade assisted by our crew. There had been a leak in a hose connection, a spark had caused an explosion and a sheet of flame had shot up between the ship and the shore which subsequently set the wooden wharf on fire. As some of the ship's tank lids were open at the time, there could have been a catastrophe of major proportions. As it was, only the paint on the hull was scorched. A kaffir was blamed for smoking on the dock.

On May 15th, 1942, we left Durban bound for Trinidad. I was out on deck with the mate in heavy seas as we turned tank valves to ballast the ship. This vital operation of ballasting the ship should have been done before we left the dock. We had almost finished when a green sea came over the bows and, before we could run for cover, we were swept off our feet. I was carried along in the torrent and fetched up against the chains lining the ship's side. The mate was as lucky as I and managed to cling to one of the vent pipes. The old man on the bridge had seen this and perhaps thought he would be making the trip short-handed. He promptly ordered us off the deck. Since I was soaked I did not need to be told twice. The ship was pitching and vibrating so violently that the old man expressed concern that the hull might be damaged if it went on much longer. Fortunately the seas moderated as we got further off the coast.

Next day, I was on the bridge by myself, the mate having gone below for his supper, when I was startled by the glare of a red light ahead of us. Thinking that it must be a ship at close quarters, I ordered the quartermaster to alter course to starboard while I fumbled for the binoculars. When the old man reached the bridge a red flare appeared. As there had been reports of U boats operating off the Cape, the old man was suspicious until we read S.O.S. sent on a flashlight. We altered course to take a closer look. At the same time the gun crew was ordered to close-up and train the gun in the direction of a light which was bobbing up and down in the water. Before long, a ship's lifeboat came into view and we saw that it was crowded with many of its occupants standing. They looked in a bad state and seas were sweeping over the boat. The ship was turned to make as good a lee as possible as we were rolling heavily. With the wild motion of the boat alongside us, it took some time before all the survivors were safely on deck.

Most of them were lascars and some so weak that they were unable to stand. They were carried into the saloon where the 2nd mate had his medical supplies spread out on the table. The last man to struggle up the pilot ladder wore the uniform of a ship's master. He was a tall, distinguished looking man and he carried a small dog under his arm. I escorted him to the bridge where he shook hands with the old man and said, "Good evening, Captain. I am the master of the 'Sudani'. Thank you for picking us up. We hit a mine yesterday. There are two more of our boats out there somewhere." He said that he and some of the other officers were having supper when the mine exploded. The stain on the front of his jacket was soup he had been eating at the time. We had rescued thirty men and one dog. They had been adrift for thirty hours and suffered from sea-sickness and exposure, but none was badly injured. We made them comfortable and they slept soundly as we headed for Cape Town. As the survivors stood on the deck of the tug that came out to take them ashore, they gave us a cheer and one of them shouted, "Hope we can do the same for you one day!"

On the 6th of June, 1942, we passed through the Boca Grande and entered Port of Spain, Trinidad. While we were taking on fuel, our gun layer and three of the Chinese firemen "jumped ship" and we sailed without them. Perhaps they had had enough of life aboard a tanker. Having taken another load of benzene in Curacao, we sailed for Freetown in West Africa. We had not gone far when the steering gear broke down and we stopped. We were in a convoy of five ships and we watched them go on without us. When it was repaired we were ordered to proceed independently to our destination. Later that day, the 2nd mate sighted a red sail ahead of us. It was a lifeboat from the American ship, "West Hartford", which had been torpedoed the night before and had sunk in seven minutes. Everyone had got away in the lifeboats but had lost contact with each other in the darkness. There were nine men in the boat. After they scrambled aboard, I went down into the boat to retrieve anything of use, including a complete buoyancy suit which was something that none of us had seen before. The old man was anxious to get under way as quickly as possible for obvious reasons and not long afterwards someone reported having seen a periscope. We made the survivors comfortable and headed for Barbados.

We arrived in Bridgetown to see a British ship at anchor in the roadstead. We wondered why she had a heavy list until we were able to see that she had three large holes in her side. She had been torpedoed six weeks before but how she remained afloat and managed to limp into port was miraculous. It was a grim reminder of what might lie in wait for us. We put off our second lot of survivors and sailed within the hour. The pilot told us that there were over six hundred survivors of sunken ships in Barbados waiting to be evacuated.

We had been at sea about six hours when we met another lifeboat from the "West Hartford". The sea was rough and we had trouble bringing the boat alongside. But this time, the old man was in no mood to pick up any more survivors and told me to tell the officer in charge to come to the bridge. The American 2nd mate looked weary as he followed me along the deck. "We were happy to see you guys come along. We have been in that goddamned boat for twenty-two hours!" The old man explained the urgency of our own situation and said that he would not take them to Barbados as we were only putting ourselves in danger. The American appreciated our situation, saying that although his men were tired, they were in good shape and could sail in the lifeboat to the nearest land, Barbados. He had brought his boat compass with him to compare with ours. He looked at our chart and said cheerfully, "O.K. Cap. We can make it." He reckoned that with a fair wind they would make landfall in about 15 hours. We gave them food and cigarettes, wished them luck, blew V for Victory on our horn and they disappeared into the darkness.

Our progress across the Atlantic was made slower by the need to zig-zag continuously in an attempt to avoid torpedo attack. It was a very uncomfortable feeling to be sitting on top of a load of benzene, never knowing when one might be blown sky-high. Not surprisingly, some of us wore our lifejackets continually. Others took a more fatalistic attitude, believing that if we were hit we would not need one! To add to our anxiety, Sparks received reports of U boat attacks, the closest being only sixty miles away.

But the trip across to West Africa was uneventful except that one of the Chinese stewards went mad. One evening he was seen standing on the catwalk looking up at the full moon, waving his hands in all directions and wailing in a high-pitched voice. It was Han Keng Ton, the Captain's "boy", who had been acting strangely for some time but as it was the full moon he had become worse. As the pumpman said, "He no good, got moon sickness." He was confined in a room by himself. Two days later several of the Chinese suddenly became ill with back and chest pains. The old man questioned them and they replied, "Wind no good." The hot, damp weather of the region may have had something to do with it.

On the 28th of June, 1942, reports came in from an American ship saying that they were being followed by a U boat. She was 100 miles away from us, which was of some comfort. The Admiralty in London must have thought that we needed protection and ordered us to look for a convoy that was in our area and bound for Britain. We made sweeps to port and starboard in an effort to find one but without success. This disgusted the old man, who gave vent to his frustrations with a colourful mix of Dutch and English swear words and ordered the mate to head for Freetown. Before our arrival every man was given quinine pills to prevent malaria.

Sierra Leone had a reputation for being an unhealthy place for Europeans. The stifling heat and damp atmosphere, combined with the thick swampy jungle, made excellent breeding conditions for mosquitoes, not just the ordinary kind but the anopheles mosquito which carried the parasite causing malaria. No wonder Sierra Leone was known as the "White Man's Grave". Some said that the white community's best defence was a large intake of good gin and that Gilbey and Booth did their best business in West Africa!

As we approached the coast, there was anxiety on the bridge as we had been unable to fix our position due to overcast skies with limited vision in driving rain, we could see nothing of the land we suspected was not far ahead. It was time to take the cover off the sounding machine and see what results we could get. On the third cast of the 30 lb. lead, we got a depth that matched our estimated position on the chart. The old man was so relieved he promised us a drink when we got into port.

Freetown Harbour was full of ships waiting to form a convoy. Two large battle wagons, the "Nelson" and "Rodney", lay at anchor and we dipped our ensign as we passed them. These massive sister ships had a different profile from other battleships as the main armament was almost all mounted on the forward part of the ship, six 16 inch guns making a formidable array of fire power. For the first time in weeks, it was possible to enjoy what the Dutch called "a farmer's night", meaning a night of normal sleep in one's bunk. However, that did not include us watch-keepers, who had to make sure that we did not drag anchor and that no unauthorized people crept aboard in the middle of the night. We had been told that some of the natives had got aboard ships at anchor and had removed equipment without the crew being aware of it. One vessel had lost her mooring lines from the fo'c'sle head which must have caused some embarrassment.

The heat was very oppressive and although we lay over two miles away from the heavily-wooded shore, the mosquitoes managed to make their way out to us. I had a mosquito net draped around my bunk but would wake up after a restless sleep to find that one or two "mossies" had left their marks on me. They were not the only insects to invade us. The area round the lights on deck was covered with beetles, moths and large flying ants.

The master of a British ship came aboard. He had spent years aboard ships on the China coast and, noticing that we had a Chinese crew, wanted to practice his Chinese with them. But he found that none of them could understand him. He knew Hong Kong Cantonese and our crew, being from Singapore, spoke Mandarin.

A day before our departure, I had to take Hendriks, the 5th engineer, ashore in the boat. He had an infected tooth which, despite his voracious appetite, must have slowed his intake considerably. He sat on the thwart ahead of me and never said a word as I steered past the throng of ships which lay between us and the wharf. One of them looked familiar. It was the old "Mandalay" looking as grimy as ever. I steered in closer to get a better look at her. A group of men stood on deck leaning over the rail and one of them I recognized as an old ship-mate, Chips, the ever-complaining Glaswegian, who always said that "this is my last trip at sea" and yet there he was two years later. I slowed down to have a chat and heard that Mr. Campbell, the kindly mate who had given me my fare home from Rotterdam, had lost his life when the "Kemmendine" had been attacked and sunk by the "Atlantis" in July 1940. Hendriks, impatient to get ashore, told me his tooth was hurting and I was wasting time.

On July 15th, 1942, we sailed in a convoy of thirty-four ships with five escorts and two days later we were off Dakar where two motor torpedo boats came out to join us. That evening, I was woken by a series of explosions. I ran out on deck to see star shells being fired over us. An attack seemed imminent. It

Steamer "Kemmendine" sunk by the Commerce Raider "Atlantis" in July, 1940

never materialized but a problem of another sort arose as men became ill with malaria. A large Dutch ship dropped astern to transfer two seamen to a sloop which had sent a boat to her. Over the next few days, five more cases of suspected malaria were put aboard the escorts.

Later that month, five of the Chinese suddenly became ill — three of the engine room crew, a seamen and a cook. They had high fevers and one of the older men was in a bad way. The mate described him as being "more dead than alive", but he was an opium smoker and the old man was unable to find out if that was the cause of his sickness or whether he had malaria.

One morning, I was on the bridge and glanced astern to see a ship suddenly veer off course at right angles and collide with a vessel in the next column. The force of the impact caused it to heel over heavily and dislodge a lifeboat which fell overboard. A signal appeared over the bridge of the runaway to announce that her steering gear had broken down. She dropped astern while the other ship, although damaged, regained her position.

July 28th, 1942, I added more in my diary: "A sad day aboard. I was on the bridge and heard a series of shots coming from our stern. I thought that someone was having rifle practice. Later, the 2nd mate appeared looking very unhappy. "I had to do it, her spinal cord was broken." He was talking about the ship's dog, Jennie, who had been aboard for three years and had survived several accidents including a fall into a tank full of benzene. The mate, whom I'd always thought was least tolerant of the dog's presence aboard, was very upset and couldn't understand why so many shots had been necessary. He said, "This is a bad omen for us."

July 30th, 1942 — "A catapult ship joined the convoy. She has a Hurricane fighter standing on a launching ramp built on her foredeck. In the event of an attack by a long-range Fokker-Wulfe bomber, the fighter can be shot off to defend the convoy and hopefully down the bomber. At any rate, it is a one-shot affair as the plane, once released, cannot be recovered and has to be 'ditched'."

August 1st, 1942 — "At about 10 a.m. I began to shiver uncontrollably and had a terrible headache. The mate took my temperature which was 39 degrees C. and sent me to my bunk. I am writing this two days later while 'bunk-bound'. It cannot be malaria as we left Freetown two weeks ago and we are now off the south-west coast of Ireland. Last night, I was startled out of a deep sleep by two heavy explosions. Thinking they were torpedoes, I ran out on deck prepared for the worst until I was told they were only depth charges."

August 4th, 1942 — "I still have a temperature but the mate insists that I do not have malaria. Whatever it is, I must 'throw it off' before we reach Liverpool. After a long trip, I certainly do not want to be in my bunk when entering port."

When we finally arrived in the Mersey River, an air raid was in progress and I went up to the bridge wearing a dressing-gown over my pyjamas. The pilot was amused by this and asked me whether it was usual for mates to wear their night attire on the bridge. The old man did not think it was funny and ordered me back to my bunk. We tied up at the oil dock and the voyage was over. We had been away for almost eight months. A bundle of mail had been thrown on my bunk and as I was reading it, the doctor walked in and told me that I had to go to hospital for "observation".

Chapter 7. Malaria and the "Groenland"

August 6th, 1942, was my twenty-second birthday and I lay in the Walton Hospital cursing my bad luck and hoping for a quick discharge and some leave. The doctors could not decide what was wrong with me. After languishing in hospital for a week in a bloody state of mind, I was pronounced fit and ready to take a train for home. It was a warm, sunny afternoon as I walked down Lord Street on my way to collect money for the train fare. I felt unsteady on my feet after being bed-ridden for so long but the urge to get away from Liverpool was strong and in a few hours I expected to be in the countryside of southern England.

I had not walked far when a sudden attack of dizziness caused me to sway and stumble across the pavement. It was a busy thoroughfare and other pedestrians must have thought that I was just another drunken seaman, a common sight in a big seaport like Liverpool. In a state of almost complete collapse and unable to walk, I noticed a car with the sign “W” on the windscreen. This was a wartime measure to indicate that the car owner was a doctor who could be summoned in case of emergency. A man was about to get into the car. I shouted and caught his attention saying that I was ill and needed help. I noticed a look of exasperation and disgust on his face as he waved me aside, muttering something about being too busy and that I should go elsewhere. Some kind passerby summoned a taxi and I must have told the driver that I had malaria because he had the sense to take me to the Tropical Diseases Hospital, which was where I should have been in the first place.

I came under the care of one of Britain’s leading specialists in tropical medicine. In the bed next to mine lay a young army officer suffering from beri-beri which he had contracted in Burma where he had served with the 14th Army. We had lots of time to chat and he told me of his experiences in the jungle fighting the Japanese. He was in one very fierce battle around the town of Arakan, after which his unit was sent in on a “mopping up” exercise during which his Gurkha batman saved his life. “I was about to enter a native hut on the outskirts of the town,” he related, “where we suspected some Japs were hiding. Suddenly I was confronted by a Japanese soldier who rushed at me with his bayonet. He was actually frothing at the mouth and made a strange, gurgling noise. I thought that I had had it as I felt the point of the bayonet slash my face. But he suddenly dropped like a stone at my feet. My batman had disemboweled him with one stroke of his kukri!” He pointed to a long scar which ran down his cheek. He was very thin and was being fed raw liver to keep him alive.

Not all the patients in the ward were suffering from war-related sicknesses. On the opposite side of the room was a pleasant young fellow of about my own age. At first, I rather envied him when his pretty fiancee came to visit. She would sit on his bed and they would chat about their future together. But at other times he would lapse into a coma and mumble to himself for hours on end. When this happened, the nurse would draw the curtains around his bed. He would keep us awake at night with his cries and I was torn between feelings of annoyance and pity. I asked the nurse what was wrong with him and she replied, "He will never see daylight again outside this hospital. He has syphillis and it is attacking his brain." About three weeks later, I was on my feet again and went home for much-needed leave.

It was wonderful to be among loved ones again and to walk along country lanes far from the sea. But I was nagged by doubts about my future, knowing that I could not go far in my profession unless I passed my 2nd mate's ticket. So I went to London and again took up residence in "Jack's Palace". But instead of attending the Nautical School there, I decided to enroll at the Sir John Cass Nautical College. It was near the Tower Bridge and had the reputation of being the sort of place where even the dullest students could be persuaded to produce results. So it was claimed anyway, but in reality it made little difference as I soon found it as difficult as before to master the problems of stability, ship's construction and related subjects. My second attempt to pass the exam was as dismal as the first, for although I passed the orals, I failed the written part. Captain Hopwood had retired and I was examined by Captain Storey who had been with the famous Union Castle Line. Although he was not as fearsome as "Old Hoppy", he was all business and grilled me for nearly two hours, then stood up and said, "I am passing you, but you are a bit weak on ship's rigging!"

He was referring to my explanation on how to lower a telescopic topmast wherein I had gone into great detail about the need to slacken the stays, remove the foremast light and then take the lifting wire to the winch in readiness to lower the mast. "Then what do you do?" he asked. "I would lower away," I replied in triumph. Captain Storey's face wore a pained expression. "Nothing would happen — you have forgotten to remove the pin on which the mast sits!" A mere detail, I thought. But failing the written exam was particularly galling because earlier on I had become friendly with a cadet from the Blue Star Line and had helped him with chart work as it seemed that I knew more about the subject than he did. We sat for the exam on the same day. He passed and I did not!

These were dark days indeed for me, caused not only by the black-out in London. I wandered about the East End of the city wondering what to do next. I wasn't keen on the idea of returning to tankers as 4th mate and even considered the possibility of joining the Royal Navy. One day, I went to the shipping pool on Leadenhall Street and was told that a small company needed a 3rd mate on a ship to be delivered to New Zealand. This sounded interesting and holding a slip of paper in my hand, I went to be interviewed by the Van Ommeren shipping company. I was kept waiting for an hour until a pompous clerk said that a "Mr. So and So" would see me now. I was shown into a small, dark room where a balding, fat man sat behind a desk. He began by telling me how careful the company was in selecting their employees — only the very best and brightest would do. His manner was offensive and condescending. He had never been to sea himself but knew what kind of men his company needed. He then asked me for my discharge book, (a record of sea service), and after thumbing through the pages said, "I see that you are a Roman Catholic." (My Christian names were evidently a give-away.) I replied that I was and wondered aloud what that had to do with my ability to do the job. He gave no response and I knew that the interview was at an end. I hadn't wanted the job anyway.

One of my best friends at the time was a dear maiden aunt who lived in a small flat in Hampstead. I would travel across the city by bus or tube to enjoy the pleasure of her company and sit down to a good meal of whatever she managed to gather from her ration book. She was as disappointed at my lack of success as I was, but made valiant attempts to try and convince me that it was not the end of the world. "Nothing worthwhile in life comes easily." she said, and that, in the end, I would succeed. "Failures strengthen the character." Maybe so, but I wondered how many it would take to do that! Christmas was not far off and I decided to spend it with my father, who by now had settled down with a lady who ran a guest house in Buckfastleigh, Devon. My sister, Gertrude was happily married to John Henle and living in a converted barn on his father's farm at Dart Bridge. John was in the army, suffering hellish conditions within the confined space of a tank. He would be fortunate to see the war through but would be badly burned when his tank was hit by a shell from a German Tiger tank. Bernard, my brother, was also in the army fighting in Germany. I thought I would stay in Devon for awhile and further my studies by enrolling at the Plymouth School of Navigation. This meant an hour's train ride and, although part of it was along the banks of the River Dart through superb scenery, it was both time-consuming and tiring. Plymouth was a shambles after receiving a lot of attention from the Luftwaffe. The city centre was virtually levelled and the shopping area shifted to a place called Manamead but there was little to buy anyway.

At first, my studies went quite well, but then I found concentration increasingly difficult and this, coupled with long hours travelling plus dwindling resources, made the decision to return to sea easy. One day, a notice appeared in the school. A crew of four men was required to man a small coaster for a short voyage from Plymouth to Cardiff. I thought it might be a good experience as well as fun, so, with three others from the school, we boarded the 500 ton ship, "Groenland". To our surprise, we were the entire crew! As the ship was in no condition to steam on her own she would be towed and all we had to do was steer her and watch the tow line. She was French and the tricolour was flying over her stern when we went aboard. Conditions aboard were abominable. Filthy bedding lay on the bunks and dirty dishes lay on the mess tables as though the last men to use them had left in a hurry or couldn't be bothered to clean them. It was a discouraging start and we were about to walk ashore, when the agent for the owners arrived at the gangway with provisions and promised to make it worthwhile if we remained aboard. We had a hurried consultation and, with some misgivings, decided to stay.

We followed the tug out of Plymouth Sound and headed down the coast towards Lands End. I did not know my shipmates but they seemed pleasant and easy going, with the exception of one fellow to whom I had taken an instant dislike. Len (his name) had adopted a superior air from the moment we stepped aboard and had made it plain to the rest of us that he was in charge. We had not bothered at the time to establish who was going to be boss, merely assuming that, as we were of equal rank, we would "pull together".

The first few hours at sea were enjoyable as we moved silently at the end of the tow line but as we approached Lands End we began to feel the effect of the Atlantic swells. The "Groenland" was completely empty as no one had thought it necessary to load any ballast. Before long, she was rolling and pitching violently. Everyone of us became sea sick except Len of course, who now had a decided "edge" over the rest of us. Although as ill as the others, I had enough experience with seasickness to be able to stay on my feet regardless of the conditions. But Len was immune and strutted back and forth to prove it. When he began to imply that we had no right to call ourselves seamen if we could not "take the weather", a shouting match started. To any impartial observer able to look at this scene from above, it would have been ridiculous. Four men, huddled in the tiny wheelhouse of a wallowing old hulk, cursing and hurling abuse at the one who was "in command"! It took us thirty hours to reach Cardiff. By then, we'd had enough of Len and the "Groenland". With little to eat, no sleep and no washing facilities during the entire trip, we were glad to get ashore. Our erstwhile "Captain" was ignored and the three of us returned to Plymouth without him.

Chapter 8. The Lucky "Murena"

I stood in heavy, driving rain on the end of the pier at Gourock, Scotland waiting for a launch to take me out to the tanker "Murena". She was just visible in the murk, lying at anchor with many other ships waiting to form a convoy. It was February 11th, 1943, and I had been given a 4th officer's job on her. She was identical to the "Macuba" so at least I would be familiar with my surroundings. But I did not relish the thought of being the "extra man" once again. The launch was crowded with men who, like me, were going out to board their ships. The water was rough and before long some of the passengers were "throwing up". A number of drunken Americans were standing near me and, before I could move clear, I received the contents of one man's stomach over my coat and onto my baggage. There was little to be said; nobody cared anyway. Surprisingly, although I felt nauseated I was not sick and managed to retain my last meal. An hour later, the launch was bobbing under the pilot ladder thrown over the "Murena's" side. I watched anxiously as my bags were hauled up and I climbed aboard.

One never knew quite what to expect on joining a new ship. There was an atmosphere aboard some ships which became apparent the minute one stepped aboard — she was a "happy ship" or otherwise. I soon found, to my relief, that the "Murena" had a friendly crew with one exception in the person of the 3rd mate who was a misfit. He came from the Terschelling Islands off the Dutch coast whose inhabitants had difficulty getting along with the rest of the country. Later, I was to hear talk that he was a Nazi sympathizer who was universally disliked and I tried to avoid him as much as possible

When I walked into the accommodation I was greeted with some indifference by the officers who were having a party in the mate's room. But when I said that I had made a voyage on a sister ship, they offered me a drink. The 4th mate's cabin was in a mess; it looked as if a dozen monkeys had been released within. Clothing, books and a variety of objects picked up in foreign ports were scattered about the room. Several darts were left stuck in the bulkhead. This said something about the previous occupant. It appeared that he had left in a great hurry.

Before we sailed, the former 4th mate came aboard to claim his belongings. He had been a cadet with the P & O line who, like me, had failed to pass his ticket and had to go back to sea before trying again. He was in a frantic rush to get ashore as he had not been happy aboard. I helped him close an obstinate case by standing on it. He was worried about the customs men as it contained a thousand undeclared cigarettes.

On the 14th of February, 1943, we sailed in a convoy of sixty ships escorted by twelve British and American destroyers and sloops. Our destination was Curacao, Dutch West Indies, for a load of benzene. I soon settled down, already being accustomed to Dutch ways. The master, Captain Edens, was a tall, handsome man in his fifties. The mate was a blond-haired fellow called De Vere; he was strongly built and spoke so loudly one could hear him a ship's length away but he was sociable enough and, like all the officers, spoke English well.

The "Murena" had more reliable engines than her sister ship and there were no stoppages at sea for repairs. As we sailed south, ships bound for Canada and U.S. ports left us until there were only thirty-two ships in the convoy. Our station was 32, which meant that we were the second ship in the third column. When we were two hundred miles south of the Azores we ran into trouble. On the afternoon of February 23rd, 1943, I was working in one of the lifeboats when the rumble and crunch of a depth charge shook the ship. U boats had found us, action stations were called, and I ran back aft to take my station at the 4" gun. The escorts dashed around us dropping depth charges and we wondered when the attack would begin. The commodore ordered all ships to take evasive action.

By nightfall the depth charging had stopped. The escorts had lost contact and we began to think that an attack had been beaten off. We sailed on in a calm sea under a full moon — ideal conditions for U boats. I was relieved at my gun station and told to go to the bridge to take over the watch so the mate could have his supper. I stood on the port wing looking anxiously at the ships around us. I could hear the slight squeak of the wheel as the quartermaster turned it back and forth and the rhythmic beat of the motors. Otherwise, all was quiet.

My attention was suddenly riveted on a white streak in the water across our bows. Seconds later, there was a flash, followed by a loud explosion on our port bow. A ship in the outside-port column was blown up by a torpedo. She disappeared in a cloud of smoke. I was just about to sound the alarm when a thunderous roar and blast knocked me off my feet. A sheet of flame and a column of water shot skyward on our starboard side. The large raft which had been secured to the shrouds on the foremast disappeared. By the time I regained my feet and walked towards the wheelhouse, the "Murena" had taken a heavy list to starboard. The old man's dog, a terrier as scared as I was, began barking furiously and snapped at my ankles as I pushed aside the canvas black-out curtains. The wheel house was in a shambles with broken glass all over the deck. The quartermaster was complaining loudly, "No steer! No steer!" The compass had been lifted right out of the binnacle and lay on the deck. The old man reached the bridge and stopped the engines. Meanwhile, the mate, Mr. De Vere, a calm and quick-thinking man, went foreward with the carpenter to assess the damage.

I glanced astern to see the ship behind in the process of altering her course to avoid hitting us. There was another mighty flash and roar. Flames and debris went shooting skyward and she disappeared from view. Moments later, another ship on our port beam was also hit. Whistles and sirens shrieked in unison, interrupted only by the thump and crash of depth charges. I found myself at No. 3 lifeboat amidst a shouting and undisciplined crew. In a smoky and murky atmosphere I recognized others who had run helter-skelter from their rooms. The chief engineer took charge of one fall and I took the other. One of the gunners cut away the canvas boat cover and cleared the boat. Then we waited for the order to lower it. When received, we lowered the boat to within 10 feet of the water and then secured it. By this time the ship was slowly being brought back to an even keel due to the mate's timely action.

We were now stopped in the water and the convoy drew away but not before a straggler almost collided with us. A ship nearby was burning furiously and three others had simply disappeared. The old man realized that although badly damaged we were in no immediate danger of sinking. About this time we put up a fireworks display of our own. The explosion had loosened soot in the engine uptakes and this caught alight, sending balls of fire erupting out of the funnel. We were a lame duck and did not need this illumination while the enemy was lurking nearby. I returned to the bridge and found that we were under way again. The old man gave me a message to pass on to Sparks which read, "To commodore of convoy. Torpedoed but will rejoin at our utmost speed." We were now on an even keel but wondered when we would receive another torpedo to finish us off. Lights were being carelessly flashed on the decks by some of the crew which further enraged the old man. He'd just been told by the mate that some of the stewards and firemen had earlier presented themselves at the lifeboats and they had been carrying personal baggage! They had actually put a boat into the water and were only stopped by the 3rd mate from casting off.

Once order had been restored, the old man gathered some of us in the chartroom for a discussion of our situation. Then he produced a bottle of whisky, gave each of us a stiff tot and said, "This will make you feel better so let's all drink a toast to the ship, 'Murena'." The 2nd mate and I were busy fixing the compass and had to remove the glass cover to gently lift the card and return it to its central pivot. The mate described the damage to the starboard side as extensive with three and possibly four of our tanks open to the sea. But the collision bulkhead was intact and it was judged safe to proceed at full speed. Apart from a good shaking up, there were no injuries reported from the crew. Throughout the night, broken beams and plating in the damaged area of the ship crashed about in the surging sea. One of our lifeboats had come adrift and was swinging about as we rolled in the swell. This was hastily secured.

We had been torpedoed in a position about 800 miles from Madeira and still had 3,000 miles to our destination. Fortunately, the weather remained good and at dawn the following day we could see the convoy ahead of us in the distance. A British sloop approached us and had the gall to flash a message which read, "Good morning! How are you?" They wanted to know the extent of the damage and when we thought we could catch up.

Twelve hours later we rejoined the convoy and counted twenty-seven ships. In all, five ships had been torpedoed. The tanker "British Fortitude" and the "Murena" were the fortunate vessels that remained afloat after being hit. Of the three ships lost, one was a small passenger ship that went down with all hands.

The commodore hoisted a signal asking ships how much accommodation could be provided for survivors who had been picked up by the escort vessels.

The days that followed were uncomfortable; the hours of darkness were the worst. I was reluctant to sleep in my room because it was so close to the waterline and I took my mattress out on deck to find a spot higher up. There was a secluded section of deck outside the old man's room and I knew that he would not object to my invading his territory, so I placed my bedding in such a way as to avoid being stepped upon. I wasn't the only one who sought comfort on the open decks. The 2nd mate slept on the "monkey island", (top of the bridge), and many of the Chinese "camped out" on top of the poop deck, (stern of the ship). Not that it would have made much difference had we been hit again. It just felt safer.

We talked about recent events and came to the conclusion that one or two U boats had waited until darkness, then surfaced and run at top speed to a position ahead of the convoy where they had submerged and waited until we were above them. They then surfaced in the middle of us and fired their torpedoes. We felt lucky to be afloat and now every turn of our screws took us closer to our destination. We managed to make 8 knots and eleven days later reached the U.S. base in Guatanamo Bay, Cuba. Navy divers went down to inspect our mangled hull and reported that although there was a 65-foot hole in our side, we were still seaworthy.

On March 16th, 1943, the low-lying islands at the tip of Florida appeared on the horizon and soon we were safely at anchor in the calm, clear waters of Key West. It was wonderful to feel safe and secure at last. The Old Man must have felt especially relieved because he held a party in his room and placed several bottles of whisky and Bols gin on the table. He became quite maudlin in his praise for the crew in getting us across the Atlantic. The men in the engine room were the most deserving of praise. To be stuck in the bowels of a ship during an attack must have been hellish and the urge to go up to apparent safety on deck, hard to resist. After two days in this peaceful haven, we met a small convoy for the short run up the coast and two days later arrived in Jacksonville, Florida.

Jacksonville was a happy choice for us; just the sort of place seamen dreamed about. It was not a large city but it had everything that we needed. It lay about 20 miles up the Saint John's River and the shipyard was within easy walking distance of the city. A new floating dry-dock had just been built and we were the second ship to go into it. Once the water had been pumped out I went down into the dock to look at the damage to our hull. A tangled mass of steel-plating, broken beams and twisted piping was mute testimony to the destructive power of a torpedo. A piece of alien steel was found among the wreckage. It was identified by a naval officer as part of the torpedo and was taken away for examination.

In contrast to being in a dry dock in Britain, living conditions aboard the ship remained relatively unchanged. We could use the toilets because pipes were welded to the scuppers on the hull, thus trips ashore for calls of nature were

Looking aft from the midship house. After a party in the Mates'' Room, the 2nd engineer would have trouble finding his way aft along the cat walk.

unnecessary. "We Americans think of everything. You are 50 years behind the times over in the old country," said the cheerful dock manager in a thick Scottish accent. "We will have you fixed up and back to sea in no time." He had left Scotland 30 years ago and never returned. Judging from what was going on around us, his boast was not an idle one. Five Liberty ships were in various stages of construction. The rate of work was staggering. During the next two months, we would see these ships take shape from the laying of the keel to the launching, all within a period of six weeks. I would look across the dock at the nearest ship and see the engine and boilers being lowered into the hull. Next day the housework was in place, the funnel and masts welded in place and she was ready to go down the ways. The yard was a hive of industry. Many of the workers were women, some of them more skilled at welding than the men. The success of building ships so quickly was thanks to the prefabrication of components which were welded, rather than riveted, at other locations and then moved to the shipyard. The hull was built in record time due to the all-welded construction. Nearly 3,000 Liberty ships were built during the war and the record time for completion of one ship was 30 days! They were built by the mile and cut off by the foot!

But shipyard activities took second place to the social possibilities ashore. It was pure joy to stroll along the tree-lined streets in the warm sunshine. The stores were full of things that were unavailable in war-time Britain. The girls looked like fashion models in their summer dresses and everyone was friendly. I had every reason to feel happy because it was obvious that our stay in port was going to be a long one. We were invited to parties, dinners at homes and drives into the country. It wasn't long before I met a very attractive girl. Her name was Diana and she invited me home to meet her mother. They lived in a southern-style house

"Murena" in drydock. Jacksonville, March 1943. View of foredeck - the stargoard liferaft disappeared after we were torpedoed.

in the suburbs. It was typical middle-class America. Rows of white houses with tidy lawns in the front, not divided by fences as in England, but open and neighbourly. Her mother was kind and talkative and I became a frequent guest for dinner. I never asked Diana about her father and she never spoke of him. Her brother was in the army and photos of him in uniform were on prominent display. She had a car and we would drive to such places as Tallahassee and Saint Augustine and return late at night when her mother would wonder where we had been. I was "walking on air" and very happy, the war seemed far away and I was in no hurry to return to it.

A letter arrived from Mrs. Thomas in Redditch, England. Her son Dick a boyhood friend of mine, had joined the R.A.F. and was now stationed in Georgia. He had got his wings and was teaching others how to fly. I got permission to take leave and made my first plane flight in a Lockheed Lodestar which took me to Bainbridge, Georgia about 100 miles away. Dick met me at the airport. Holding his hand was a pretty, dark-haired girl whose car was parked outside and she drove us to the base. "I've organized a flight for you tomorrow and we have a party laid on for tonight. I hope you feel up to it," Dick said. He was wearing his R.A.F. uniform but the wings didn't look quite right. When I remarked on this, he replied, "These are Yankee wings on loan until the R.A.F. ones are available. We call them 'tin uns'."

The base was enormous. Long rows of Quonset huts lined the road leading to the hangars. In the distance, a squadron of training planes sat, parked and silent after a day's exercise. I was introduced to Dick's fellow officers, both American and British, and sat down to a service meal of gargantuan proportions. I wondered how men were expected to fly after consuming all that was available. The party was held off-base in a tavern in Bainbridge. It was a boisterous affair with many of the "local talent" attending. Dick seemed very popular and had a different companion from the girl who had accompanied him to the airport. Next morning I had a slight hangover. The idea of taking a flight anywhere did not appeal to me and I said so. But Dick was made of sterner stuff and would not hear of it. I was ordered to get into a jeep and collect a parachute. As the girl who issued the chute helped me into it, she assured me that I was in for a great ride. "If you have to jump out, all you have to do is count to five, then pull this ring. Have a good flight!"

I climbed into the rear seat of a Harvard trainer, the seat normally occupied by a student flyer, and we were soon roaring down the runway. Dick's voice came through my head set, "I want to show you what this aircraft can do, so hold tight." This order was superfluous as I was already gripping whatever was at hand. The plane climbed steeply until we reached a height of a few thousand feet. Then the nose of the plane dropped suddenly and we went into a power dive at full throttle. I held on for dear life and reminded myself this was fun as the force of gravity seemed to leave my stomach elsewhere. Looking over Dick's shoulders, I watched in mounting terror as the ground rushed up to meet us. Then, when tree tops appeared at the same height as us, the infernal machine swooped upwards. The next manoeuver was even more unnerving. The plane was put into a steep banking turn as one wing suddenly dropped and I was viewing the base from a very acute angle. There seemed to be a real chance of my falling out altogether. I glanced at the ring of my chute and grabbed the stick in front of me. This brought immediate response on my headset from Dick. "Get your hands off the bloody stick, I can't move it!" We flew over the highway and he shouted, "Hold on! I'm going to buzz that car." We went into a steep dive. I could see a car directly ahead of us and seconds later we shaved the roof. I wondered what the driver must have said, what the flying rules were and whether my friend would survive this kind of madness. It was a memorable week end. It ended with another party where I drank Budweiser beer with some of Dick's co-fliers and their girl friends.

My romance with Diana had blossomed to the extent that I began to harbour thoughts of marriage. But then she asked me what I intended to do for a living when the war ended. I hedged a bit and said that I thought that the sea life seemed to agree with me. This reply put a damper on our relationship. She did not relish the idea of becoming a sailor's wife!

By the 1st of June, 1943, repairs to the ship were almost completed. It had taken longer than expected for two reasons: the completion of the Liberty ships took priority in materials and labour and the repair of a tanker was more complex and time-consuming than that of a cargo ship. A week later, the "Murena" was afloat once more and ready for sea. We had a rousing send-off. Two of our Dutch engineers had married local girls and there were tearful dockside farewells. These girls must have wondered when they would see their husbands again. We had made many friends during our stay in Jacksonville and they hooted their car horns as the ship moved out into the river. The old man blew a few blasts on our horn and we headed for sea.

The run up the coast to New York was made more interesting as well as safer since we took the inland route, going through the Baltimore-Maryland Canal. It was a tight squeeze as the "Murena" was close to the limiting size.

The oil dock in Bayonne, New Jersey was a fair distance from Manhattan. The lure of the bright lights was like a magnet but a long journey in the subway lessened its appeal. Once again, the Immigration Authorities placed restrictions on shore leave for the Chinese. This bothered them and there was grumbling. The Chinese steward was particularly upset and when he saw me dressed in my shore-going clothes he asked me to do him a favour. He handed me a small parcel to deliver to his cousin in Chinatown. It seemed like a reasonable request although I should have known that finding any address in a maze of streets in that section of New York would be difficult. The steward gave me a piece of paper with his cousin's address and, as few people in Chinatown understood English, I soon realized that a large part of my shore leave would be spent on a futile search. I showed the slip of paper to a dozen people and was about to give up when a man in the back of a food store came forward and offered to take me to the place I was looking for. We arrived at a door in a side alley and knocked on it. As I had observed before in the Orient, the occupants of dwellings liked to scrutinize visitors through a peep hole before opening the door. It was opened and the parcel was taken by a furtive individual who darted inside and closed the door. Not a word was spoken and I hurried away. Sometime later I mentioned this episode to one of the other mates. He smiled wryly and asked me whether I had any idea what was in the parcel. I told him that I did not. In his opinion the steward had used me to deliver opium! "If you had been caught by the police, you would have spent a long time ashore!" he said with a grin.

After an uneventful Atlantic crossing we headed for the top of Scotland and entered the Naval Base at Scapa Flow. Some of our fuel was required in Russia because as soon as we had dropped anchor a small tanker came alongside us. She was called the "Green Ranger" and she was fitted with an unusual device designed to fool the enemy. A false funnel, which emitted smoke when required, had been built on the fore-end of the vessel and a bow wave had been painted on her after-end to give the illusion that she was going the other way! She was destined to sail on the dangerous run to Murmansk. Our stay was brief and we went to Loch Ewe, a remote anchorage on the West Coast of Scotland.

My request for early leave had been granted on the condition that I escort some of our Chinese crew across the highlands of Scotland to Inverness where we would board a train for London. The journey was an ordeal. The bus provided was an ancient vehicle which spluttered and wheezed as the driver constantly shifted gears over humps and holes in the road. The scenery was lovely but with the clatter and roar of the motor, combined with the never-ending chatter of the

Chinese, it was impossible to enjoy it. I sat in the front near the driver who seemed inclined to talk but had to shout in order to make himself understood. As he was unable to converse with anyone but me, he insisted I stay where I was. "It helps pass the time," he said. I was extremely glad to reach Inverness after a bone-shaking trip of seven hours. The train to London took a further eight hours but in relative comfort. I said good-bye to the Chinese crew and headed for Dick Thomas' parents' house in Redditch.

Mrs. Thomas thought that the East End of London was an unsuitable place for me to study for exams. She had friends who lived in Dulwich which was considered a residential area. Ronald and Angela Alport were the kindest of people and quite prepared to put up with me and put me up! He had an important job with the Bank of England, (he was a Director), and Angela was a handsome and elegant lady who spent her time doing charity work. She was also a chain-smoker who used a cigarette holder in the belief that this device rendered her habit harmless. She puffed relentlessly throughout the day and part of the night and her consumption of the weed was so great that Ronald had to bring home a box of one hundred of the best Ronson cigs almost every night. They lived in a comfortable flat surrounded by trees overlooking a park. During the lengthy bus ride to the navigation school I would sit on the top deck studiously reading a technical book in an effort to prepare for yet another attempt to pass my ticket.

After hours and hours of effort, for reasons completely inexplicable to me, I once again failed to pass the exam! To say that I was mortified would be putting it mildly. My father must have been exasperated also. So much so, that he never asked me why I had failed which was just as well. It was a painful experience.

Chapter 9. "Jamaica Producer"

The "Jamaica Producer" was lying in dry-dock in Avonmouth when I joined her on the 25th of October, 1943. She had a hole in her port bow from a collision with a Canadian corvette off the entrance of Halifax harbour. She was a fast, single-screw vessel of about 5,000 tons with accommodation for almost 100 passengers and a crew of about 60. She had been built to carry bananas from Jamaica to Britain but since this was no longer considered essential in wartime, she was now on the New York run bringing back frozen meat. It was the first time that I had sailed with a British crew. They were mainly from the Avonmouth, Bristol area and some of the stewards and firemen were from Jamaica. How different they were in mood and manner from the men from India and China. Indeed, there was a difference in the crews from Liverpool, London, Wales and the Geordies from Tyneside. During the next few years, I got the impression that the toughest, most intractable crews were the men from Liverpool. They were known as "Scouses" and the most difficult of them were the Liverpool Irish, who seemed to thrive on agitation of some kind and liked to settle arguments with their fists. They were, however, good seamen and their toughness in enduring wretched conditions afloat on the older ships encouraged owners to sign them on.

During the war, with so many men in the Armed Forces, there was a shortage of experienced seamen. This meant that some ships put to sea with a complement made up of "the dregs" — men who would not have been accepted in peace time. Many of them had signed on to avoid being called up to go in the Services. They would have been misfits among any collection of men. Malcontents who, having avoided service in the army or navy, drifted into the merchant navy. But there were also seamen of the "old school", men who knew no other work and who came aboard with their worldly possessions in one kit bag. The only home they had was the ship and when they signed on the articles some could only mark the paper with an X because they were illiterate. When they had to go ashore between ships they would live in the sailors' home. If that didn't suit them, they would put-up in a whore house until their money ran out and they had to look for another ship. There was much to admire in these men who led such nomadic lives.

The seamen on the "Jamaica Producer" lived in cramped quarters up forward in the focsle, which was a disgrace considering the ship was not old and the accommodation for passengers and officers was above average. She was not a happy ship. The mate, a Welshman called Jenkins, was at odds with everyone. The master kept to himself and was only seen on the bridge when entering or leaving port. He was like some other war-time masters who were recluses, seldom seen by the crew except for the stewards who brought meals up to their cabins. But the 3rd mate of the "Jamaica Producer" was quite the opposite — a gregarious fellow whose sole interest was the passionate pursuit of female passengers. His room was next to mine, (I was 4th mate), and he had gone to great trouble to convert it into a seductive boudoir with soft cushions on the settee and subdued lighting. He had also replaced the drab bunk curtains with coloured ones he had bought in New York. His name was George and he called me "Win", not so much to be friendly but because he needed my co-operation in sneaking female friends into the officers' accommodation, which was strictly forbidden.

When I first joined the "Jamaica Producer" I noticed a platform on the top of the bridge which supported a Perspex dome. I had seen others like it on other ships and had wondered what they were. Once we were at sea, I realized that this mysterious gadget was capable of picking up targets (as we called them) that were not visible to the naked eye. A voice pipe in the wheelhouse communicated with operators in a room below. At the sound of a whistle, the mate on watch would put his ear to the pipe and receive a message such as, "This is 271, Target bearing green, 35 degrees, range 18 miles." "271" was later to become Radar, the greatest invention of the war. The installation was under constant guard by Naval personnel and not even the master was allowed to see it. We were told not to talk about "271" with anyone other than fellow officers.

When the ship was lying in Avonmouth I persuaded the mate to give me a day off so I could visit a relative in Bristol. While there I heard that the "Mauretania Bar" was worth seeing. The walls of the lounge were lined with wooden panels taken from the public rooms of the grand old lady of the Atlantic, the Cunarder "Mauretania". She had gone to the breaker's yard before the war.

I dallied too long in Bristol, missed the train back to Avonmouth and "stuck" for the night, was looking for a cheap hotel when I met some Canadian fire-fighters from Calgary. They were in Bristol to assist the local brigades in fighting fires caused by air raids. They insisted that I accompany them to the fire hall where they would find me a bed for the night. They were a generous, cheerful lot and they gave me a meal and a cot to sleep on.

Our passengers on the "Jamaica Producer" were a mixed lot: Jewish refugees from Poland and Germany mixed with foreign trade officials and military people bound for Washington. Among them was the attractive wife of a Russian diplomat. George, the 3rd mate, had watched their tearful embrace as she and her husband stood on the dock before she walked up the gangway. We had not been at sea more than two days before George had enticed her into his cabin. There was a good deal of gossip about their trysts in secluded parts of the ship, and by all reports, (mostly from the stewards), she couldn't speak a word of English! Not that it deterred George — he was a "past master" at communicating with the ladies. On the trip back from New York there were a number of single and married women, some with children. George was particularly good with kids. That was his strategy. He could be seen in the passengers' lounge bouncing babies on his lap. The mothers loved him, some of them more than others. He kept the 8-12 watch and I was on the 4-8, so he had to arrange his illicit meetings for a few minutes after midnight. "Win, do me a favour. Keep a look-out for me. If you see the old man or the mate, let me know. I have a date when I come off watch. Give me the all clear so I can bring her up to my room." It went against the grain having to lose sleep in order to please George, but he was willing to trade this service in return for keeping a watch aboard for me while I went ashore in New York. He was never caught in these off-duty activities, which was surprising since the heavy smell of perfume pervaded the officers' quarters during the early hours of his romantic rendezvous.

Crossing the "Pond" in a 10 knot convoy was frustrating when we were capable of 16 knots and it took us nearly two weeks going in a westerly direction in rough weather. One evening, the ship was rolling heavily and I was sent down to check on any gear on the open decks that might have worked loose. On my way back to the bridge, I took a detour to see how many passengers were still having supper in the dining saloon. Most of them were too sick to leave their cabins but some of the hardier ones were loath to miss a meal. I looked into the saloon at the very moment the ship took a heavy lurch to starboard. Immediately the place became a shambles. In heavy weather the tables and chairs were secured to the deck by means of a chain. The sides of the tables had fiddles (boards on hinges) to prevent crockery from falling off. But this roll was heavier than usual and the chains on one or two tables and chairs came adrift and slid with passengers across the saloon, landing in an undignified heap. One old dear, gripping a table frantically, had a look of terror on her face as she went sliding to the side.

It was on our second trip to New York that I, too, had a brief romance, although not of the same intensity as George's. Most of the passengers were Jewish refugees. Margo was dark-haired and pretty. I happened to be walking aft to read the log on the stern when she asked me in halting English when I thought we would arrive in New York. I asked her where she came from and she related a sad story of persecution and hardship. She had lost her parents and had escaped from Germany with the assistance of the Red Cross. She was put aboard a ship going to neutral Sweden and eventually got to England. She longed to see America and was going to live with an aunt in Brooklyn. I would meet her on the promenade deck as I did not have the nerve to invite her to my room. Jenkins, the mate, was always on the prowl; he had already warned me not to fraternize with passengers. He had words with me when he walked past my room and saw me writing in my diary. He asked what I was writing about and whether I was jotting down positions and courses. "Do you realize," he yelled, "that information could be useful to the enemy?" I assured him that I had not done so but his threat to confiscate my diary was enough to discourage any further writing.

Before we docked in New York, Margo asked me to come and visit her and gave me her address. It was a few days before Christmas, 1943, and bitterly cold when we secured to the wharf in Brooklyn. Our decks were covered with ice. The skyscrapers of Manhattan were just visible through the sea smoke, (caused by the air being colder than the water), and I wondered if it was worth the hour long subway ride to reach there. I reminded George that he owed me some shore time and I decided to visit Margo. Brooklyn was heavily populated with recent Italian and Jewish immigrants and everyone I spoke to for directions knew no English. It was late in the afternoon before I finally reached a shabby apartment in a run-down area and knocked on the door. A middle-aged woman opened it and I asked to speak to Margo. She did not understand me and called for someone else. This brought a fat woman, dressed in black, who looked at me suspiciously and in a thick accent asked me sharply what I wanted. I replied that I had come to see Margo. While the women chattered in Yiddish, Margo appeared in the background. She looked unhappy and I realized that I had misjudged the situation. We exchanged a few words and I left quickly and never saw her again. I often wondered later whether life in America came up to her expectations.

In the spring of 1944, I left the "Jamaica Producer" and after a few weeks at school I made another attempt at my ticket. This time I passed. It was almost anticlimactic. As one cynic put it, "He got it for good attendance!" It had taken three years, three navigation schools, countless hours of study and four tries but now, at long last, I could say that I was competent to sail as 2nd mate of any vessel afloat!

Chapter 10. Argentina

The clerk behind the desk at the shipping pool told me that a ship bound for South America needed a 3rd mate immediately. On May 22nd, 1944, I boarded the "Empire Buckler" in the West India docks within a few hours the pilot was aboard and we steamed down the river bound for Buenos Aires. She was a war-built, 10,000 tonner driven by steam, a coal burner and capable of 11 knots. The master was a quiet Londoner by the name of Grant, who had lost his previous command when his ship hit a mine. The 2nd mate was an amusing character called Doyle. He was Irish and, like so many of his countrymen, was a good story teller. But he often broke the golden rule at sea; he seldom was able to relieve the watch on time. When my watch ended at midnight, I would have to send the apprentice down several times to try and shake him out of a deep slumber. He would eventually stumble on to the bridge like a man in a trance and by the time he was awake enough to take over the watch it would be well past midnight. Then he would have the gall to begin yarning about adventures in various parts of the world. He was so entertaining that he would keep me enthralled for as long as an hour until I would finally realize that I was losing valuable bunk time.

By now the U boat war had turned round in the Allies' favour and we crossed into the South Atlantic unmolested and arrived at the River Plate twenty five days out of London. Buenos Aires was a seaman's Mecca and referred to as one of the most sinful seaports in the world. Even the jaded traveller did not need to look very long to find something to satisfy his needs. I did not feel any great desire to explore the "flesh-pots" of the city and instead contacted some people whom I had been told to "look up". Mr. and Mrs. Swann were members of the large British community in Argentina. He worked in the banking business and they lived in a comfortable hacienda in the suburbs. I was taken on a tour of the city which was considered one of the best-planned and most attractive in the world. It could be likened to a wheel, the centre being a plaza in which stood an obelisk and the streets fanning out from there to form a circle. The Calle Corrientes was the main thoroughfare and shopping area. The best-known shops were Garthe and Charves, and Harrods which catered to the rich. The flashy night-spot named Taberis was on Calle Florida. It boasted the "best floor show" and the admission fee was more than a month's wages for a seaman. The Swanns took me to one of the best restaurants where the food was as good as any I had ever tasted.

The ship lay in Puerto Nuevo and warships of the Argentine Navy were anchored nearby. One day I watched a ceremony taking place on the quarter deck of a cruiser. The sailors wore blue uniforms identical to those worn by British Tars which was not surprising as the Argentine Navy was established and trained by Britain. A band struck up some military music as be-medalled admirals, commodores and captains stood to attention and saluted the blue and white ensign. My attention was caught by a contingent of soldiers marching along the dockside. I did a double-take and could hardly believe my eyes. These men were in German uniforms and goose-stepping in the Nazi fashion. It could have been a parade in the streets of Berlin. The Fascist regime of Juan Peron was in power and the army had been patterned on the German model. Although Britain had a strong influence in Argentina, Germany had a stronger one and the Peronistas were hoping for a German victory. Seamen from the wrecked "Graf Spee" were feeling quite at home in Buenos Aires and even went on parade through the streets cheered by large crowds of well-wishers. The Americans had powerful business interests in Argentina, particularly in the meat-packing industry. But there was strong resentment against them and during our stay in port, hardly a day went by without anti-U.S. riots when store windows were smashed and cars overturned.

One hot afternoon, I witnessed the way the tough "Vigilantes", (Argentinian Police), dealt with unruly citizens. I was on my way back to the ship walking along the Retiro when I heard shouting. A man was on the ground, a Vigilante was dragging him by his feet while another beat him on the head with a long stick. Passersby didn't seem to take much notice. Buenos Aires could be hazardous for seamen too. Between the docks and the city, there was a sort of "no man's land" of grass and bushes where hundreds of predatory homeless lived. In order to reach the docks, seamen had to pass through this area and it was better to be with a group rather than alone. But one evening I had left my companions ashore to return to the ship and was walking quickly towards the safety of the dock gates. Some distance behind me was a group of seamen who had obviously spent all their time and money in the bars. But the sound of their merriment suddenly turned to frantic shouts of "Marineros! Marineros!" (Dock Police). I looked back to see them being attacked by a gang of thugs who had been lurking in the bushes. I did not wait to see the outcome and ran the rest of the way to the ship. The City Police had a novel way of dealing with drunken seamen. They threw them in jail overnight to sober them up, then put them to work sweeping the streets and clearing manure from the police stables. Some men derived great pleasure from watching their shipmates working off their hangovers in this manner.

Seamen were attracted to the notorious areas known as the "Arches" and the "Twenty-fifth of May Street" where the cheap bars and prostitutes relieved them of their money. The "Liverpool" and "Bristol" bars were known to mariners world-wide, especially the crews of the regular traders such as the Blue Star and Royal Mail lines. Another famed institution was the British Apprentices Club. It was founded by Canon Brady, an Irish priest determined to steer innocent young apprentices away from temptation once their ships reached Buenos Aires. The club was strategically located between the docks and the bars. It offered good, clean fun. No alcohol was allowed on the premises. Dances were organized and only girls selected from good Catholic homes attended. The boxing contests were the most popular activity at the B.A.C. Boys from the ships in port who fancied themselves in the art of self defence could square-off against each other in the ring. The Canon, who was pretty tough himself, would referee the bouts.

After two weeks in port we had almost finished loading a full cargo of frozen meat and related products for Britain. I was on deck watching the last slings of meat come aboard. It was noon and the 2nd mate was still ashore. I was beginning to think that we might have to sail without him, (which would have meant an unexpected promotion for me), but on looking up the dock I spotted a forlorn figure staggering towards the gangway. It was Mr. Doyle and he was barely coherent. I assisted him up the gangway and along the deck towards his room. On the way he stopped to lean over the side to empty the contents of his stomach. Having spent some time retching miserably, he suddenly straightened up and with a cry of anguish said, "Where's me teeth? I've lost me fuckin' teeth!" There was nothing to be done. His false teeth had dropped into deep water and by the time he had sobered up we were heading down the Rio de la Plata, bound for Britain. Later, he began to appreciate his loss, having to chomp on his gums for a month before seeing a dentist. At Freetown we joined a convoy for the last leg of the voyage home. Two weeks later we were back in London.

Chapter 11. April and Rosie

I was about to go on leave when I was laid low by a second attack of malaria and was taken ashore to the Connaught Hospital in the East End of London. I was put in a ward with three men who had been injured by a land mine dropped by a German plane. Germany had by this time started firing buzz bombs aimed at London and a few passed close to the hospital. The air raid sirens would go off and soon we would hear the intermittent splutter of a jet engine. It had a very distinctive sound which was nerve wracking as once the spluttering stopped, we knew that it was on its way down. Three or four seconds of silence would be followed by a loud bang.

My stay in hospital was made easier by visits from April, the girl I had met three years earlier when studying for my ticket in the East End of London. One visit coincided unexpectedly with one from my dear Aunt Ursula who had never heard about April. For one reason or another, I was reluctant to mention girl friends to a maiden aunt. Aunt Ursula had a heart of gold but was apt to be critical and disapproving. I knew this, having once told her about an American girl I had met called Diana. "How nice," she said, "but what a pagan name!" My initial unease during this hospital visit was soon dispelled. "Auntie, this is my friend, April." If there was disapproval she did not show it.

On my feet once more, I went on leave to Devon. My father was now doing what he had always wanted. He was a farmer, working 100 acres of mixed farming in beautiful South Devon. After a short stay, I returned once more to London feeling content that my father was happy.

After placing my name in the Shipping Pool as being available for sea service, I moved into Jack's Palace hoping for a few days grace before being called. I slept in a dormitory with four men who were studying for tickets. One night I was woken up by a sharp stinging sensation on my back. Realizing that I was not alone, I jumped out of bed, turned on the light and began a search for the cause of a maddening itch..This disturbed the other occupants who began to curse, demanding to know the reason for the commotion.A quick inspection of the sheets revealed a bloated bed bug which had raised several bumps on my person.. After despatching the bug, I put it into a matchbox, turned off the light and went back to sleep.

In the morning I went to see the Manager, Captain Bone. He was a retired army man who liked to be accorded the respect due to a man of his rank, even though he was running a marine establishment. "Look at this, I found it in my bed" I said as I opened the box a few inches from his nose. The Captain's usually reasonable demeanour changed, his voice took on an accusatory tone, "Thats impossible, where did you get it"? Realizing that I was suspected of trying to bring disrepute to Jack's Palace I lifted the tail of my shirt to reveal the tell-tale bites, just as Mrs Bone appeared on the scene demanding to know what all the fuss was about. She took a more sensible attitude telling me to come into the office. In a hushed tone she said "You must not tell a soul, it must be kept secret, otherwise there will be trouble and we will have to close down"

I wasn't sorry when at the end of November, 1944, I was offered a 3rd Mate job with Prince Line of London. They insisted that I take a course on the gyro compass before joining one of their ships. I did not mind this as it meant a week in London at the company's expense. During this time April and I renewed our friendship. She was a quiet and gentle girl and I began to think about a possible future together. But I was bothered by stories I had heard from residents of Jack's Palace that she was known to hang about that establishment. It was suggested that she was determined to ensnare a likely prospect among the aspiring officers who stayed there.

We would go for walks in the parks or take bus rides to the West End to see films. One day she told me that April Anderson was not her real name. It was Rosemary Atkinson. I asked why she thought it necessary to adopt another name but she became evasive and acted as though she, herself, didn't know the reason. She was an unusual girl in another way too, for although she had always lived in the East End of London, she spoke with no trace of a Cockney accent, indeed with no particular accent at all. I found her enigmatic, however she was good company and I needed that. She wanted me to meet her parents.

We boarded a bus for Stepney and were soon in a very dismal area, made even worse by heaps of rubble between houses where bombs had fallen. Rosemary led me to a house which was indistinguishable from the ones on either side of the row of dreary brick housing. We entered a narrow, dimly-lit hallway beside a staircase and went on into the kitchen. A sad-looking, untidy woman sat at a table littered with dirty dishes. "Mum, this is Anthony. We have just been to the pictures." Mum looked neither pleased nor surprised and didn't bother to remove the cigarette that dangled from her lips, but mumbled something about, "Rosie always bringing boys home." She was probably in her mid-thirties but looked much older. Rosie took my hand and said, "Come and meet Granny." Granny lay in a bed so large it filled the room. The bedclothes looked dirty and an unpleasant odour filled the air. I shook a bony hand and said hello. Poor Granny appeared ready to expire at any moment. Back in the kitchen, Mum was making a cup of tea, her pale, pinched face in contrast with Rosie's fresh complexion. There was very little space — a jumble of cooking utensils and empty jam jars lay on a sideboard, clothing hung on nails driven into the wall and a bucket of coal stood beside a smoky stove. A collection of bric-a-brac was placed in every available spot. Old Players cigarette tins, picture cards of popular footballers and a bottle of sand from Clacton-on-Sea competed for space on the shelves. While we sat talking about goodness knows what, Rosie's Dad walked in. I could not have made much impact upon him as he never said a word.

The buzz bomb attacks on London had ceased but they were followed by the V2 rockets which fell out of the sky without any warning at all. I was near

Aldgate tube station on a rainy morning when I was startled by a terrific crash. A rocket had landed on a clothing factory a few streets away. Sixty women working there were killed. The gyro course was due to begin on Monday and I decided to spend the weekend with Rosie. She had arranged a picnic with friends on Hampstead Heath. I liked Alf and Edie immediately. They were cheerful Cockneys with a fund of good stories. Alf worked at Claridges, one of the poshest hotels in London. As we lay on the grass eating sandwiches, he told us about the famous film stars he had met, which ones tipped well and the ones who didn't tip at all. We watched the antics of Londoners romping in the grass, gazed at the barrage balloons floating in the sky over the city and chattered about nothing in particular.

On Sunday evening Rosie and I had supper at Alf and Edie's flat in Wanstead. As the evening wore on I became anxious about the gyro course I had to attend next morning. It was late and a long bus ride to my lodgings lay ahead. But Edie urged me to stay overnight, sleeping arrangements having already been made. Although Rosie and I had hugged and kissed often enough, matters had not gone beyond that. I found myself in bed with Rosie, not in a state of passion, but one of funk and panic while listening to giggles and grunts coming from Alf and Edie's room. I lay immobile and wretched in a state of moral rectitude. Goodness knows how Rosie must have felt — I didn't ask her. I slunk away in the very early hours and we never saw each other again.

Chapter 12. The "Egyptian Prince"

The "Egyptian Prince" was a small, general cargo ship of 5,000 tons. She had been built for the Prince Line's Mediterranean fruit trade but the requirements of war were such that she had been on the North Atlantic run from the beginning. Bridge watches in bad weather were uncomfortable because the wheelhouse was only partly enclosed, the after-part was entirely open to the elements. That may have been fine and airy in the balmy waters of the Med, but we were bound for Montreal in January, a decidedly uncomfortable prospect which meant wearing heavy clothing and oilskins on watch in the Western Ocean. She was a triple expansion steamship, coal fired and she could make 11 knots in good weather. Her accommodation was as spartan as one might expect aboard a twenty year old ship.

I joined her in Avonmouth on the 3rd of January, 1945. Captain Hennessy seldom ventured out of his room and when I knocked on his door to report my presence aboard, I waited for a minute or so and heard the clinking sound of bottles being moved. The door opened and I was confronted by a handsome, middle-aged and dishevelled woman whom I took to be the master's wife. She told me that her husband was resting, took my discharge book and closed the door. The mate was a bearded, taciturn Channel Islander called Barker. His name appeared on the ship's articles with N.D. (non domiciled), written after it, which meant that he was exempt from income tax. The 2nd mate was Michael Wardle, who hailed from Mansfield, Notts. He was fond of telling me that Mansfield held the distinction of having more pubs per capita than any other town in the land. Since he, too, was an alcoholic, his home town's reputation may have been a contributing factor. One of the three apprentices was a lanky lad by the name of David Ffollkes who had almost finished his time and needed only a month of sea time before going for his ticket. He wanted watch-keeping experience and was put on the 8-12 with me. I was pleased to have his company and assistance as he was a bright fellow and eager to learn. I soon realized that in some areas he knew a good deal more than I did. But to his credit, he never took advantage of this, and so we ran an efficient watch and both of us profited.

We were part of a fifty-ship convoy and on the second day out, the commodore ordered all ships to carry out a practice shoot. Our 4 inch gun was manned by naval gunners but the normal procedure was that the junior mate acted as the gunnery officer. All I had to do was shout, "Open Fire!" when the gun layer gave me the nod. Our orders were to aim our shots down between the columns of the convoy so as to clear the other ships. Our course was altered slightly to make this easier. Conditions were far from ideal — misty rain with a moderate to heavy swell. The signal went up on the commodore ship and soon the sharp crack of guns could be heard again. My ears plugged with cotton-wool, I focused my binoculars astern to pick up the splash of each shot fired at an imaginary target. All went well for the first few rounds until one hit the top of a swell and ricocheted to one side, uncomfortably close to a ship about one mile away. Angry cries of "Cease fire!" bellowed through a megaphone from the bridge brought the exercise to an end.

There was always activity on the bridge at noon when we estimated our position and hoisted the appropriate flags on the yard arm. All the other ships would do the same with the exception of an American Liberty ship nearby. Then the commodore would hoist a signal requesting the American's position and, after a significant delay, the signal would go up giving a position very close to our own. Inevitably, we began to suspect that the American ship did not bother to work out a position but merely waited until signals appeared and copied them! We did hear that the U.S. Merchant Marine was desperately short of men and that officers were being sent to sea as junior mates after only three months training in an academy. They were known as "ninety day wonders"!

We reached the St. Lawrence intact. It was my first sight of Canada and it looked cold and bleak with a snow-covered landscape. A strong gale whipped up a rough sea off Anticosti Island but once we picked up the pilot off Father Point, the shoreline became interesting as the mighty river became narrower. Our stay in Montreal was pleasant and I enjoyed being in a city where there was no blackout and the stores were filled with goods unobtainable in the U.K. I had been given a shopping list by friends back home and attempted to fill it. We loaded a general cargo and then moved to Halifax to wait for a convoy. While lying in Bedford Basin we heard the news that President Roosevelt had died. We were in mid-Atlantic when the war in Europe came to an end. The ships in the convoy blew their whistles and the escorts fired off rockets in celebration. For the first time in four years we turned on our navigation lights. On reaching the United Kingdom, Captain Hennessey was replaced by Captain Montgomery, who was a likeable man but did not enjoy being at sea which he described as "a wasted life".

I made one more trip on the "Egyptian Prince." We loaded seed potatoes in Avonmouth for Dubrovnik in Yugoslavia. We had entered the Meddy when the signal came diverting us to Naples. The city was full of American troops and supplies were being unloaded at a record rate. There was a chronic shortage of berthing space, and the problem had been partly solved by the use of up-turned hulls of capsized ships. We secured alongside one of these wrecks. The U.S. army engineers had built ramps from the shore to enable heavy trucks to run up onto the wrecks. While secured in this manner we had to leave in a hurry one day and put to sea when a gale made it hazardous to remain in port. We dropped anchor in the Bay of Naples but there was little shelter, the wind increased, we began to pitch heavily and the anchor cable parted. We were obliged to get under way, steam into deeper water and ride out the gale until it abated and we could return to the harbour.

Naples was a war-weary city and there was little reason for spending time ashore. But there was one memorable occasion when we were asked if we would like to attend the opera. It seemed surprising that a city still suffering from the effects of war could stage an opera. But the Italians' love of music transcended other needs and Naples had the second best opera company in Italy. Not knowing what to expect a few of us went. We walked along grimy streets to the San Carlo Opera House. Once inside we were astonished at its lavish and ornate splendour. The walls of the theatre were lined with individual boxes decorated in gold plaster. We had seats "up in the Gods". The theatre was full to bursting point and we were treated to a first class production of "Madame Butterfly".

We left Naples and steamed across to Spain where we loaded oranges. Our first port was Burriana, a small place north of Valencia. We arrived off the breakwater on a beautiful sunny morning and waited for the pilot. When he arrived on the bridge and began shouting orders to me at the telegraphs and to the quartermaster at the wheel, the old man became alarmed for the safety of the ship and decided that the pilot was drunk. He was promptly ordered off the bridge. The old man took the ship into the harbour and dropped anchor. This upset the port authorities and all shore leave was subsequently forbidden. Armed guards were stationed at our accommodation ladder. They were a ragged lot — one or two were without boots with their feet wrapped in sacking. Our arrival had coincided with a festival in the town and we were the only ship in port. Eventually the old man was allowed ashore to clear the ship and, at the same time, make peace, and he invited the Festival Queen to visit the ship. We stood in awe and wonder as the beauty arrived on deck with her entourage. Flowers and kisses were exchanged (officers only), and they went into the saloon for drinks.

We completed loading in Valencia and sailed for Liverpool. Running up the Irish Sea before a southwesterly gale was particularly unpleasant on a partially open bridge as the smoke from our funnel would envelop the watch-keepers. Aboard the ship were two men of whom I was particularly fond. They were seamen from a bygone era. The bosun must have been close to seventy but for all his advanced years he could work harder than the able seamen in his care. He was a man who had been on sailing ships as a boy. One had only to look at his large, gnarled hands as he opened up the lay of a rope when splicing it to know that his life had been a hard one. He seldom raised his voice in anger — he didn't need to as his very presence was sufficient to keep the crew in order. The other man was Greek and the ship's carpenter. He, too, was an elderly man but unlike some ships' carpenters who were called "wood butchers", our Chips was an excellent craftsman. As good wood was generally in short supply, he would select pieces from the dunnage and fashion splendid sea chests and articles of furniture which he would give to the old man and chief engineer. He was also a skilled model maker and before I left the ship, he had completed a large model of a windjammer on which he had served.

It was important in those days not only to be a good seaman but to look like one too. The wearing of wrist watches or gloves invited derision. Even in the coldest weather, men would not cover their hands as it was considered unseamanlike, and the only way one could get the feel of a rope and do a job properly was with bare hands. A true seaman always carried a knife. Not on his belt — that was considered too showy — but in his pocket. French berets were a popular form of headgear as they were unlikely to be blown away in the wind. A sou'wester was essential in heavy rain. Sea boots were also necessary but I was warned to be extra careful when wearing them whilst climbing down a ladder into a hold, as many men had fallen to their death that way. If a man fell overboard with sea boots on, he had to get rid of them quickly as it was almost impossible to swim with them. At sea it was not the custom to close cabin doors unless they were exposed to the elements and the weather was bad. If the occupant was asleep either the curtain across his bunk was drawn, or the door was put on the hook. Doors were only closed in port when there was risk of entry by thieves. A closed door at sea would have invited suspicion, and been considered an unsociable act.

After a few days' leave, the company sent me to one of their new ships as 3rd mate. The "Highland Prince" was a 10,000 ton, utility-built, cargo ship and I joined her in Glasgow but was only aboard for a week when they again sent me on leave.

Chapter 13. Cook's Ruhr Tours

My friend, Dick Thomas, was now back in Britain and attached to a squadron of Halifax bombers based in Norfolk. He had made one or two operational flights over Germany before the war in Europe came to an end. He was now married to Nan, a clergyman's daughter, and they invited me to come and stay in their cottage for a few days. When I got there he said, "You're coming flying with me again. I've arranged a flight over Germany." I was taken aback by this announcement, having vivid recollections of the previous flight a few months earlier, but he was not a man who would take "No" as an answer and as he said, "A Halifax bomber is a more substantial plane than a Harvard trainer." Now that the war was over, the R.A.F. had arranged flights over Germany for the ground crews who had done so much to keep the bombers in the air, so that they could see for themselves the damage to the industrial areas. These flights were known as "Cook's Ruhr Tours".

Early one fine morning, I jumped on a bicycle and rode three miles to the airbase. Here a girl in the W.A.A.F. helped me into a parachute and I climbed into a four-engined Halifax bomber, code named "T for Taire". With Dick at the controls, we took off into a clear blue sky and headed south with about ten ground crew. I sat behind Vivian, the Jamaican co-pilot, until we were at a certain height and was then allowed to take his seat beside the pilot. We flew over the Thames estuary before turning east. It was an exhilarating experience looking down on the water shimmering under the bright sunlight. With four Rolls-Royce engines roaring at full throttle we could only communicate with each other via our head-sets, and Dick began to give a commentary on what we could expect to see over Germany. I realized how the crews must have felt when on a bombing mission and coming under heavy flak. When we reached the coast of Holland, Dick brought the plane down so low that we were skimming across the fields at no more than 200 feet. Horses and cattle scattered at our sudden approach over the tranquil countryside.

Before long we were over the Ruhr. This was the very heart of industrial Germany. We looked down on Dusseldorf where the massive Krupps "Maschinenwerke" lay in ruins, the giant dies clearly visible among the rubble. The R.A.F. and U.S. Air Force had wrought great destruction here. We flew over Essen, Emden, Duisburg and on to Cologne. The spire of the famous cathedral rose among the ruins and we circled it at close range before turning south to Bonn and heading home. By the time we touched down in Norfolk we had been in the air for six hours and I had begun to feel queasy. Also, because I had removed the uncomfortable head-set, I was half-deaf. This made me unsteady on my feet so that the ride back to the village on the bike was as much of an adventure as the plane trip!

My sister's husband, John Henle, had just left the Army and he and Gertrude were still living on Dartbridge Farm in Devon. It was a wonderful place to go after living aboard ship for weeks on end. There were eight children in the

Henle family and one of the daughters, Celia, had joined the Wrens. She was very attractive, especially in her Wren uniform. She was jolly company and with my increasingly frequent visits to the farm, we soon became close friends. She was later stationed at a Royal Naval Air Station in Scotland and I made several trips to visit her. In July of 1945, we became engaged to be married.

Shortly afterwards, I was sent to Liverpool to join the Liberty ship "Samdaring" as 3rd mate. She was loading a cargo of military supplies for the Far East. We had signed on a crew of Irishmen, some of them were Liverpool-Irish and some were from neutral Eire. They did not get along with each other, as subsequent events proved. One day I was given the job of bailing out one of the cooks who had been accused of stealing ration books, a serious offence. I went to Walton Jail with the required money and caught a glimpse of the inside of a grim prison. The cook was very glad to see me. He had spent the night in the company of men accused of violent crimes and was in fear of his life. On return to the ship in a taxi he told me that he had only taken the ration book because his family wasn't getting enough to eat. A likely story, which I didn't believe because theft of ration books was commonplace as they could be sold for a good profit.

Time was running out if I was to be married before the ship sailed. The ship went to Loch Long on the west coast of Scotland to complete loading heavy equipment. The wedding date was arranged, I got special leave and Celia Henle and I were married in Buckfast Abbey, Devon, on August 18th, 1945. I had only been given four days leave so, after a short stay with Celia's aunt in Paignton, we travelled to Loch Long to spend the rest of our honeymoon aboard the ship. That was not as bad as it might sound for the weather was glorious and the countryside along the shores of the Loch was ideal for pleasant walks and long conversations.

Chapter 14. A Long Voyage Around the World!

On the 25th of August, 1945, the "Samdaring" sailed for Bombay. The war in the Far East had come to an end three weeks earlier and there seemed every reason to believe that the trip would be a short one. Our cargo of tanks, personnel carriers, etc., was already redundant. It would surely be unloaded and the ship would return to the control of the Prince Line for commercial trading. I had seen Liberty ships being built several years earlier when I was in Jacksonville, and it was something of a novelty to find myself aboard one. Many of these ships were taken over by the Ministry of War Transport and given the prefix, "Sam", to their names. Unlike most British ships, they were of all-welded construction and the entire crew was housed amidships. They had an ugly, utilitarian appearance and were supposedly disposable ships, i.e., only good for one voyage. Even their strength was in question as there were stories about all-welded Liberty ships not being able to stand up to the weather and simply breaking up. I spent over two years on two of these ships and on one Pacific crossing we were hove to in terrific seas with no subsequent damage to the ship.

Captain Bernard Simons was the Master. It was his first command. He was a nervous, rather ill-tempered man who preferred his own company in the isolation of his cabin abaft the chartroom. The First Mate was a first class seaman and shipmate by the name of Henry Pusey who was later to become an extra-master

On the wing of the bridge of the "Samdaring" in Bombay, 1946. I had run out of razor blades.

and instructor at Southampton Sea School. He was a tower of strength to all aboard and had qualities of leadership that the master lacked. It was just as well the mate was a man of such character because the crew were a troublesome lot and we were in for a long and unpleasant voyage. The 2nd mate, Dave Wylie, was an affable Londoner and an ex-metropolitan policeman.

Many of the seamen came from neutral Eire. Among them was a man named Byrne who stood 6 feet 6 inches tall and seemed to be as strong as a lion. However, subsequent events proved that he was as timid as a pussy cat. The firemen, stewards and cooks were from the Merseyside and some of them were Liverpool Irish. One would have thought that these two types of Irishmen would get along well. But such was not the case. We hadn't been at sea a week before several fights had broken out between them. This posed a problem for the officers. We were used to British-built ships where the crew were accommodated in the foc'sle, forward or aft. Any disturbances among the crew would go unnoticed but when a fracas occurred on the "Samdaring", in close proximity to our accommodation, it became a matter of concern. It became apparent that the chief cook was the main troublemaker and the toughest man aboard. His name was Alexander and he was an ex-boxer who loved using his fists to settle arguments. He beat up one of the Irish seamen while the giant Byrne looked on but was afraid to intervene.

By the time we reached Bombay the south-west monsoon had brought torrential rain to the city. It was unpleasantly hot and humid but once the cargo had been unloaded there seemed every likelihood that we would return home. But the ship was due for dry-docking and three Indian contractors came aboard to do business with the old man. I was busy correcting charts at the time and overheard the bargaining. The contractor who offered the most baksheesh was given the work to clean and paint the hull. The old man made several thousand rupees and was generous enough to pass some of them on to the mate and, in turn, this bonanza filtered down to Dave Wylie and me.

A section of the dock area in Bombay lay in ruins and we wondered why. In 1944, the Canadian-built "Fort Stikine" loaded with nitroglycerin had caught fire and blown up with such force that another ship lying across the dock was also destroyed. A shanty town of slums outside the dock was also levelled. The civilian death toll was over a thousand.

We left Bombay with a cargo for Singapore that included several hundred tons of beer for thirsty soldiers there plus 2,000 tons of ammunition. Why the latter was needed in South East Asia, now that the fighting had ended, nobody seemed to know. We heard later that the tanks, gun carriers and other unwanted vehicles which we had delivered to Bombay were loaded aboard landing craft which took them a few miles offshore where they were pushed over the side!

We arrived in Singapore to find the port so crowded with ships that we had to anchor with many others awaiting their turn to unload. We now realized that there were hundreds of ships like ours, loaded with war materials which nobody needed. With the dropping of the atom bomb on Hiroshima hostilities had come to an end sooner than expected. The mighty engine of war when running at top speed could not be brought to a sudden stop and supplies continued to pour in to where they were no longer needed.

Weeks of frustration lay ahead and to make matters worse, morale aboard the ship was at an all-time low. As there was a military curfew ashore, no leave was allowed and crew unrest came to a head on Christmas Eve. Each man was entitled to one can of beer a day and some of them had stashed this away for a binge at a later date. This was supplemented by cases of beer pilfered from the No. 4 hold. We knew this had been going on as empty cases would appear among the garbage, or in the water alongside, but we did not know how the culprits were able to gain access to the lower hold.

The first indication of trouble came when one of the firemen appeared outside the 2nd mate's door. He was drunk and required medical attention for a deep laceration on his face. Shouts and curses arose from below deck. It was after midnight and the uproar continued to escalate. The sound of chairs, crockery and other things at hand being smashed to pieces mingled with the sound of body punches being exchanged. It was futile to intervene. I ventured halfway down a ladder leading to the crew's quarters to take a look. About twenty men were engaged in a pitched battle. One of them was half-naked, blood streaming down his face and torso. He had just been hit by a man brandishing a brass nozzle taken from a hose. Alexander, the cook, was in the thick of it, beating a man senseless. I returned to my room and locked the door. Sometime during the early hours they ran out of steam and the riot was over. While all this was going on, the old man had called Singapore radio requesting assistance from the naval or military police. They replied that as we were merchant marine, it was a civilian matter and we must resolve our own problems. The civil authorities had more than enough to do as Singapore had not yet returned to a state of order after four years of Japanese occupation.

After nearly a month at anchor it was our turn to enter Keppel harbour and unload the cargo. The 2nd mate, Dave Wylie, became sick and was transferred to the hospital ship "Gerusalemme" lying at anchor. I went aboard and stood at his bedside but he could hardly speak. Nobody knew what was wrong with him. He was sent home and I became 2nd mate. Three weeks later the new 3rd mate arrived. He had just passed his ticket and was anxious to put his knowledge to practical use.

As soon as the Chinese dockers uncovered the hatch boards over No. 4 lower hold we discovered that a large number of beer cases had been broken open. The mate and I went down to take a closer look and found that a small plate had been removed from the shaft tunnel which ran through the lower hold, thus allowing entry to the cargo. Obviously it was an "inside job" but the culprits were never found. The dockers began wholesale pilferage on their own and a large number of cases were broken into. Attempts to stop it were met with blank stares from the stevedore boss. He was asked to control his men, heated exchanges took place and for a time we thought we had managed to stop the theft. But a sling load of beer would land on the dock and be broken into in full view of everyone. When the army soldiers heard that the dockers were helping themselves to their beer, guards were sent to the godowns (dockside sheds) to protect it. A few days later a docker was caught in the act, shot and killed. This resulted in a strike and all work stopped until the guards were removed. The mate reckoned that about a quarter of our load of beer had been stolen!

Nobody wanted the 2,000 tons of ammunition so we sailed with it still aboard. We were needed in Rangoon where huge numbers of military vehicles

A Sikh driver in a Punjabi regiment. I had asked him whether he thought my beard was up to snuff.

from the 14th Army had to be taken elsewhere. We arrived in Rangoon to find the city in near chaos and very different from the bright and bustling place I had last seen in 1937. It had a decayed and neglected look. I walked along streets strewn with rubbish, broken carts and discarded tyres. Shops had been deserted and windows smashed. On one corner I saw an emaciated man on all fours picking through a mound of stinking garbage. The once-smart Mayo Marine Club was deserted; the lawns had long since disappeared under a cover of weeds. It had been used by the Japanese as a shipping control office. Allied bombing had reduced some of the wharves and cargo sheds to ruins, and there was little space to park the long lines of army vehicles waiting to be loaded. There were thousands of troops in the city and theft of military material by civilians and soldiers alike was widespread. Trucks loaded with supplies of all kinds would simply disappear. We heard about an army officer who came out of his quarters to find his jeep missing. Red-faced with anger, he flagged down a passing jeep and climbed in demanding to be driven to the military police. En route, he complained about the audacity of the thief, not realizing that the jeep he sat in was his own!

The city was under a curfew at night and sometime shots could be heard as thugs and dacoits (gang members) went on a rampage of looting and murder.

The mate and I were taken by two British army officers to see the countryside round Rangoon. We drove along dusty roads past lush jungle where only a year before there had been fierce fighting. We came to a white bungalow on a hill overlooking a lake. It was a beautiful setting but the building was derelict with stone floors covered in rubble and paint peeling off the walls. It had been an exclusive country club for "pukka sahibs" in pre-war times, explained one of our guides, but the Japanese had found another use for it. They used it as a brothel for army officers. We wandered through the rooms and out on to the verandah, and I tried to imagine how it must have looked when the sahibs and their memsahibs had last sat there — sipping pink gins and downing "burra pegs" (large whiskies).

We left Rangoon, bound for Singapore, with a load of surplus army vehicles. Two army officers came with us — Major Coleman and his aide. Major Coleman was a judge advocate, one of several sent to Singapore to try Japanese soldiers accused of war crimes. A war crimes commission had been set up to investigate atrocities committed against civilians and prisoners of war, and thousands of suspects were being held waiting to be "processed". On the run to Singapore we got to know the major. He was a cheerful chap who seemed only too pleased to sit down and have a beer with us. Clad in khaki shorts and tattered shirt he would stretch out on the settee in the mate's room and play a mouth organ; his favourite tune was "I Wish You Were A Paper Doll". He didn't give the impression one might expect of a judge! He was chided by the steward for wearing a singlet instead of a shirt when sitting down to a meal in the saloon. We got the impression that he had been in the jungle too long.

As before, Singapore harbour was crowded with ships, and we anchored in the Approaches within sight of the wreck of the "Empress of Asia". Her masts stuck out of the water like bean poles. Japanese planes had sunk her during the fall of Singapore when she had tried to escape with a load of Australian troops fleeing the burning city.

On May 16th, 1946, Sparks received a message from Singapore Radio. He gave me the news that my first child, a girl named Veronica, had been born — the first of a long line of progeny!

Before Major Coleman went ashore, he told us that if we wanted to attend a war crimes trial over which he would preside, he could arrange it. When viewed from seaward, the green-domed Justice Building was most prominent. Six trials were in session simultaneously. One of these was drawing to an end and the mate and I went ashore to attend the last day. When we entered the court the public gallery was already full of Chinese. They had a particular interest in the case since the crimes had been committed against their people. The mate and I sat to one side near the proceedings. In front of us was a young Dutch woman dressed in white. We were told that she had lost her parents who died from ill-treatment in a civilian prison camp in Singapore. Judge Coleman walked in; this time he was dressed in proper uniform. The seven accused Japanese soldiers were marched in and stood in line, each of them with a white card on his chest with his number on it. A Japanese officer stood with the prisoners. There were two interpreters, one for the accused and one for the Chinese. There had been excessive brutality during the interrogation of Chinese civilians suspected of aiding the Allies. Evidence was given about lighted cigarettes being pushed into people's eyes. Men and women had been beaten with iron rods. Several people had been held in a confined, dark and airless cellar eventually dying from suffocation. It was a shocking story of callous cruelty.

There was an atmosphere of tension and dread as the case came to its inevitable conclusion. Of the seven accused, all were found guilty except one who was not present when the crimes were committed. The judge sentenced them to death by hanging. I looked at the prisoners as the verdict was translated. None of them flinched or showed a trace of emotion. I supposed that they expected it. Each man had given the same classic defence: "I obeyed orders." Some time later, British soldiers, whose barracks lay near Changi Jail, told us that throughout the night they had heard the thump of the trap doors as three Indian hangmen "processed" the condemned.

We made two more trips to Rangoon to load army material. Vehicles were needed in Chittagong which was about 20 miles up the Kharnipuli River. It was a ramshackle town of slums as bad or worse than any in Calcutta. Vultures stood on the banks of the stagnant river waiting for something to float by.

We had now been away from home for a year. There were strong feelings of discontent aboard due to the long periods of inactivity, weeks lying at anchor waiting for orders and the apparent inefficient handling of our movements by the office "wallahs" ashore. Nobody was more frustrated than the mate. He had toyed with the idea of leaving the sea, now there was no doubt in his mind. "I've had it, this life is not fit for a dog!" he said, and he wrote a letter to the owners in London. In it, he told them that their ship was being badly managed, that we had 2,000 tons of ammo aboard that had been loaded nearly a year ago and that nobody ashore seemed to know or care about this. He urged Prince Line to seek the ship's early release from Government control. We officers signed it and hoped that perhaps it might reach someone who could cut through the red tape.

The mate and I thought of a way to improve the ship's morale, now at an all time low. We would organize a sports club. Some money was held in a "slush" fund to buy tobacco and beer for the "slop chest" and there was enough in hand to buy equipment. The crew were in favour of the plan and football and cricket were the sports chosen. I went aboard a ship lying nearby and persuaded the crew to part with netting and cricket bats. The rest of what was needed I bought from an Indian-owned shop in Singapore. Matting was laid along the foredeck and netting strung up to prevent balls from going overboard. Cricket and football teams were selected and games were organized against teams from other ships. This meant finding suitable places ashore where games could be held. Our new 3rd mate was in charge of that, a job he did not expect to be doing when he had come aboard a few months earlier.

All this seemed to make our lives less boring until one evening the intractable cook, Alexander, provoked another fight. This time he got the worst of it. An able seamen called McPhee had come aboard to replace a sick man. He was a good footballer and tough enough to beat up Alexander who then looked for a way to get his revenge. He waited until most of the crew were asleep then threw overboard all the sporting equipment. This time he had "shot his bolt" and the old man took action at last. Alexander was put ashore and locked up. We were without a cook, not that it made much difference, the food was deplorable anyway. The old man was unlucky to have had a crew of troublemakers on his first trip as master.

As 2nd mate I was in charge of the medicine chest. For reasons unclear to me, the chief steward had been entrusted with drugs such as sulpha and antibiotics, and these were locked up in his room. I dispensed medicine under the master's authority for such ailments as prickly heat, abrasions, bowel problems (castor oil and black-draught were effective purgatives), removal of foreign bodies in the eyes and so on. One day, I needed drugs to treat a patient and went to the steward's room to get them. I was met with a blank refusal to hand them over. The master became involved as we now suspected mischief on the steward's part. His room was searched, the medicine cabinet opened and found empty. It then transpired that he had sold the drugs in Singapore for a good profit!

Stewards on British ships were generally held in low esteem and it wasn't entirely undeserved. It was common knowledge that some of them flogged the ship's stores, or were in cahoots with a supplier ashore who delivered less stores to the ship than the company paid for. No wonder they were called "belly robbers" by underfed crews. The steward had other means of raising some spare cash through the ship's "slop chest" which supplied tobacco, cheap clothing and various other items which seamen needed at sea. All a man had to do was sign a receipt for the goods, sold by the steward at a good profit, and the money was deducted from his wages.

But stewards were not the only ones guilty of shipboard larceny. Some chief engineers "cooked the books" to show that more fuel had been consumed than was actually the case. For example, the chief would sign a receipt for 1,000 tons of bunker coal but in fact only 950 tons would be loaded. The ship owners would pay for 1,000 tons and the coal merchant and the chief would pocket a nice "bonus". This sort of fiddling sometimes back-fired on the chief if the ship encountered bad weather and the daily consumption entry in his log book could not hide the fact that the fires were burning coal at an alarming rate. However much as he fudged the figures, there was a very real chance that the ship would run out of fuel before reaching port. When this happened it was sometimes necessary to cut up the wooden derricks and whatever else they could find to burn in order to reach land.

In the days when the master fed the ship from his own money, many were the stories of chicanery and miserliness, but when I first went to sea those practices had largely disappeared. Once, the master of the Henderson Line tramp steamer "Henzada" had been caught overloading his ship. We heard about it on the "Mandalay" because we were on the same salt run from Aden to Calcutta. Apparently the "Henzada" was found to be loaded below her marks by a few hundred tons. Questions were asked. There had been collusion between her old man and the agent in Aden. They stood to make a handsome profit as salt was a valuable commodity.

As we entered Singapore for the third time, the pilot pointed at a Liberty ship at anchor: her decks were deserted and for good reason. She was the "Samfreedom", ironically named in view of the fact that her entire crew including the master were in jail for theft on a grand scale. No doubt her crew had suffered the same frustration as we had at having to wait at anchor for so long. The "Samfreedom" had had a large consignment of beer and cigarettes and the interminable delay must have seemed a terrible waste to her crew. They decided to go into business for themselves. They made arrangements with unscrupulous Chinese merchants ashore to rendezvous with the ship at sea. The "Samfreedom" waited for darkness before weighing anchor and slipping out of the harbour and steaming down the Straits to a position well clear of the land. She then stopped and waited for one or two junks to come alongside and receive as much cargo as they could carry. In 1946, the shipping situation in South East Asia was in a state of chaos as hundreds of ships lay off ports loaded with cargoes that were no longer needed. The shipping authority could not possibly monitor the movements of all the ships, so the "Samfreedom" was able to reappear off Singapore as if nothing untoward was going on.

In June, 1946, we steamed up the coast of Burma to a port which nobody knew existed. It was shown on the chart as Kyaukpyu, a mere indent on the coastline. We dropped anchor a mile from the shore and wondered why we had been sent there as there appeared to be nothing but an unbroken line of jungle along the shoreline. But a road led inland to a place where there had been heavy fighting and there was equipment which had to be taken out. We lay for two long weeks in this god-forsaken spot. Loading was difficult and slow as only two small barges were available to ferry the vehicles out to the ship. We delivered this load and the ammunition which we had carried for so long to Vizagapatam, a small port on the East coast of India. This was a pleasant change, for although it was hot and dusty, it had been untouched by the war and the town was an interesting place to walk around. One day I watched a Hindu ceremonial procession coming along the narrow road where I stood. It was led by men beating drums and they were followed by a large ornamental box carried on a platform. The box had windows on its sides. As it passed me I looked in and was surprised to see a child dressed in highly-decorative clothing. I could not tell whether it was a boy or a girl but it did not appear very happy. I was told that the child was revered as being god-like.

We sailed for Labuan on the North West coast of Borneo. The ship was almost empty except for 2,000 tons of flour which the Australian troops needed. I had always wanted to see Borneo; there was something mysterious about it. I had read about the Dyak tribesmen and of James Brooke who a hundred years ago had left his ship and gone to live with the natives. He became Rajah Brooke of Sarawak after helping the Sultan of Brunei suppress a revolt, and his kingdom became part of the British Empire.

Mount Kinabalu at 12,000 ft was visible from nearly 100 miles offshore, and twelve hours later we dropped the hook in the secluded harbour of Labuan. The water looked so inviting some of us went in for a swim, but the Australian sergeant who had come aboard to see the mate about our cargo ran to the ship's side and bellowed out that we should get out right away as it was not safe. Sometime earlier a Japanese prisoner had been allowed to go swimming and was splashing about near the wharf. Men working nearby heard shouts and were in time to see him being dragged under by some creature. His body was never found.

I was ashore with Sparks one afternoon and we found a shack which sold soft drinks. While we were slaking our thirst an elderly white man, dressed in tattered clothing, came and sat down beside us. He was eager to talk and wanted to know if we carried passengers as he wanted to get out of "this hell hole". We told him the "Samdaring" was a cargo ship and that the old man would not allow passengers aboard. He seemed resigned at this piece of news and told us about his experiences in a Japanese prison camp. Before the war he had worked for an engineering firm in Rangoon. He had been in Burma for twenty years and was married to a Burmese woman. He had been ostracized by the whites so he lived in the native quarter of the city. When the Japanese took over he had expected that he would receive better treatment than the other Europeans because he was living with the Burmese. But he had been herded into a prison camp with the other whites, the men in one building and the women in another. Their clothing was taken away, leaving the men with only a loin cloth to wear. The purpose of this was to humiliate them and to show that white men were no better than the natives. For the first few weeks the prisoners were treated relatively well. The camp commander was a civilized man who provided food and medical care. He told the prisoners that he regretted having to confine them in such poor conditions, but it was his duty and even his own men were no better off. But the commander was replaced by a brutal man and overnight conditions changed for the worse. Prisoners were beaten for the slightest infraction of the rules. Their food ration was cut and communication with the women was forbidden. Any attempts to escape were punishable by death. When British soldiers reached the camp at the end of the war, almost half the inmates had died and he felt lucky to be alive. He had not seen his wife since being separated in the camp and did not know what had happened to her.

Our cargo of flour was piled on the dock as there was nowhere else to store it. The Aussies did not need it as they were leaving. The rains came and the lot became soaked and useless. A small rust covered vessel came alongside. She was a water boat manned by Japanese which a few months earlier had replenished the ships of the Imperial Fleet. After she had tied up alongside us we noticed a lot of activity about her decks. Not all of it was human: she was swarming with rats, and before long some of them came aboard the "Samdaring". Earlier I had adopted a cat and now instead of chasing cockroaches she had more formidable quarry to deal with. I was woken one night by a strange squeaking sound. There was sufficient light to see that my cat had cornered a blunt nosed rat almost half her size. Startled, I cried out in alarm, this was enough to distract the cat and in an instant the rat darted out of the room to find refuge elswhere. The rats stayed with us until we reached Britain where the extermination team came aboard with cyanide canisters to fumigate the ship.

We left Labuan with a small load of supplies for Sandakan on the North East coast of Borneo where a notorious death march had ended. Over three thousand men had been forced to march across the top of Borneo through dense jungle. Many were so weak from malnutrition and disease that they were unable to walk and were shot. Those who fell by the wayside were clubbed to death with rifle butts. By the time the march was over only seven hundred men were alive.

When we heard the news that we were to load military supplies in Singapore and take them to Japan, a wave of optimism swept the ship and I eagerly searched for the charts for that area. We entered the Inland Sea without a pilot as apparently no one was available. My confidence as a navigator was given a boost when on my afternoon watch I was left to take the ship through the Inland Sea on our way to Kure. We tied up in the Naval Dockyard amidst wreckage caused by heavy bombing. Across the dock from us an aircraft carrier lay on its side. Several midget submarines lay in a dry dock, strewn about like discarded toys. The mate and I went aboard a wrecked cruiser. Her decks were littered with pieces of metal — she must have received a direct hit as part of her stern was missing.

The small town of Kure did not appear to have suffered much damage. I went there one hot afternoon and was surprised to find that the shops were well stocked with the things I had seen in Osaka in 1938. Beautiful silk kimonos, delicate chinaware and bowls made of lacquer. The people were neither friendly nor unfriendly — they simply ignored me and as the atom bombs had been dropped only months before, their attitude was understandable.

The Australian Army was in charge of the docks and most of them had seen action in Burma and Malaya. They had little sympathy for the Japanese soldiers unloading our cargo who received no pay and were given very little to eat. They would hang around the galley and ask for left-overs. To their credit they were not sullen or resentful, and were probably only too pleased that the war was over. In typical Japanese fashion they worked hard and the cargo was unloaded in record time. The mate saw a golden opportunity to get extra work done on the ship and asked the Aussie boss for some Japanese labour. He was told that he could have as many men as he wanted — all he had to do was feed them. There must have been over fifty men chipping and scraping the decks, washing bulkheads and sweeping the holds. The cooks were given extra pots in which to cook rice and the result was that the "Samdaring" was cleaner than she had been for months. A few understood English and they told me how glad they were that the war was over.

Hiroshima after the bomb - utter devastation

Before we left Kure, the Aussie in charge of the dock took the mate and me in his jeep to Hiroshima. The road ran along the shore of the Inland Sea and it took us an hour to reach the devastated city. As we approached, a scene of utter ruin lay before us. The bomb had been dropped ten months earlier, but already the resourceful inhabitants had managed to provide themselves with rudimentary forms of shelter. Amidst the rubble were thousands of packing-case shacks. Hiroshima had been a port city of 200,000 people which had remained relatively untouched until the morning of August 6th, 1945. It was warm and sunny; people were going about their daily lives not suspecting that a terrible weapon was about to be used on them. The incoming plane was so high that it was unlikely anyone saw it. A house painter stood on a ladder working on the side of a building. The bomb exploded 100 feet above the ground and the shadow of his pulverized body was etched against the wall.

We parked beside one of the few buildings left standing. It had been a department store and the bare, steel ribs of the dome made it look like a bird cage. Tables were laid out inside the gutted interior and it was business as usual. I bought a lacquer bowl which seemed delicately beautiful amidst so much destruction.

I wasn't sorry to leave Japan as our stay had been depressing. The old Japan which I had seen eight years earlier had gone for ever. We had orders to proceed to Hong Kong with a part load of army vehicles that were no longer needed. We went alongside in Kowloon and the mate and I went for a drink in the Peninsula Hotel, which boasted the longest bar in Asia. By now most of us were thoroughly sick of the Far East and when we heard that we were bound for Vancouver, Canada, to load lumber for Britain there was much rejoicing aboard. In port with us was the trampship "King Stephen". We had been in Singapore with her and had exchanged books and magazines with her crew. Her mates invited us aboard for a drink. She was also bound for Vancouver and was due to sail on the same day as we were. Naturally we challenged her to a race.

Our passage across the Pacific was a long one. We chose to take a great circle track which proved to be a mistake. Near the Date Line we ran into bad weather, and being in ballast, the ship became almost unmanageable and we were hove to for a day. We were in contact with our pals on the "King Stephen". She had wisely taken a more southerly route and was 300 miles south of us and enjoying fine weather. She reached Vancouver a day ahead of us. So, after 27 days at sea, we steamed under the Lion's Gate Bridge. It was my first visit to Western Canada and it was wonderful to be back in the Western Hemisphere.

We were glad to be in the English-speaking world again and Vancouver offered everything that we had gone without for so long. There was no shortage of anything, and for the first time in months we enjoyed real butter, fresh vegetables and even fresh milk. Best of all, I had relations in Kelowna whom I had never seen, and I managed to get a few days leave to go and visit them. It was the first time that I had been able to leave the ship for over a year, and as I sat in the old colonial parlor car aboard the train, and gazed out upon vast forests and splendid mountains, the thought entered my mind that perhaps I should come back here to live. The train rattled along beside a magnificent lake and into Kelowna. I was met at the station by at least a dozen relatives and a rousing reception which I had not expected. They were all part of my mother's family and their kindness and hospitality during my stay in Kelowna was extraordinary.

By mid-September we had finished loading and were now homeward-bound with a full load of lumber, a journey of 8,000 miles via Panama which would take a month. I spent many hours pacing back and forth on the wings of the bridge pondering over my future. Did I really want to spend the rest of my life at sea? Or should I start a new life doing something else in Canada?

On the 24th of November, 1946, we docked in Hull, England. We had been away for 15 months. I went home to see my wife, Celia, and daughter, Veronica, who was already six months old. Whatever the hardships of life at sea, long absences from home were the most difficult to bear, particularly for married men. After a voyage of this duration there was exquisite pleasure in being with my family once again.

Chapter 15. The " Samtucky" to Vancouver

I now had more than enough time to sit for my first mate's ticket and in the spring of 1947, I moved into the Seamark Club, which was near Tower Bridge in London. It was a a residence for seamen studying for certificates at the nautical school nearby. It was run by Mrs. Kirby, a kindly woman, who laid down strict rules about drinking on the premises and rowdy behavior. No strange women were allowed in without her approval.

It was while staying at the Seamark Club that I heard that Frank Owen, the assistant editor of the Daily Mail, needed a skipper. He owned a 35 foot motor cruiser and had planned a trip down the Thames to Southend and back. It seemed like a good idea even though I had no knowledge of the river, never having been further up the Thames than Tilbury. I asked a young Port Line cadet to come along to help me on the cruise. He had no river experience either. Frank Owen had brought along a friend and they were accompanied by their wives and several bottles of liquor. We set off from Chelsea Pier and it soon became apparent that we were in for a lively trip. There was heavy traffic moving in all directions and as our passengers "whooped it up" in the cabin, the cadet and I had to keep a sharp look-out as we sped down river with the tide. We assumed that the rules of the road applied here as elsewhere. But it was a hair-raising passage as tugs, barges, lighters, pleasure steamers and small coasters shot past us from all angles. Before long, our passengers wanted to go ashore and insisted that we stop at Dagenham where there was a pub near the jetty. After a spell ashore, they were barely able to scramble back aboard and one of the women lost her shoes overboard. Eventually we reached Southend near the mouth of the Thames and by then our passengers were sound asleep. The cadet and I were tired too, and after an uneventful return up river with our subdued and hung-over passengers, we were relieved and happy to step ashore.

I had heard that, whereas a 2nd mate's ticket was tough, a mate's ticket "was a piece of cake!" It wasn't long before I discovered that although it may have been true for some, it was not true for me. Stability and ship's construction were the subjects which still eluded me. I passed the orals but failed the written exams. This resulted in further soul-searching about starting a new life in Canada. Celia and I discussed the idea but we could not yet make a definite decision. She was not particularly enthusiastic about going to Canada and her parents felt that I should leave the sea life and find a shore job.

Meanwhile, our money was running short and there was no alternative but for me to return to sea. On August 23rd, 1947, I took the train to Avonmouth and walked aboard the "Samtucky" as 2nd mate. She lay in dry dock for a long-overdue hull inspection. She was identical to the "Samdaring", except that she had some new hull plating to repair the damage inflicted by a torpedo off the east coast of Canada. I was pleased to hear that we were bound for Vancouver for a load of lumber. Our crew was from the Bristol area and after a day's work they went home, so a night watchman was hired. He was an elderly ex-seaman who was in the habit of spending an hour or two in the pub before he came on duty at nightfall. On several occasions when he came into the accommodation to announce his presence, he would smell of alcohol. He was not much use as a watchman as he fell asleep soon after arriving aboard. But no one was hard-hearted enough to get rid of him. One warm evening as I sat talking to the mate in his room, the cadet rushed in to tell us that the watchman had suffered a terrible accident. We went out on deck and looked down into the dock. A dark figure lay prone in a pool of blood directly beneath the gangway, which, because of his state of intoxication, he had missed and fallen 50 feet to his death.

I took special leave and was at home when my second child and eldest son, Andrew, was born in Ashburton on August 27th, 1947. Once again, the possibilities of my staying at sea, finding a shore job or emigrating to Canada were discussed with no clear decision reached.

We sailed from Avonmouth on September 3rd 1947; we had taken on about 4,000 tons of sand ballast. During the previous months, two Liberty ships had come to grief as a result of being insufficiently ballasted. One of them, the "Samkey" , was also bound for the Pacific. Her last reported position was east of Puerto Rico and she was experiencing heavy weather. She was never heard from again.

Our master was Captain Ewan Ellis, a tall Welshman in his fifties and a thorough gentleman in every sense. He told me that he had been to sea for over thirty-five years and estimated that in that time he had spent six years at home! The mate was a canny Scot by the name of James Coldwell. He was an avid reader and brought aboard a large tin trunk full of books to prove it. He said, "If I have to be at sea for months on end, I may as well improve my mind." The 3rd mate was Johnny Williams. He had been a cadet on the "Worcester" and had won a sextant for high marks. He and I became good friends and at last I felt I had joined a happy ship even if it possibly turned out to be my final trip!

Before we entered Vancouver harbour we had to dump our ballast overboard into English Bay. When that was finished we shifted to an anchorage closer to Stanley Park. On the middle watch in the early hours a westerly began to freshen. I was busy taking shore bearings and became alarmed when I noticed that the lights on the Lion's Gate Bridge were gradually disappearing behind the rock bluff. We were dragging the anchor and if we had not lifted it in a hurry and steamed to sea, we would have grounded on the beach at Stanley Park. We spent the next day steaming up and down the Gulf of Georgia until the gale blew itself out.

Another visit to Kelowna to see my relatives was enough to convince me that we must come to Canada. I spoke to the pilot who took us up the river to New Westminster. He suggested that I apply for a job with the Union Company

Captain Ellis "A thorough gentleman"

who owned a fleet of ships which plied the coast of British Columbia. Several of them were lying alongside the dock when I arrived and asked to speak to the Superintendent. He was a busy man but after glancing at my papers, told me that if I came back to Canada during the coming summer he would give me a job. The die was cast; all I had to do now was convince my family that it was a good move, pack-up our belongings and emigrate to Canada.

While we loaded lumber in Vancouver two of the firemen "jumped ship" . It was easy enough to find work ashore that paid more than they made on the ship. But they had to avoid detection so most of them took off for the interior of British Columbia. A year later, when I was 3rd mate on one of the Union Company ships, I recognized one of the men who had deserted the "Samtucky" and hailed him by name. He immediately put his finger to his lips and said, "I am Smith now!" He was working on the same ship as I was and asked me not to say a word to anyone as the Royal Canadian Mounted Police were after him. I told him that he should think about giving himself up rather than having to live a double life. Some years later I met him again. He had thought about what I had said and decided to go to the police. He was glad he had as he had been granted conditional immigrant status, kept his job, reverted to his original name and had then been able to make a down-payment on a house.

The trip back to Britain was unremarkable except for an incident in Portland, Oregon, where we docked to complete our load of lumber. Among the crew we had a few hard-case troublemakers who had caused problems both aboard and ashore. One particularly rough seaman had picked a fight in a bar and had landed in jail. We hoped that we could sail without him because he was useless to the ship. But the police did not want him either and he continued to make trouble aboard. Before we had signed off in Newcastle the old man showed the mates the crew list, and asked us to mark the name of any man who we thought was unfit to work aboard merchant ships. We had put a black mark against three names. Presumably these names were circulated throughout shipping offices in the country. It was a necessary measure to rid the merchant service of undesirables, so many of them men who had gone to sea to avoid being conscripted into the armed services. There was even the story of a war-time judge who gave a convicted felon a choice — he could either go to prison or join the merchant navy!

Noon sights aboard "Samtucky"

I, too, had a choice. It was time to "swallow the anchor" and find my destiny in Canada. I had spent eleven eventful years aboard eleven ships and sailed under the British, French and Dutch flags. Perhaps that would be sufficient to satisfy my wanderlust as the prospect of being away from home and family for months on end was not a happy one. Like many other people in Britain I felt that our future lay elsewhere. I would take the job with the Union Company in Vancouver and, once we had settled down, I would find a shore job.

It did not work out that way as I was destined to serve under five more flags over the next forty-four years. However, those events and stories will have to wait until the next book!

Other titles available from Navigator Books:

ORMONDE TO ORIANA
Nelson French

The author joined the Orient Line as an Assistant Purser in 1947. He was appointed Purser in 1954 and thereafter served in every ship in the Orient Fleet. There are whole page illustrations of most of them. Migrants to Australia and world cruises are here. He was involved in the commissioning and the Maiden Voyage of the previous "ORIANA".

234x153, illustrated, paperback,
ISBN: 0 902830 58 9 ***£9.99***

ORMONDE
to
ORIANA

ORIENT LINE
to
AUSTRALIA AND BEYOND
A PURSER remembers

Nelson French

Navigator Books

- -

THE RACE TO THE CAPE
Norman Hodson

Fully illustrated with whole page photographs of the Union Castle Liners, this is the story from the joining of the Union Line and the Castle Line, of the early days of competition on the South African route; to the time of "Every Thursday at 4pm a Union Castle Liner leaves for the Cape."

210x145, illustrated, paperback,
ISBN: 0 902830 42 2 ***£8.99***

The Race to the Cape
a story of the
UNION CASTLE LINE
1857 - 1977

Norman Hodson

NAVIGATOR BOOKS

NEVER FORGET, NOR FORGIVE
Captain George T. Cooper, R.N.

From the sinking of H.M.S. "EXETER" by the Japanese in the Java Sea, this is the story of the survivors of her crew at the hands of the Japanese in Prisoner of War camps, of the inhuman treatment and hardships endured. A gripping books that will add to your understanding. Read this and understand why Captain Cooper says, "Never forgive".

234x153, illustrated, paperback,
ISBN: 0 902830 53 8 ***£9.99***

- -

FIFTY YEARS AT SEA
Captain John Delaney Nash

The years at sea of Captain John Delaney Nash, F.N.I., from joining the Eagle Oil Shipping Company as a Deck Cadet in 1927. He served throughout the war in tankers supplying H.M. Ships at sea, one of the most hazardous jobs of the war from which he survived unscathed. He then joined B.R. as Master of R.M.S. "DUKE OF ARGYLL".

210x148, illustrated, paperback,
ISBN: 0 902830 41 4 ***£8.99***

MASTER IN SAIL
Captain William Murchison

Tales of a seafaring family going back to 1884 in Toscaig between Lock Torridon in the North and Lochcarron in the South. Stories of poaching from Arduie past Cruachrie Point, rounding Cape Horn with the foresail and lower topsails on the fore main and mizzen, so fascinating you wish it could go on forever.

234x153, illustrated, paperback,
ISBN: 0 902830 58 9 ***£9.99***

BY A SLENDER THREAD
Barrie Skelcher

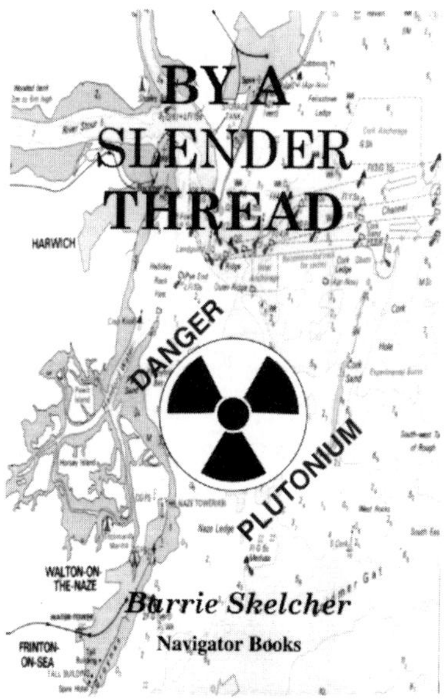

Could terrorists steal plutonium from an Atomic Power Plant and make a bomb? This question is often asked and an answer is provided in this novel.

It is written by a nuclear physicist who is also a yachtsman and the yacht chase is fascinating in detail and excitement.

Could it happen? You must read it to know.

234x153, cased,
ISBN: 0 902830 46 5 ***£9.99***

A DASH OF SALT
Stuart Beck

The life of a marine artist, technical illustrator and graphic designer that started as a boy in New York Harbour on the bridge of a cargo steamer of which his father was captain.

Illustrated with drawings by the author who is a Member of the Royal Society of Marine Artists and whose work is permanently exhibited at the National Maritime Museum and the RNLI Museum at Poole.

234x153, illustrated, cased,
ISBN: 0 902830 13 9 ***£14.99***

- -

THE BERMUDA TRIANGLE
Mystery No More
Richard Silvester

The author has researched the fields of hydraulic and coastal engineering for some 40 years, in all parts of the world. He has always been fascinated by the power of whirling water or air, which he intuitively realised was the cause of the ship and plane disappearances in the Bermuda Triangle. Once he was convinced, he searched the literature to prove his hypotheses.

234x153, illustrated, paperback
ISBN: 0 902830 68 6 ***£9.99***

SAFETY AT SEA
Dave Welbourne

Too many amateur yachtsmen risk their lives, and the lives of their families, by being unaware of the sort of advice offered in this book.

The sea is a tough place and disaster strikes the best of us - but you've got a chance if you know what to do.

210x148, illustrated, paperback,
ISBN: 0 902830 48 1 ***£4.99***

- -

TROOPSHIP MEMORIES
Geoff Charlewood

To have served anywhere at sea during the war was fraught with anxiety and the Japanese theatre of operations particularly so following the loss of "PRINCE OF WALES" and "REPULSE".

The author's account of years of trooping in "NEURALIA" must bring back memories to many thousands. Many ships mentioned.

234x153, illustrated, paperback,
ISBN: 0 902830 62 7 ***£8.99***

THE ILLUSTRATED DIARY OF A THAMES PILOT
John Foot

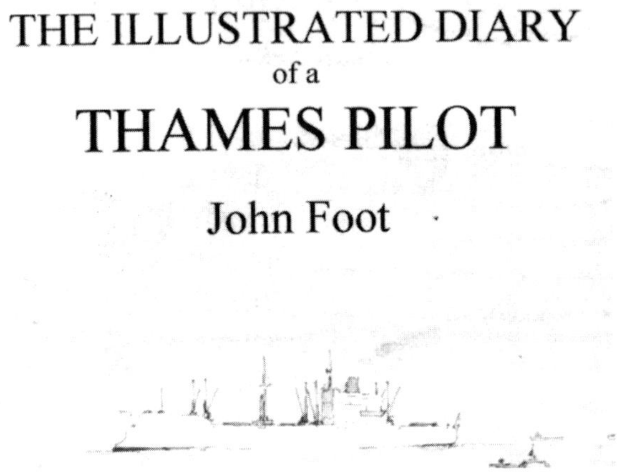

Fascinating stories of the author's early life at sea until he qualified as a Thames Pilot. The author is an artist of considerable ability and there are charming drawings throughout the book. The pilot's experiences with "STEFAN BATORY" and "MONTE ULIA" alone are worth the price of the book but there is other fascinating detail.

174x246, illustrated, landscape, cased,
ISBN: 0 902830 51 1 ***£9.99***

SINGLE HANDED THRO HOSTILE SHORES
David Alexander

The crew of a Catalac catamaran set out on a 1,500 mile delivery trip to Durban harbour, past hostile shores, and one by one the crew have to leave for various reasons and the author is left to make the trip on his own. One of the engines fails, problems arise, the islands north of Madagascar are not friendly. A fascinating story of problems overcome and lessons learnt.

210x148, paperback,
ISBN: 0 902830 61 9 ***£4.99***

A TRAMP ABOUT THE WORLD
Peter Biddick

What life was like as a Merchant Navy cadet in the great days of shipping. The experiences of the author who joined a rough tramp company at the tender age of sixteen up to the time when he left as Second Officer on passenger and cargo ships.

Humorously told, will bring back memories.

210x143, paperback,
ISBN: 0 902830 24 4 ***£8.99***

FROM ENGINE ROOM TO ADMIRALTY
Tommy Brown

The great days of the Royal Navy as seen from the engine room. Naval supremacy needed engine room and gunnery supremacy too.

A fascinating record with many references to famous ships long since consigned to the breaker's yard.

234x153, illustrated, paperback,
ISBN: 0 902830 57 0 ***£11.99***

NO SAFE HAVEN
George Glenton

The role of the small, armed tramp ships that kept the Army supplied with munitions and fuel from Alamein up through Italy in the Second World War. An epic story of endurance of the Allied Merchant Fleet in the Mediterranean, carrying their dangerous cargoes from the Barbary Coast to Bari during 1942 and 1943. With many illustrations of famous ships that were sunk.

234x153, illustrated, paperback,
ISBN: 0 902830 44 9 ***£9.99***

H.M.S. "BEDOUIN"
And The Long March Home
Percy Hagger

The story of Tribal Class Destroyer "BEDOUIN" up to her sinking while escorting a Malta convoy in the Mediterranean. The actions are well described with the naming of the ships involved which will revive memories for thousands of matelots who were there. And then the survivors of "BEDOUIN" go into captivity in Italy and Germany, vividly described.

234x153, illustrated, paperback,
ISBN: 0 902830 28 7